UNMASKED

UNMASKED

Inside Antifa's Radical Plan to Destroy Democracy

Andy Ngo

CENTER
STREET

NEW YORK • NASHVILLE

Center Street
Hachette Book Group
1290 Avenue of the Americas, New York, NY 10104
centerstreet.com
twitter.com/centerstreet

First Edition: February 2021

Center Street is a division of Hachette Book Group, Inc. The Center Street
name and logo are trademarks of Hachette Book Group, Inc.

The publisher is not responsible for websites (or their content) that are not owned
by the publisher.

Library of Congress Control Number: 2020951079

ISBNs: 978-1-5460-5958-5 (hardcover), 978-1-5460-5956-1 (ebook)

Printed in the United States of America

LSC-C

Printing 1, 2020

To my father, Ngo Quoc Binh

CONTENTS

Introduction

"WHOSE STREETS? OUR STREETS!" the crowd of left-wing protesters chanted as they marched in the heart of downtown Portland, Oregon, in June 2019. Some of them wore red shirts and bandanas to broadcast their allegiance to Marxism. They paraded red flags printed with a rose logo, a symbol of the Democratic Socialists of America. They were joined by dozens of people dressed head to toe in black. These were the radical anarchist communists. Most of them wore masks—long before the COVID-19 outbreak made them a norm of public life. Many also wore helmets and carried melee weapons. Together, the crowd of around four hundred brought traffic to a standstill—by now a regular occurrence in the City of Roses, as Portland is known by. As usual, the police stayed away. They knew whom the streets belonged to.

Working as a journalist with a phone and a new GoPro camera, I slowly made my way toward the front of the crowd. Some of the protesters recognized me. They glared and whispered in the ears of their comrades. Luis Enrique Marquez looked right at me. The 48-year-old Rose City Antifa member has been arrested so many times at violent protests in Portland over the past few years that he no longer bothers to wear a mask. Still, I ignored the stares and continued forward. By this point, the crowd's chants had changed.

"No hate! No fear!" they began shouting.

Before I made it much farther, someone—or something—hit me hard in the back of the head. I was nearly knocked to the ground from the impact. Never having been in a fight, I naively asked myself in the moment: "Did someone just trip and fall into me?" Before I could turn around to look, a sea of bodies dressed in black surrounded me. In the background, I could still hear the crowd chant, "No hate!"

Ironically, all I saw next—and felt—was the pure embodiment of hatred.

Staring at an amorphous mob of faceless shadows, I froze. Suddenly, clenched fists repeatedly struck my face and head from all directions. My right knee buckled from the impact. The masked attackers wore tactical gloves—gloves hardened with fiberglass on the knuckles. It's likely some of them used brass knuckles as well. I put my arms up to surrender, but this only signaled to them to beat me more ferociously. Someone then snatched my camera—my evidence. I desperately tried but failed to hold on to it. The masked thief melted into the crowd, a function of the "black bloc." Another person ran up and kicked me twice in the groin. Someone bashed me on the head from behind with a stiff placard or sign.

The attack left me dazed and bloodied. I was bleeding from my ear and had open gashes all over my face. My eyes were beginning to swell with blood. I thought the beating was over, but next came the hailstorm of "milkshakes," eggs, and other hard objects at my face and head.

The mob roared in laughter as I stumbled away. A crowd of cameramen surrounded and followed me. I thought they were going to offer to help, but they just took photos and video.

"F—king owned, bitch!" shouted a local transsexual antifa militant and a member of the Satanic Portland Antifascists.[1] I walked away, half blinded, to the county courthouse across Lownsdale Square before losing my balance. Later, in the emergency room of the Oregon Health and Science University hospital, I found out my brain was hemorrhaging.

Outside of the Multnomah County Justice Center, the building that houses the Central Police Precinct, the Sheriff's Office, and courtrooms, I was nearly killed by a violent mob. At no point did police intervene to help. Mobile phone footage recorded by Jim Ryan, a news reporter with the *Oregonian*—Portland's newspaper of record—captured part of the beating.

While I was in the emergency room, the video was being watched hundreds of thousands of times on social media. My name began to trend on Twitter across the United States, even though most people had no idea who I was. Even liberal mainstream media outlets like the *New York Times*, the BBC, and CNN could not ignore what happened. In contrast to the narrative Americans had been sold that antifa are merely "anti-fascists," the video showed a mob of mask-clad extremists beating a journalist in the middle of a major American city with impunity. It confirmed what some had been warning for years: antifa is a violent extremist movement that attacks all kinds of targets under the guise of "anti-fascism."

Though my assault that day received national and international attention, I was hardly the only one to be brutally attacked. Adam Kelly, 37, was hit from behind with an overhead swing by several masked militants as he attempted to help an older man being beaten on the ground next to the Pioneer Courthouse. One of Kelly's attackers used a baton to strike him on the head. The impact could actually be heard on video. Kelly's head injury required twenty-five staples to close. He and I were treated in the same emergency department, but we didn't know it at the time. He was lucky to survive.

Gage Halupowski, a 24-year-old Portland resident, was convicted and sentenced for the attack against Kelly. To date, he remains one of the very few antifa extremists in the United States sentenced to prison time. Tellingly, antifa groups refer to him as a "political prisoner."[2]

In total, eight were injured that day. Three, including myself, required hospitalization. Rose City Antifa, the Portland antifa group, claimed responsibility for the attacks.

"The events of this weekend are what we mean by community defense," the organization said in a statement on its website.[3] "This is exactly what should happen when the far-right attempts to invade our town." This was a rare moment of honesty for an antifa organization that otherwise spreads disinformation and propaganda. If it isn't clear yet, violence is a feature, not a bug, of antifa's ideology. In fact, they venerate violence. Since 2015, untold numbers of victims, including other journalists, have been doxed, beaten, robbed, or killed by antifa militants. Few of them receive media attention—or justice.

For whatever reason, the violence on June 29, 2019, in Portland became one of the watershed moments that brought national attention to antifa violence and the left-wing politicians who enabled it despite many people having been victimized before me. For example, two Marine reservists visiting Philadelphia in November 2018 were jumped after being mistaken for Proud Boys by antifa. Alejandro Godinez and Luis Torres, who are Latino, told investigators they were called racial slurs during the unprovoked attack and robbery. Tom Keenan, Thomas Massey, and Joseph Alcoff were later arrested after they were identified in a video recorded earlier in the day at a nearby antifa protest.[4] Alcoff is the son of a feminist professor and worked as a progressive Democratic lobbyist in Washington, DC.[5]

Those attacks flew under the radar at the federal level, but President Donald Trump finally weighed in soon after my attack. "Portland is being watched very closely," Trump wrote on Twitter. "Hopefully the Mayor will be able to properly do his job!"[6]

Part of the city resembled a failing state that day, with masked thugs patrolling the streets openly and freely with weapons. The authorities were unable to secure order and protect citizens per commands that limit police engagement with left-wing protesters and rioters. This has been the norm in the City of Roses.

In fact, the normalization of antifa violence in Portland could be summed up in how a local left-wing journalist described the events of June 29. Even with all the violence, now—*Washington Post* writer Katie Shepherd called it "mostly unremarkable."[7] She was actually right, just not in the way she meant. Political violence involving antifa extremists had become so routine in the city that by 2019 the near-killing of three citizens was considered a banality. But what happened in Portland didn't stay there. Nor did the violence end at severe head injuries. As antifa continue to be whitewashed and ignored and their existence denied, their appeal and membership grow. So does their adherents' willingness for violence. After months of coronavirus lockdowns in early 2020, race riots erupted in May in response to the death of George Floyd during an arrest by Minneapolis police. In the name of Black Lives Matter (BLM) and with the help of antifa, rioters and looters torched buildings, raided stores, and attacked law enforcement in dozens of cities. This resulted in over two dozen deaths.

Despite what was happening before our eyes, left-wing politicians and media denied antifa played a role. House Judiciary Committee chairman Jerrold Nadler (D-NY) called the movement "imagery" during a congressional debate.[8] And even though the public could plainly see masked militants openly planning and carrying out riot operations, we were still told there is "no evidence" of organized antifa.

"Who caused the violence at protests? It wasn't antifa," declared one gaslighting *Washington Post* "fact-checker" analysis, for example.[9]

In 2018, I was one of the few journalists writing about antifa and warning the public about what was happening in Portland. I had only been a journalist for a few years, and my older mentors in the field told me to pick a new beat. "Antifa is an old story. They're irrelevant. Move on," I was told by one trusted editor. Against their advice, I continued writing and speaking about the subject. Thanks to brave editors and producers at the *Wall Street Journal* and Fox News, respectively, my reporting was given a large national audience.

What my mentors failed to see at the time was antifa's sophisticated strategy to destabilize society using propaganda, radicalization, violence, and even electoral politics. It was always wrong to reduce antifa to a ragtag group of street hooligans. Behind their violence is a plan to destroy the nation-state, America in particular, to bring about a revolution that leads to their vision of utopia. In 2020, the country experienced a taste of this when a relatively small group of committed radicals incited and carried out massive damage to life and property in the name of "anti-racism".

ON AUGUST 4, 2020, I gave testimony to the U.S. Congress about the threat antifa poses to American life and liberty. I was invited to speak by Texas Republican senator Ted Cruz, who chairs the Senate Subcommittee on the Constitution. I came with a nonpartisan message. Being a Portlander who has reported extensively on antifa for years and witnessing their daily violence firsthand, I knew that local and federal authorities weren't taking the threat seriously. Not only had it led to preventable deaths, anitfa militants were now openly organizing uprisings from coast to coast.

I knew that the high-profile nature of giving testimony to the Senate meant that I would be subject to another round of death threats. But I couldn't ignore the opportunity to speak with Democrats for once. The threat of antifa cannot be solved through just one party.

Hawaii senator Mazie Hirono, one of the highest-level Asian American politicians, cochairs the subcommittee with Senator Cruz. I wrote my remarks hoping she and her Democratic colleagues would understand, even just a little, that antifa are not simply "anti-fascist" as they claim. I cited evidence from court documents, government press releases, law enforcement, and my own research to show that antifa are violent and seeks to destabilize the United States through domestic terrorism. My comments were ignored by the Democrats. Not one asked me any questions or even acknowledged my presence there. Senator Hirono for her part repeated headlines from the *Guardian* and other leftist sources that erroneously say that antifa have "killed no one."[10] Before the three-hour hearing was over, she stormed out of the room. "I hope this is the end of this hearing, Mr. Chairman, and that we don't have to listen to any more of your rhetorical speeches," Hirono told Senator Cruz when he asked her if she would denounce antifa.[11] At that point, no other Democrats were in the hearing. They had either physically left or logged out if they were attending virtually. A few weeks later, antifa militant Michael Reinoehl went on to kill in Portland.

UNMASKED IS THE end result of years of reporting on antifa, even before I understood what they were. It has taken me on the streets of Portland, Seattle, New York, London, and more. As any good journalist should know, you don't want to become part of the story. However, whether I wanted to or not, antifa decided to make me part of *their* story. After my 2019 beating, I became antifa's public enemy number one. They've sent me death threats, stalked me, and even showed up at my family's home on several occasions. They have threatened to shoot me and to set me on fire. They've released my exact whereabouts in real time on social media. They've threatened my friends. The criminal threats are reported to local police, but no one is ever held accountable.

By 2020, antifa grew to become a near-household name in the United States following months of street violence and property destruction. President Trump moved to have his administration treat them as a domestic terrorist organization after promising to do so for a year. Predictably, this prompted a new wave of countless reports, op-eds, and essays defending or whitewashing antifa.

Few of the people who write about them actually know what this movement is and what its goals are. In fact, misconceptions, misinformation, and disinformation abound about antifa in both left-wing and right-wing media. On the right, antifa are portrayed as street hooligans—violent but also weak, gender-confused "soy" boys and girls. On the left, they are characterized as brave heroes who defend their communities against white supremacists and fascists. Neither side captures what antifa fully are nor the true threat they pose to liberal democracy and the American republic.

So, what exactly are the "antifa," and what do they want? Antifa—pronounced "an-tee-fa" and short for "anti-fascist"—is a relatively new American phenomenon, but their ideology and violent strategies have been honed and refined for decades in Europe. Simply put, antifa are an ideology and movement of radical pan-leftist politics whose adherents are mainly militant anarchist communists or collectivist anarchists. A smaller fraction of them are socialists who organize through political groups like the Democratic Socialists of America and others. Labels aside, their defining characteristics are a militant opposition to free markets and the desire to destroy the United States and its institutions, culture, and history. Contrary to what many on the right believe, they are not liberal, though that does not mean they haven't made inroads in transforming and radicalizing the Democratic Party.

What unites this group of leftists is its opposition to so-called fascism, though importantly, what is defined as fascism is left wide open. This is intentional as it allows antifa to justify all manner of violence and extremism in the name of opposing "fascism." However, not all of its followers participate in violence. In fact, most don't and instead work on delegitimizing liberal democracy and the nation-state through "charity" and relentless propaganda. Since Trump's election win, the manifestation of antifa in the United States and Canada (and to a lesser extent in other Western countries) has mutated into a unique contemporary breed of violent left-wing extremism. Influenced by BLM, intersectionality, and other vogue left-wing theories from academe, American antifa have become a more virulent strain that appeals to the mainstream left.

Antifa are no longer a fringe group of radicals wreaking havoc in a handful of cities in America. They've seen tremendous success through finding fellow travelers in education, journalism, the legal profession, and politics. The United States is being attacked in all directions by a movement few understand or recognize.

The political street violence involving antifa in the United States serves as a harbinger of American society—the canary in the coal mine of our coming disorder—even possible civil war—if we allow their actions and ideology to be further normalized. American media constantly warn us about the rise of right-wing violence and the lethal threat posed by white supremacy. No honest person denies there are indeed violent far-right militants in the United States, as documented by federal law enforcement, but their numbers and influence are grossly exaggerated by biased media. Antifa receive a tiny fraction of the news coverage of the far right, and yet I would argue their increasingly violent tactics and ideology pose just as much, if not more, of a threat to the future of American liberal democracy. In these pages, I will show why.

Through analysis of never-before-seen antifa documents, *Unmasked* reveals some of the key players behind this movement and the strategy they've developed to recruit, train, and radicalize followers and the public. Street violence is only one part of their planned revolution. We ignore or whitewash antifa at liberty's peril.

Antifa brawl with right-wingers in the middle of a street in downtown Portland on June 30, 2018. Photo: Chelly Boufferrache

A tweet by the Colorado Springs Antifa

A Portland bronze statue of George Washinton was toppled by BLM-antifa rioters in June 2020. Photo: Andy Ngo

CHAPTER 1

Insurgency

I N MAY 2020, when much of the American population was still under compulsory stay-at-home orders due to the coronavirus pandemic, Black Lives Matter (BLM), with the aid of antifa, moved into action.

George Floyd's death on May 25, 2020, in the custody of Minneapolis police officers ignited an already volatile anti-police political climate set in place by the recent deaths of two other black men. Antifa groups and accounts on social media played a key role in amplifying false narratives and outright lies about these men in support of BLM.

On May 6, 2020, Indianapolis police shot and killed 21-year-old Dreasjon "Sean" Reed. That day, Reed recorded a livestream of himself fleeing police in a high-speed car chase. The Indianapolis Metropolitan Police Department said they tried to pull him over for reckless driving before he sped off.[12] Reed's Facebook livestream showed him armed with a distinctive gold-and-black pistol during the chase. At some point, Reed pulled over and continued to run on foot; his gun can be seen tucked under his waistband. After an exchange of fire, Reed was shot dead by a police officer, who is also black. Reed's death and edited video clips were used as propaganda to incite anger and hatred online. On the petition website Change.org, a campaign was started to "demand justice" for Reed.

"Yesterday, excessive use of violence ended the life of [an] unarmed man by the name of Sean Reed," the page read.[13] "I, and all who sign this agree that those officers should be charged with murder, because it fits the definition of the word."

The campaign garnered over 100,000 signatures. On Twitter, tweets claiming Reed was unarmed and "murdered in cold blood" went viral. The falsehood was amplified by a network of left-wing influencers with millions of followers, such as teen gun control advocate David Hogg.[14] And per usual, media stories poured fuel on the fire by leaving out key details in news story ledes and printing old photos of Reed rather than recent ones showing him proudly engaging in illegal activities. Even worse, news reports failed to mention that one of his last uploaded videos showed him committing a drive-by shooting with a handgun matching the one he used against police.[15]

Facts be damned, the public narrative was the familiar refrain that an innocent black person had been brutally murdered by racist, bloodthirsty police. For days, demonstrators gathered in Indianapolis to protest law enforcement.[16] Anti-lockdown protesters had been threatened with fines and even jail time by mayors and governors for violating public gathering rules. Yet no one took issue with the massive crowds of people demonstrating in the name of BLM.

The narrative around Reed's death, with the aid of biased media, was used as the groundwork for exploiting American sensitivities on race. On the fringe left, antifa-aligned accounts on social media saw an opportunity to use his death as fodder for police hatred. It worked. Around the same time, activist networks began blasting a short segment of a video that showed Ahmaud Arbery, a 25-year-old black male, being shot by a white father and son vigilante duo in Glynn County, Georgia.

Gregory and Travis McMichael said they suspected Arbery of being a returning burglar in their neighborhood. They accosted Arbery on the street while waiting for police to arrive. Video recorded of the street confrontation showed Arbery rushing in and fighting Travis, who was armed with a shotgun. Arbery is then shot and killed. The incident occurred on February 23, 2020—months earlier—but the release of the video in May and the narrative that Arbery was a jogger who was murdered for being black reignited a national crisis on race and policing.

Though Arbery's death did not directly involve police, Gregory, the father, was a retired law enforcement officer. Local prosecutors did not bring charges against the men, though following the release of the video and street protests, the Georgia Bureau of Investigation arrested the pair on charges of felony murder and aggravated assault. Again, antifa accounts saw an opening to spread disinformation about the case to radicalize the public toward their cause. Photos of a man at a small 2016 Ku Klux Klan march in Georgia were misidentified as Gregory McMichael. The posts circulated in viral posts on Twitter and Facebook, leading Georgia Followers, a popular news and culture site, to tweet the photo and a false news report to its 1.5m followers.[17] (The story was later removed from the site instead of properly noted as being factually incorrect in an editor's note.)

The American public was now primed for mass resistance and violence against law enforcement. Glued to social media due to lockdown orders, all they needed was a reason to get out. That reason came in the death of George Floyd Jr. on May 25, 2020.

Floyd, a 46-year-old black man with an extensive criminal history, died while being arrested by police in Minneapolis after allegedly using counterfeit money. Shocking video recorded at the scene showed Officer Derek Chauvin pressing his knee on Floyd's neck while he repeatedly stated that he couldn't breathe. Three other officers stood nearby.

Floyd became unresponsive and died. The Hennepin County

medical examiner found that he died as a result of the "combined effects of...being restrained by the police, his underlying health conditions and any potential intoxicants in his system."[18] There was no evidence found of traumatic asphyxia or strangulation in the county's autopsy. It was later revealed that Floyd's blood contained a fatal level of fentanyl.[19]

The reaction to the video was swift and unprecedented. Condemnation over the officers' conduct poured in from the political left and right. Within twenty-four hours, all four police officers were fired from the Minneapolis Police Department. Chauvin was charged with third-degree murder (later upgraded to second-degree murder) and second-degree manslaughter. His ex-colleagues, J. Alexander Kueng, Thomas Lane, and Tou Thao, were arrested and charged with aiding and abetting second-degree murder. The Federal Bureau of Investigation and the U.S. Department of Justice announced investigations into Floyd's death.

Though the legal process was moving at lightning speed, others saw Floyd's death as an opportunity to push through an ambitious political agenda to spark uprisings against the state and its institutions. The wall-to-wall coverage of Floyd's death along with online agitations by race-baiters sparked mass protests that devolved into some of the worst rioting seen in Minneapolis's history. From May 26 to 29, the city was convulsed by massive riots that reduced neighborhoods to rubble. But the process, from window breaking to the wholesale looting and destruction of buildings, is not always as organic as it appears. In fact, the riots in Minneapolis and other cities give insight into the workings of antifa's riot plans and how they manipulate large mobs into doing their bidding.

THE FIRST BUILDING to be torched in Minneapolis was the Auto-Zone store on East Lake Street, adjacent to the Third Police Precinct, the site of early violence the previous day. One viral video recorded at the store showed a male dressed head to toe in black breaking windows one by one using a sledgehammer. He was wearing a gas mask and carrying a black umbrella, a tactic appropriated by antifa from Hong Kong protesters to block cameras. He spray-painted "Free shit for everyone zone" on the doors of the AutoZone. According to an affidavit written by an investigator in the Minneapolis Police Department weeks later, the looting and fire that followed "set off a string of fires and looting throughout the precinct and the rest of the city."[20]

Sgt. Erika Christensen wrote: "Until the actions of the person your affiant has been calling 'Umbrella Man,' the protests had been relatively peaceful. The actions of this person created an atmosphere of hostility and tension."[21]

Videos captured at the scene in the evening showed the auto parts store entirely engulfed in flames. Soon after, a Target store in the area was broken into and looted. Rioters were seen sprinting in and leaving with trolleys filled with electronics, shoes, and clothing. Others used hammers to break into cash registers and safes. A woman in a wheelchair who tried to block an exit of the store to slow looters was beaten by a mob and sprayed with a fire extinguisher.

Police did not respond to the scene.

The violence in that part of the city quickly spread to the rest of Minneapolis. Overnight, dozens of businesses were vandalized, looted, and destroyed. An affordable housing unit that was under construction was set on fire, becoming fully engulfed in flames that reached high into the sky. The heat from the fires "melted" nearby cars. By morning, some thirty businesses had been vandalized or destroyed.

But the violence was far from over. Like clockwork, it repeated again even as Mayor Jacob Frey, a demure Democrat, declared a state of emergency in the city on the third day of unrest. O'Reilly's, another auto parts store, was targeted by a small group of masked vandals dressed in black who broke windows. After that, other rioters ransacked and ultimately destroyed the store.

As businesses were looted throughout the city, rioters surrounded the Minneapolis Police Third Precinct. The mob was so large the mayor gave an evacuation order to the officers trying to defend the station. After they fled in vehicles, the mob promptly stormed the building and set it on fire. Some even made it out with stolen police equipment. For hours, the city burned and citizens experienced what true anarchy and chaos looked like. The state could not or would not protect its citizens, leaving business and property owners in particular to fend for themselves.

As violence continued for the fourth day in Minneapolis and began to spread to dozens of other American cities, I was immediately drawn to images of mysterious masked vandals dressed in black breaking windows. In the grand scheme of mass riots, broken windows seem minor, but as noted by the Minneapolis Police affidavit, the act set off a "chain reaction" that led to looting and arson. Think of it as James Wilson and George Kelling's "broken windows theory" in a different context. Antifa know the effect that smashed windows, breached businesses, and fires have on crowd mentality. Each act serves as blood in the water. It can turn protesters into rioters. That's why antifa teach this in their literature that is disseminated widely online and in real life.

In the extreme anarchist literature think tank known as "CrimethInc," one of their most popular manuals is "Why We Break Windows: The Effectiveness of Political Vandalism." The booklet, available free to print as an online PDF file, argues breaking windows is an act of protest against capitalism, white supremacy, and the police, and should be actively practiced:

> To smash a shop window is to contest all the boundaries that cut through this society: black and white, rich and poor, included and excluded. Most of us have become inured to all this segregation, taking such inequalities for granted as a fact of life. Breaking windows is a way to break this silence, to challenge the absurd notion that the social construct of property rights is more important than the needs of the people around us.[22]

If this sounds familiar, it's because in 2020 numerous mainstream left-wing commentators began criticizing the very notion of property rights. "Destroying property, which can be replaced, is not violence," said *New York Times* reporter Nikole Hannah-Jones in a CBS News interview in June 2020.[23] Hannah-Jones won a Pulitzer Prize for her involvement in the error-laden "1619 Project" in the *New York Times Magazine*, which argues that America's true founding is in its enslavement of Africans. BLM cofounder Alicia Garza had earlier stated this sentiment.

"We don't have time to finger-wag at protesters about property. That can be rebuilt. Target will reopen. The stores will reopen. That's assured. What is not assured is our safety and real justice," Garza said in an interview in *New Yorker* magazine in June 2020.[24]

The word "violence" is being systematically remade to conform to their worldview. Looting and arson aren't violence, they argue. And yet physical violence directed at their opponents is also not violence but rather "self-defense."

The CrimethInc manual on breaking windows goes on to explain that taxpaying businesses are fair game to target because that ends up hurting police, who rely on public funding. The intellectualizing of their arguments tries to mask the ruthlessness of their worldview. They don't care whom they harm, what livelihoods they destroy, as long as it furthers their political agenda.

And if the sociopathy of the booklet wasn't clear enough, the anonymous author argues that, at the end of the day, window smashing creates work opportunities for laborers who otherwise would be wasting their time doing something else. "Anyone who truly desires to see an end to property destruction should hasten to bring about the end of property itself. Then, at last, the only reason to break windows would be thrill seeking," the manual states.[25]

In the days after the riots broke out first in Minnesota and then elsewhere, a flurry of headlines sought to discredit Attorney General William Barr and President Trump, who stated that there was some evidence for antifa involvement in the riots.

"As Trump blames antifa, protest records show scant evidence," declared the Associated Press.[26]

"Federal arrests show no sign that antifa plotted protests," echoed a *New York Times* report.[27]

These headlines filtered down through dozens of other reports and into the mouths of left-wing commentators on television. What the writers of these reports seemed not to understand is that antifa is a phantom movement by design. It is leaderless and structured to be functional through small, independent organizations, known as affinity groups, and individuals. Only the ideology needs to be propagated for lone wolves or groups to be inspired. Part of that ideology involves extensive training on "digital security," that is, using encrypted tools, apps, and web browsers to completely evade detection by authorities and others. It is no surprise that scant evidence materialized in the early days of the investigations into accused rioters. Antifa are trained to hide their political affiliations.

As demonstrated with window breaking, it only takes a small group of people—even just one person—to set off a chain reaction. It makes sense that the overwhelming majority of those arrested at random are not aligned with antifa ideology. They don't need to be in order to play a role in the riots. The smashing of businesses' windows serves as an open invitation to opportunist looters and rioters to wreak havoc. That's the genius of antifa's riot strategy: they only have to light the match.

Uprisings

While many recoiled at the shocking scenes of violence in Minnesota, a segment of the American population expressed open support for the riots. The Minnesota Freedom Fund (MFF), a far-left organization, raked in over $35 million in donations with the help of celebrities like Drake, Chrissy Teigen, and Steve Carell.[28] (The MFF later admitted to only spending $200,000 on bail bonds.[29])

Antifa groups across the United States expressed support for the Minnesota riots. "Solidarity from NYC to all the real folx in Minneapolis tonight!" tweeted New York City Antifa on May 27, 2020.[30] Antifa Seven Hills, an antifa group based in Richmond, Virginia, tweeted out donation links for protesters and rioters in Minneapolis.[31] The Portland chapter of the Youth Liberation Front (YLF), a new antifa group, tweeted, "From Portland to Minneapolis, for youth liberation! We will see you on the streets."[32] Their tweet included emojis of a black flag and fire.

Seeing the resounding success of the riots in Minnesota and given the support from media elites, these and other antifa groups across the United States began to organize their own "solidarity" riots. On May 28, 2020, the Colorado Springs Anti-Fascists tweeted an announcement that it was organizing three days of "solidarity actions" at the state capitol.

"You DON'T have an excuse not to go. If you're watching the riot porn, you owe Minneapolis radicals a favor by standing in solidarity with them. #ACAB," they tweeted. Similarly, antifa in Portland plastered posters across the city announcing a "I can't breathe" protest for May 29 also in "solidarity with Minneapolis." The YLF promoted the event on Twitter and picked up additional steam with promotion on an antifa blog named *It's Going Down*.[33] "Solidarity" sounds benign, but it is a far-left dog whistle for repeating the same direct action. In this case, violence.

The choice to call the violence in Minneapolis "riot porn" also provides a window into the antifa worldview. That's how they view the destruction, looting, and carnage that destroy lives and result in deaths. In Minneapolis, an alleged looter was shot dead by a pawn shop owner whose business suffered serious damaged during the riots. Two months later, a charred body was discovered in the ashes of another business that was burned down during the riots.

In Oakland, an officer with the Federal Protective Service was killed while protecting federal property. Dave Patrick Underwood,

53, died and a second officer was injured in a drive-by shooting. Steven Carrillo, who is Hispanic, was later charged for the shootings. He is accused of being part of the boogaloo movement, a fringe anti-government movement wrongly described as "far-right" in the media. In fact, boogaloo followers have much in common with antifa in that they seek to accelerate mass anti-government violence in order to destabilize the state.

In St. Louis, Missouri, David Dorn, a 77-year-old retired police captain, was killed by looters. In Davenport, Iowa, Italia Marie Kelly, 22, was shot in the back and killed after leaving a protest. Her younger sister recorded an emotional Facebook video blaming protesters for the violence. "A protester shot my sister! A protester!" she cried. "You are so mad at the police that you are hurting everyone else."[34] After fourteen days of riots, there were at least nineteen dead.[35] Most of the victims were black.

The scale of the destruction to neighborhoods in Minneapolis and other cities after each night of rioting is truly difficult to overstate. Videos recorded the morning after showed scenes reminiscent of Syria or Yemen. In Minneapolis, entire buildings laid in waste on the ground, leaving behind burned-out frames. But antifa members salivated at these scenes of mayhem. By their own admission, they wanted the fires to continue.

"We are on the verge of a global revolution that can finally rid the world of police, along with the systems of anti-blackness and capitalism they uphold," tweeted the New York chapter of the Revolutionary Abolitionist Movement (RAM) on June 2, 2020. The group identifies as a revolutionary anarchist organization "fighting for a stateless, anti-capitalist, and prison-free world."[36]

On September 4, 2020, they spearheaded a march through lower Manhattan carrying a banner that read "Death to America." They then smashed the windows of numerous properties and businesses.[37] Like antifa elsewhere, they were dressed in black bloc and used large umbrellas to shield one another when they were vandalizing property. Within a short time, they did

$100,000 in damages. One of the eight arrested at the riot was from Portland.

Though lesser known and without "antifa" in the name, RAM is in fact an antifa group. It has even articulated its political agenda in ten points—the clearest articulation published by any antifa organization.[38] Point one: "Liberation will be won by any means necessary." "By any means necessary" is adopted by many extreme left-wing groups as a dog whistle to their members that violence is a necessary part of their agenda. Point two: "We will destroy the state, police, military, corporations, and all those who run the American plantation." Antifa and far-left groups intentionally use words related to slavery to radicalize those sympathetic to their message. They believe that Americans, particularly nonwhites, are still "enslaved" because of work, capitalism, and the criminal justice system. Points three through nine dictate that they will abolish free markets, property ownership, the rule of law, and national borders. But the most chilling part is the final step: "Militant networks will defend our revolutionary communities. Liberation begins where America dies."

Before May 2020, I never thought antifa could ever come close to achieving this goal. I am asked often in interviews: "Do you think antifa will win?" I always say no—if winning means their ultimate goal of abolishing America. The United States has the strongest military in the world, a robust rule of law, and a strong civil society. If Yemen is on one end as a failed state, the United States is on the other. And yet, as the riots broke out in late May, I began to wonder if I needed to reevaluate my position. For the first time in my life, I witnessed major American metropolises struggle and fail with protecting the most basic right of citizens: the right to life and property. For days on end, those victimized by rioters never received help even as they repeatedly called 911. Further events in Seattle, Portland, and elsewhere demonstrate the balkanization of geographic areas into "no-go zones" for police and outsiders.

The riots in Minneapolis and other cities in May were also used to set a new precedent, a new normal for America. Anytime there is a police-involved shooting of a black person, no matter the circumstances, the response will be mass violence.

On June 12, 2020, Rayshard Brooks, a 27-year-old black man in Atlanta with a criminal history, passed out drunk in the drive-through lane of a Wendy's restaurant. Two responding officers from the Atlanta Police Department (APD), Garrett Rolfe and Devin Brosnan, woke Brooks and spoke cordially with him for about forty minutes. When Brooks's blood alcohol level showed he was intoxicated, the officers attempted to handcuff him. Brooks brawled with the officers and stole a taser from Rolfe. Brooks fired the taser at the officer before he was shot. Brooks died at hospital. The following day, Rolfe was fired by APD and Brosnan was placed on leave. Despite Brooks assaulting police, stealing a weapon, attempting an escape, and firing a taser at one of the officers, Rolfe was charged with murder, five counts of aggravated assault, and other charges by the district attorney. Brosnan was charged with aggravated assault. If Rolfe is convicted, he may face the death penalty in Georgia.

Like clockwork, Brooks was made into the next BLM and antifa martyr, even though he had an extensive criminal history that included domestic violence, theft, child cruelty, and more.[39] One day after the shooting, BLM rioters amassed at the Wendy's where Brooks was killed. They burned down the restaurant and set fire to cars in the area. For weeks, they shut down nearby streets using makeshift barriers. Some of the rioters patrolled their zone armed with rifles. Mayor Keisha Lance Bottoms and the city tolerated the lawlessness in the name of racial justice. And tragically, as in the George Floyd riots, another innocent person was killed. This time, it was a child. On July 4, 2020, 8-year-old Secoriea Turner was shot and killed in a car that was attempting to turn around in the occupied protest area near the Wendy's.[40] Julian Conley, a black male, is the suspect in the homicide.

By mid-August 2020, mass BLM and antifa violence broke out yet again in the Midwest. In Kenosha, Wisconsin, a former auto-manufacturing center, Jacob Blake was shot by police after fighting with cops in a residential area. He had shrugged off being hit with a taser round and reached inside his vehicle, where there was a knife. This was all caught on camera. Blake, who is black, had a warrant issued for his arrest by the Wisconsin Circuit Court for a felony sex crime and other charges related to domestic abuse. The criminal complaint for that May 2020 incident accuses Blake of raping a woman with his hand in front of her child.[41] According to police scanner audio on August 23, officers responded to the same woman's residence after she called 911 and said Blake was at her home again. Blake's criminal history also includes assaulting police, resisting arrest, carrying a firearm while intoxicated, and use of a dangerous weapon.[42] Even though he survived the shooting, the response was again mass carnage and looting in the streets of Kenosha. Democratic vice presidential candidate Kamala Harris later visited Blake and said she was "proud of him."[43]

When rioting first broke out at the scene of Blake's shooting, rioters threw rocks and bricks at police, hitting one in the head and knocking him out. The city declared a state of emergency, but it did nothing to quell the violence. Masked BLM-antifa rioters set the Kenosha County Courthouse and nearby city dumpster trucks on fire. The sky was bright from flames and billowing smoke. Rioters then set a car lot on fire. Those flames spread next door to the Bradford Community Church, a Unitarian Universalist church that displayed "Black Lives Matter" on its signage.

Businesses were looted through the night, and numerous other buildings, including a museum, suffered damage. One shocking video clip recorded by independent journalist Drew Hernandez showed rioters armed on the street stopping a Sheriff's Department armored personnel carrier. Multiple gunshots can then be heard.[44] Other video showed rioters picking up large chunks of concrete from the group to smash businesses and building windows.

The following day, Wisconsin governor Tony Evers, a Democrat, called in the National Guard. A county curfew went into immediate effect. But even that wasn't enough. By nightfall, rioters, who were joined by antifa black bloc militants carrying umbrellas and shields, gathered near the courthouse and began attacking police with projectiles and firework explosives.

Rioters moved throughout the city, looting and smashing up a furniture store, a used car lot, and other businesses. As in Minneapolis, rioters burned down buildings after they were done robbing them. Among buildings torched to the ground were the Wisconsin Department of Corrections and the Danish Brotherhood Lodge. Elijah Schaffer, a conservative YouTube journalist who documents protests around the United States, says he instantly recognized antifa in the Kenosha riots.

"Black bloc were present in significant numbers," Schaffer says.[45] They waved an antifa flag and carried out shield formation tactics he witnessed in other cities. "Black bloc was largely responsible for lighting the Wisconsin Department of Corrections building on fire, which is now rubble. They broke off the wood barrier on the back door as well as started a fire near the front."

Hernandez, one of the first journalists on the scene of the Kenosha riots, says he also recognized antifa. "It was the same tactics as Portland."[46] Antifa rioters dragged around stolen trash bins to start fires in the street. He says antifa militants enticed black youth to participate in violence by giving them supplies to start fires.

On the third night of rioting, it became deadly. A 17-year-old allegedly shot three people, killing two. Footage recorded by Hernandez and others showed Kyle Rittenhouse, who was armed with a semiautomatic rifle, being chased and attacked by several men. Rittenhouse appears to have shot the first man chasing him outside an auto store, killing him instantly. An armed mob then chased the teen down a street. When he tripped and fell to the ground, several people charged at him but were quickly shot in succession, on the videos. One masked man who was hitting him with a skateboard was shot in the chest. He fell over lifeless and was the second to die. Another man armed with a pistol rushed toward the teen. Rittenhouse shot him in the upper arm, causing a huge chunk of flesh to be blown off.

Police responded minutes later after the shooting was already over. The teen shooting suspect was arrested the next day and charged with first-degree intentional homicide.

BEFORE OUR EYES, antifa and BLM-antifa were burning city after city. People died needlessly. Livelihoods were destroyed overnight. Those who said that these organizations could never achieve their goals in any significant way (myself included at one point) underestimated the speed at which antifa can work. With the momentum building, extremists began traveling to different cities.

One of them was Matthew Banta, a confirmed antifa militant connected to the Fox Valley Antifa group of northeastern Wisconsin. Using several monikers, such as "Commander Red," Banta posted masked photos of himself engaging in antifa activities in Wisconsin. In the photos, he wears patches that have the insignia of antifa's two flags logo.[47] In early August 2020, Banta was part of a group of antifa who marched in Waupaca, Wisconsin. There, he allegedly aimed his loaded semiautomatic rifle at an officer before brawling with him and causing injuries.[48] Photographs of Banta's arrest show he was wearing an antifa patch.[49] He was quickly released on a $10,000 cash bond for the felony charges. By the end of the month, Banta was in Green Bay, Wisconsin, at another violent BLM-antifa protest. Police say he brought a flamethrower, military-grade smoke grenades, fireworks, and antifa propaganda to the downtown protest, which was declared an unlawful assembly.[50] Banta was with a group of people who were armed with bats. He was charged with obstructing an officer and two felony counts of bail jumping. Within less than forty-eight hours, he was bailed out again.

Banta wasn't the only one who traveled around Wisconsin in response to the Jacob Blake shooting. Of the 175 arrested in Kenosha after a week of deadly unrest, 102 had addresses in other cities.[51] Some of those people included extremists from the

Pacific Northwest. Riot Kitchen, a Seattle group that provides food and supplies to rioters, drove a minivan, truck, and school bus to Kenosha. They were arrested by local and federal police. In their vehicles, officers found riot gear, illegal commercial-grade fireworks, controlled substances, and full gasoline canisters.[52] Riot Kitchen was one of the pop-up antifa mutual aid groups I encountered when I was in Seattle in June 2020.[53] In the largest city in the Pacific Northwest, militant antifa networks actually created their own separatist revolutionary commune. In a six-block zone close to downtown, far-left activists occupied an area where they said America ceased to exist. The Capitol Hill Autonomous Zone, or CHAZ, had its own declared territorial borders and private militia on guard.

A National Lawyers Guild volunteer wears records police at a Portland antifa riot in 2018.
Photo: Andy Ngo

In Seattle, I was pointed out in a crowd. Photo: Andy Ngo

CHAPTER 2

The World's Newest Nation

O N JUNE 8, 2020, staff and officers of the Seattle Police Department (SPD) frantically loaded what they could from their East Precinct onto cars and a rented moving truck. The East Precinct is located in the heart of the Capitol Hill neighborhood in Seattle, a densely packed business and residential area popular with artists, leftists, and the city's LGBTQ community.

For days, the neighborhood was marred by scenes of intense violence by rioters intent on overtaking the East Precinct similar to what was done to the Third Precinct in Minneapolis. Night after night, hundreds of antifa and BLM militants lined the streets, throwing rocks, concrete chunks, and incendiary devices at officers, leading to multiple injuries.[54] By now, police were banned from using tear gas to disperse rioters. A few days prior, Police Chief Carmen Best relented to political pressure from the Mayor's Office to ban the SPD from using the crowd control tool despite its effectiveness. Mayor Jenny Durkan, a Democrat and former U.S.

Attorney in Washington state appointed by Barack Obama, had given numerous concessions to the far left in the wake of George Floyd's death.

A week and a half prior, on May 30, 2020 multiple SPD cruisers were smashed and set on fire by rioters dressed in black bloc. In the chaos, some of the rioters stole weapons, including AR-15s, from the vehicles. There were no police in sight. Harrowing footage recorded at the scene showed a security guard for a local Fox News affiliate charging in with his handgun to disarm one of the militants who stole a rifle. The unnamed Marine Corps veteran did this twice, successfully taking back the stolen rifles from two black bloc militants.

Despite the ultraviolence of the Seattle riots, police were prohibited from using the best tool they had for crowd control: CS gas. Also known as tear gas, CS gas is used by law enforcement agencies around the world. As soon as one is exposed to the gas, which is dispersed from canisters, the eyes, nose, throat, and skin experience intense irritation. Through the course of my protest and riot reporting, I have been exposed to it at various times and intensities. I describe the feeling as walking into a plume of pepper. Each breath brings more pain. Fortunately, the extreme discomfort and irritation are temporary—the effects usually clear within about twenty minutes of leaving the area. It is favored by law enforcement because it works extremely well at clearing crowds and has a low chance of actual bodily injury compared to other tools, like batons. But the SPD were now banned from using it. Although a federal judge later suspended the ordinance, the directive from the city effectively prohibited its use. The consequences for police were severe: they suffered broken bones, eye injuries, and burns from rocks and IEDs thrown by mobs of rioters.

No longer able to push back the nightly onslaught from black-clad rioters in Capitol Hill and facing pressure from the mayor's office to pull back, Seattle police boarded up and abandoned the East Precinct. Within hours, militant BLM and antifa protesters declared ownership of most of the neighborhood. They named their new six-block territory the Capitol Hill Autonomous Zone or CHAZ. (It was later renamed by some as Capitol Hill Occupied Protest, or CHOP.)

No laws or rules applied here except for one: "No cops allowed."

Against all logic and reason, CHAZ was allowed by the city to run its course for more than three weeks. It was a large-scale experiment in anarchy, chaos, and brute-force criminality. Various Occupy-type protests have occurred across the United States since the original occupation in Manhattan in 2011, but CHAZ is noteworthy for taking control of such a large and densely populated territory. Toward the end of its twenty-four-day run, there were numerous assaults, robberies, an attempted rape, six shootings, and two homicides.

When the SPD evacuated from the station on June 8, 2020, masked protesters stole city property—barricades, fencing, and more—to create makeshift barriers. These barriers became the official walls around CHAZ. A movement that has border abolishment at the core of its ideology immediately set up its own border to keep out outsiders. To fortify their barricades, armed volunteer allies moved in. They operated as a private militia complete with their own uniforms.

"We need more people with guns at the CHAZ," tweeted Seattle Antifacists.[55] It received hundreds of retweets. Many of those who showed up wore patches to signal they were part of the Puget Sound John Brown Gun Club. The far-left militia-type organization is named after radical slavery-era abolitionist John Brown. It is a regional offshoot of the Redneck Revolt, a far-left militia. Conservative investigative media group Project Veritas infiltrated the North Carolina chapter of Redneck Revolt in 2018. An undercover journalist caught the group preparing for revolutionary armed conflict.[56] These groups provide volunteer armed security for antifa and BLM events. In 2019, a member of the John Brown Gun Club carried out a firebombing attack on an Immigration and Customs

Enforcement (ICE) facility in Tacoma, Washington. He was killed by police.

Despite the group's link to violent extremism, its armed members were celebrated in the CHAZ for "protecting" the residents. On the first night that police withdrew from Capitol Hill, masked militants harassed and assaulted the press. Brandi Kruse, a reporter with local news station Q13, was accosted and hit with an umbrella. One of the people who surrounded her was Nicholas James Armstrong, a transsexual antifa militant who uses the pseudonym "Nikki Jameson." I recognized Armstrong immediately because she had threatened me for months online and at one point tried to rally people to my physical location when I was grocery shopping in Portland. Using numerous monikers like "@WABlackFlag," Armstrong tweets extremist content in support of antifa. In January 2020, she wrote: "We can't wait till someone gets sick of this guy's [Andy Ngo] shit and rearranges his face proper. It's inevitable really but the anticipation is killing us."[57]

In 2019 Armstrong was legally barred from owning dangerous weapons, including guns, in King County, where Seattle is.[58] Despite that, she was one of the armed security at CHAZ. I saw her patrolling the zone with a revolver on her hip.[59]

In Portland, I made the decision to go to CHAZ. There's a lot of reporting one can do from a distance away, but at some point, it requires being on the ground. But I was scared. Terrified, actually. Ever since I was beat by antifa in June 2019, one of the debilitating psychological consequences is anxiety in crowds. I had never suffered from enochlophobia, a fear of crowds, but everything changed after the attack. For my own safety, I stopped documenting antifa riots and gatherings. I hated giving antifa what they wanted—fear—but they've made it very clear they want to beat me again and this time finish the job.

But a friend of mine urged me to go. CHAZ was spread out over six blocks. This was a large chunk of territory in contrast to the small, densely packed antifa riot zones in Portland. I thought about it and decided I couldn't live in perpetual terror. I packed up a small suitcase filled with random black bloc–style clothing and departed for Seattle.

When I arrived and made my way past one of the "checkpoints," a few of the guards looked at me. My heart sank with each step I took. I knew that if I was interrogated and my cover was blown, I would receive no help from police or anyone else. A source in the SPD had already warned me that they were instructed to stay out of CHAZ. I'd asked him, "What if there's an emergency inside?" He replied that the victim would have to come out or be "brought out" for help. And just as quickly as the guards looked at me, they looked away. I was fully masked up in black bloc in the summer heat, so they viewed me as one of their own. I walked farther into the fortressed autonomous zone. A sign posted on one of the barriers read, "You are now leaving the USA."

In the week I spent undercover at CHAZ, I was able to observe the operations that sustained the chaos for weeks. Although I wasn't privy to the innermost details of "comrades" who'd been vetted, as leaders and organizers, I was trusted enough for them to occasionally let their guard down in conversations. In many ways, being at CHAZ was like being among jihadists. To each other, they showed a lot of care and camaraderie in the form of mutual aid, and compassion but opponents to their political agenda needed to be destroyed.

While there were many kinks in running their so-called autonomous zone (no running water was an issue), what was clear were the dedication and training some of the organizers had for "safety." This was most visible in the security apparatus, which was responsible not just for providing armed guard at checkpoints but also for "de-escalating" fights and responding to emergencies. In short, they operated a lot like police but without professional training, or accountability.

The head of CHAZ's security, at least for part of the time, at night was a short female called Creature. All the security volunteers used monikers when referring to one another. She wore a white helmet to be easily identifiable in crowds. Creature and the rest of her team communicated using walkie-talkie-type devices and earpieces. They were each assigned across various zones within CHAZ. Some of them openly carried weapons like rifles, handguns, batons, or knives. When I saw Creature, she was responding to a health crisis of one of CHAZ's residents.

On a street intersection just outside one of the border checkpoints, an inconsolable, screaming woman sat on the ground. CHAZ security wanted to move her so that their vehicle could pass through the road. In fact, these medical crises became quite common at CHAZ as vagrants and others flocked to the zone's tent encampment where free food was provided. Another person had allegedly overdosed earlier in the week and was transported to hospital by an ambulance.

Before Creature could get a handle on the screaming woman, she received another urgent call on her walkie-talkie. I couldn't hear what was said, but she promptly left the area to rush to another part of CHAZ. I tried following her, but she melted into the crowd. At nighttime, brawls between residents were common. Security often tried to act as mediators, but they were usually unsuccessful.

The security team's operating base was in the open-air eating section of the Rancho Bravo Tacos restaurant, where they had set up a large tent. The business seemingly allowed or tolerated CHAZ security to set up camp there in exchange for peace. Signs posted all over the base declared, "NO PHOTOS. NO VIDEOS." A sign next to it listed Venmo names for cash donations for "medical and food supplies." Another sign listed the contact information for the National Lawyers Guild, a far-left legal group that provides pro bono help for militant leftists and antifa.

Though CHAZ claimed to have no rules, what quickly developed was a complex code of conduct that varied from area to area within the zone and even with the time of day. For example, those in the garden area, who were mostly white, needed to make sure they did not "recolonize" the space. Signs around the gardens reminded people of this. There was even a separate garden for "black and Indigenous folks" after concerns arose over there being too many whites in the area. The gardens featured residents' attempts at growing herbs and vegetables. Though freshly planted, most of the plants had wilted within a day or two.

On the outside, reports from legacy media outlets focused heavily on the alleged "block party" atmosphere of the occupation, repeating a talking point from Mayor Durkan. "The Capitol Hill Autonomous Zone #CHAZ is not a lawless wasteland of anarchist insurrection—it is a peaceful expression of our community's collective grief and their desire to build a better world," she tweeted on June 11, 2020.[60] Durkan along with Governor Jay Inslee, both Democrats, had gone to great lengths to emphasize the "peaceful" nature of the occupation. In a CNN interview with Chris Cuomo, Durkan infamously said CHAZ could be a "summer of love."[61]

Of course, when media crews arrived at the gates of CHAZ during the day, this might have been believable. In the daylight hours, they would have seen people having barbecues in the street. People would bring their children to make street art. Others walked their dogs. Ben and Jerry's even set up a truck that passed out free ice cream scoops. Left-wing news site *Daily Beast* published a report by Kelly Weill headlined, "Local Businesses Love the 'Domestic Terror' Zone in Seattle, Actually."[62] It claimed to authoritatively "debunk" President Trump's claim that CHAZ was run by "domestic terrorists" by interviewing a few select business owners who were neutral or supportive of the occupation.

For sure, there was some support by locals for the occupiers. CHAZ's Little Big Burger, a fast-food chain, changed its toilet door code to "1312," a dog whistle for antifa's "ACAB" slogan. (Each number corresponds to a letter in the alphabet.) But many others— I would argue the majority—were silenced through fear and intimidation. At night, a whole different side of CHAZ emerged when the media crews and outside visitors left.

Because there was no agreed-upon leadership in CHAZ—which

was intentional—those who naturally rose to the top did so through force or intimidation. For example, Seattle-area rapper Raz Simone (real name Solomon Simone) patrolled CHAZ on some nights with an armed entourage that functioned as a sort of mini-militia. Some in the media dubbed him the "warlord" of CHAZ. Simone, originally from Georgia, has a criminal record stemming from charges related to cruelty to a child and other offenses.[63] He became infamous for conducting his patrols while carrying a semiautomatic rifle and sidearm. One livestream video recorded Simone handing another male a semiautomatic rifle from the trunk of a car.[64] Another video recorded him assaulting a cameraman.

Simone relished in the media attention but also rejected the violent depictions of him. "I'm not a Terrorist Warlord. Quit spreading that false narrative," he tweeted on June 10, 2020. "The world has NEVER been ready for a strong black man. We have been peaceful and nothing else. If I die don't let it be in vain."[65]

Not everyone in CHAZ recognized Simone's police-like presence, but no one was willing to stand up to him and his group. For one, the optics of confronting a black male in a space for "black lives" would have been problematic.

While CHAZ was ostensibly created to be an explicitly "anti-racist" zone, it ended up segregating along racial lines. Most of CHAZ's black residents and black visitors did not follow antifa's anarchist-communist ideology. Some actively took issue with antifa's destruction and vandalism of the space. The white anarchist, socialist, and communist radicals mostly stayed together in their spaces. As for Simone's disputed leadership, there were severe consequences to those perceived as challengers or threats. Independent Los Angeles–based conservative journalist Kalen D'Almeida recorded Simone and his armed crew having a meeting shortly after midnight in June. He was spotted filming with his phone by one of Simone's men. That man assaulted him and demanded he turn over his mobile device.[66] When D'Almeida refused, Simone's entourage tried to drag him to the security tent at the taco restaurant. D'Almeida identified one of his assailants as DeJuan Young. Young later became one of CHAZ's shooting victims in a different dispute. He was never charged or arrested.

"He repeated himself several times, 'You're going to hand over your phone or I'm going to knock you the fuck out and take it from you,'" D'Almeida said. D'Almeida escaped by hiding in a construction site outside CHAZ until police responded to his 911 call. "I ran from the autonomous zone and multiple people attempted to drag me back to their interrogation tent for questioning." I saw D'Almeida soon after the assault. His jacket was filthy, and he was rattled. He was lucky to make it out of CHAZ with only minor scrapes and bruising. Other journalists were also attacked at CHAZ.

Dan Springer, a reporter with Fox News, was trapped in his car and surrounded by rioters who jumped on the vehicle. On another occasion, he was followed and kicked out of CHAZ. As much as CHAZ was an experiment in anarchy and chaos, it was also a successful experiment in propaganda making. What journalists were allowed to record was heavily controlled by the residents there. For example, in one instance a black man carried an American flag through the zone. He was immediately accosted and followed by a large mob, including masked black bloc antifa, who shouted racist invectives at him. "Race traitor! Race traitor" one man yelled repeatedly on a bullhorn. "Fox News will use this," another person yelled after rioters tried to steal his flag. This became a relatively common refrain in CHAZ anytime fights broke out. CHAZ supporters were not interested in reality. They wanted the media to broadcast to the world a fabricated utopia.

THOSE UNFORTUNATE ENOUGH TO have homes within CHAZ had no say over their new overlords. Residents discreetly voiced their concerns to local media. Some moved out temporarily. There were reports of gunshots and "screams of terror" at night.[67]

On one day I was there, a resident inside an apartment building came out twice to ask protesters to leave the alleyway where the apartment entrance is. They brushed him off. The alley had been severely vandalized with graffiti and extremist messages. It also houses a back entrance to the police East Precinct. At night, volunteers guarded the alley after antifa expressed a desire to break inside the precinct to burn it down. According to the police chief, there were "credible threats" to burn down the building. It was later reported that she was briefed on intelligence from the FBI.[68]

Business owners, however, did not have the luxury of leaving on a whim. Every business and property inside CHAZ was vandalized with graffiti. Most messages said some variation of "ACAB," "Black Lives Matter," or "George Floyd," but other messages called for the murder of police. These were the least of their problems, however.

Faizel Khan, the owner of Cafe Argento, told the *New York Times*: "They barricaded us all in here."[69] He didn't dare speak out to media until weeks after CHAZ's demise. "[T]hey were sitting in lawn chairs with guns." His testimony to the paper comports with what I witnessed myself. Though there were thousands in CHAZ during the day, actual business was incredibly slow. Customer traffic was severely impacted from the street blockades. People could only travel in and out by foot. CHAZ residents had no need to purchase food or drink given that there were more than a dozen "free" food stations across the zone. Donations from outsiders were dropped off around the clock, and people gifted so many pizza deliveries that CHAZ residents began turning down offers of free pizza slices.

IN THE EARLY HOURS OF JUNE 14, 2020, a hip-hop dance party in the middle of CHAZ was disrupted when someone announced that a fellow resident was being held "at gunpoint." The man rallied the crowd, and within seconds, everyone ran after him. After several blocks of running, we arrived at Car Tender, an auto repair shop. Within minutes, the mob rushed the gate of the business, breaking it easily. They threatened to ransack and destroy the business. The rumor of someone being held at gunpoint turned out to be baseless. The business's security had detained Richard Hanks, 21, who allegedly broke inside and was trying to start a fire. Jason Rantz, a Seattle-based conservative radio host and journalist, interviewed the business owners.

"The son, Mason, told me they called 911 over a dozen times and they refused to send officers to come pick Hanks [the suspect] up because SPD was told they couldn't go into the CHOP zone," Rantz says. "Mason told me over 100 people, several armed, showed up outside their business yelling at them to turn Hanks over or they'd burn the business down. They tore down the fencing around the building and stormed the yard so Mason and his dad ended up releasing Hanks to the crowd."

By miracle, bloodshed was narrowly averted. A large team of CHAZ volunteers successfully de-escalated the explosive situation by forming a human chain. It was the only time I witnessed CHAZ volunteers actually ending imminent conflict. Most of the time, rioters gave into their base instincts and were uncontrollable. For example, a street preacher was pinned to the ground during one day and forcibly "deported."

Though mass violence was averted the night of the break-in at Car Tender, the business's address was put on a list on the Cop Blaster website, which purports to track police brutality and "snitches." His shop has been subject to frequent harassment and threats ever since. A private security firm that volunteered to help the business later said they found a cache of weapons, including a semiautomatic rifle and loaded magazines, hidden in a nearby bush.[70]

ONE GLARING BLIND SPOT in the mainstream media coverage of CHAZ was how the space gave platform to violent extremist ideologies. Reports about CHAZ's political agenda focused shallowly on "racial justice" and "defunding the police" rather than its explicit calls to kill cops and overthrow the government. Hundreds of graffiti messages and images lined the zone showing dead pigs wearing police hats.

"No work. No cops. End this stupid fucking world," read one message. "Voting keeps you tame. All politicians are the same," read another. Around CHAZ, antifa had also marked their territory. The red-and-black flag of anarchist-communism was painted on several buildings. There were also stickers plastered around for the "Anti-Fascist Action" group. I even saw Rose City Antifa member Luis Marquez with his friends at CHAZ. For those who ignored the ubiquitous graffiti, they could also read some of the posters and signs. "COVID-19 is the virus. Capitalism is the pandemic," declared one sign posted around CHAZ. One large handwritten poster stated "Death to capitalism!" It blamed capitalism for racism and poverty.

Political groups also moved in to capitalize on the opportunity to recruit new members. The Democratic Socialists of America (DSA) featured prominently via a booth. The DSA has been given a veneer of mainstream respectability with the popular rise of Sen. Bernie Sanders and Congresswoman Alexandria Ocasio-Cortez, two politicians endorsed by the party. But reading their manifesto makes clear they are traditional socialists with the explicit agenda of "abolishing capitalism."[71] Another group that set up in CHAZ was the Seattle Revolutionary Socialists, who share a similar agenda to the DSA but are more explicit about their regime change ambitions. Tellingly, there was no Democratic Party presence at CHAZ. As leftward as the Democrats have swung in reaction to Trump, the party is still viewed as too moderate for the revolutionaries who want the abolishment of police, capitalism, and the United States itself. They mean it when they chant: "No Trump, no wall. No U.S.A. at all!"

Beyond political parties, extremists set up tables where they distributed extremist agitprop, literature, and instruction manuals printed from anarchist think tanks or zine collectives. By the end of the day, they'd all be given out to anyone who walked by, including children and youth. In one booklet titled "Blockade, Occupy, Strike Back," instructions are given on how to use human shields against police and how to make rudimentary "bombs" using light bulbs and paint.[72]

"A large crowd, especially of 'ordinary, everyday people,' is our first line of defense against a police attack," the manual reads. "If the police build barricades, the crowd will be between us and the cops, rather than outside police lines." As riots continued in Portland and elsewhere in the following months, antifa militants used these instructions in their riot formations. Additionally, light bulb paint "bombs" were routinely used to attack police.[73] They primarily served the purpose of obscuring cops' vision. Those who don't wear riot gear are cut by the shattered glass.

Another booklet given out at CHAZ was titled "Against the Police and the Prison World They Maintain."[74] It features short essays on why police, capitalism, and the state must be destroyed by any means necessary, including through violence. One section explains how the media are enemies used to "pacify" revolutionaries.

"Our contempt for the media is inextricable from our hatred of this entire world," the booklet reads. Attacks on journalists who were accused of not toeing the line were commonplace in CHAZ, and generally any event organized by the far left. They justify it by claiming "self-defense" to protect their identities from being unmasked through photos or video footage.

Another booklet distributed at the table stood out for its front cover artwork: a stark black-and-white image of a balaclava with the title, "Accomplices Not Allies."[75] The manual lists the problems of having "allies," for example, academics and nonprofits, in the movement who are unwilling to participate in criminal direct action.

AS CHAZ CONTINUED INTO its second week, pleas from those who live and work inside Capitol Hill were ignored by the mayor and city council. Even subtle public jabs from the now former police chief Carmen Best were ignored. Best stated that police response times in the area had "more than tripled" because the SPD was down a station for a large area of the city. What was previously a five-minute response time for emergencies was now taking up to eighteen minutes.

"Emergency calls, which often means somebody's being assaulted, sometimes it's a rape, sometimes it's a robbery, but something bad is happening if it's a top priority call, and we're not able to get there," she told media at the time.[76]

Not only did the city of Seattle refuse to restore order, they actually provided periodic upgrades to CHAZ. On June 16, 2020, the city brought in concrete street blockades that also doubled as graffiti canvases. The city maintained cleaning services, wash stations, and portable toilets for the occupiers. Despite claiming to be an "autonomous zone," CHAZ was a welfare state parasitizing off Seattle taxpayers.

A few days after CHAZ's establishment, an arsonist attempted to make good on the threat to burn down the East Precinct. On June 12, 2020, a person was recorded on CCTV pouring an accelerant on debris on the side of the precinct and setting it on fire. Others in the area ran in and quickly put out the flames using extinguishers. They could be heard on video telling someone to move the gas can. Thirty-five-year-old Isaiah Willoughby was later arrested and charged by federal authorities following an investigation by the Bureau of Alcohol, Tobacco, Firearms and Explosives (ATF).[77] Willoughby had run for Seattle City Council in 2018. The early signs of violence continued. On June 20, 2020 livestreamed video captured the sound of multiple gunshots inside CHAZ. Video showed a frantic response, with people sprinting around and yelling about a shooting. Horace Lorenzo Anderson Jr., a 19-year-old black male, was treated by "street medics" at the scene and transported to Harborview Medical Center. He later died. Anderson's older brother told livestreamers he was prevented by "street medics" from seeing his dying brother, who they were treating inside their tent at the Mexican restaurant.

"They hid my little brother from me for the longest—I thought my little brother was at a hospital," the unnamed brother told cameramen at CHAZ.[78] "I didn't see where they had my little brother at until about 9 o'clock this morning. The table was covered in blood."

SPD released a statement saying that the city's medics were unable to respond because of a violent and hostile mob. "Officers attempted to locate a shooting victim but were met by a violent crowd that prevented officers safe access to the victims," they wrote.[79]

Horace Lorenzo Anderson Sr., the deceased victim's father, said the family had been left in the dark with little contact from police and no contact from Seattle politicians. He shared his grief in an interview with Fox News's Sean Hannity.

"My son needed help, and I don't feel like they helped my son," he said, referring to CHAZ's volunteer "street medics."[80] He later received a phone call from President Trump, who expressed his condolences.

The gun violence didn't end that night. The following day, a third black male was shot. An unnamed 17-year-old was transported to hospital and survived. Per CHAZ's rule of "not talking with the pigs," the teen declined to cooperate with SPD in the shooting investigation. And just two days later on June 23, another black male was shot. He survived but also refused to speak with police.[81] Despite the three shootings that left one man dead, the city continued to tolerate CHAZ's lawlessness. Meanwhile, Mayor Durkan proposed a $20 million cut to the SPD budget.[82]

THERE WAS NO SINGULAR VISION or goal in CHAZ. The occupation was made up of several far-left ideological factions: anarchists, communists, anarcho-syndicalists, Marxist black nationalists, and so on. One manifesto posted on blog site Medium demanded the abolishment of the criminal justice system.[83] "The Seattle Police Department and attached court system are beyond reform," the statement read. "We do not request reform, we demand abolition." Jaiden Grayson, a young black woman who developed a large following in CHAZ, told filmmaker Ami Horowitz: "Respond to the demands of the people or prepare to be met with any means necessary. . . . It's not even a warning. I'm letting people know what comes next."[84]

She did not elaborate further, but what came next was more deadly violence. As the city cowed in the face of extremists in CHAZ, a fourth shooting broke out. In the early hours of June 29, 2020, a white Jeep driven by two young teens made the fatal mistake of going inside the autonomous zone. What exactly happened remains unclear because witnesses refuse to cooperate with law enforcement, but security video recorded the sound of a dozen shots being rapidly fired. After a few minutes of silence, another eighteen rounds were fired. The Jeep ended up crashing into a barricade.

What we know is that a 16-year-old black male was taken from the scene to hospital where he was pronounced dead. A 14-year-old passenger sustained serious injuries but survived. Photos and videos of the aftermath showed grisly details. The vehicle was riddled with bullet holes, allegedly fired by CHAZ's "security." One round was fired clean through the windshield on the driver's side. This is likely the shot that killed the teen driver. Inside, the seats were soaked with blood.

When police responded to the crime scene, they found signs evidence was missing, removed, and tampered with. No one was willing to speak. One video recorded moments after the shooting showed a group of CHAZ residents picking up bullet shells and instructing others to do the same. "Once you see any shells on the ground, pick those up and pocket them. Take them home," said one man.

Online, a clearer picture emerged through posts by antifa-sympathetic accounts, including possibly from those inside CHAZ. Before the identities of the victims were known, online antifa-sympathetic accounts claimed CHAZ security had "neutralized" a threat from white supremacists.

"2 guys in a stolen SUV shot up #CHOP tonight," tweeted user "@MaliceBD." "They came through and fired ~15 shots, then maybe 15 mins later, drove across Cal Anderson field and opened fire again...and got fucking MURKED [murdered] by security on the ground. This is the SUV they were driving. Beautiful shot placement."[85] To date, no video or evidence shows shots originating from inside the vehicle.

"@MaliceBD" continued: "I know I shouldn't glorify death and violence but tbh [to be honest] if you try and shoot at innocent people then you deserve to get fucking dealt with."[86] Those responding to the viral tweets thanked CHAZ security for "protecting" the residents there. "Congratulations! I'm proud of you Anarchists, Makes us ML's [Marxist Leninists] look like old men proud of their Sons or Grandsons, Keep up to [sic] good work!" tweeted "@JaredComrade."[87]

It later emerged that the victims of the shooting were two unarmed black males. Marty Jackson, a street medic, told an NPR affiliate that CHAZ security shot at the vehicle and that one of the victims was instantly killed from a headshot wound.[88] Despite claiming to be a refuge for blacks from white racists, CHAZ ended up with a 100 percent black victim shooting rate. To date, only one suspect was named in all the shootings. A warrant was issued by the SPD for the arrest of Marcel Levon Long, who is accused of murdering the first shooting victim, Horace Lorenzo Anderson Jr.

After four shootings, two homicides, and a growing chorus of anger from residents in the form of a class action lawsuit, Mayor Durkan finally relented and issued an executive order to forcibly dismantle CHAZ. On the morning of July 1, 2020, around one hundred SPD officers joined by other law enforcement agencies moved in quickly on foot and bicycles to evict the remaining occupiers. Rioters attempted to obstruct police by moving junk into the street and knocking over porta potties. It was futile. Within thirty minutes, CHAZ's three-week siege was finally over. All it took was a police force given the directive to do their jobs effectively.

Though CHAZ had died, its ghost lived on. In the weeks after the zone was forcibly dismantled, antifa black bloc rioters returned weekly to Capitol Hill to vandalize property, break into businesses, and attack police. On July 23, 2020, a large group of antifa marched around the neighborhood carrying bats and pipes.[89] After smashing several businesses, they started fires. Journalists who recorded the carnage were threatened. Police were ordered away, and no arrests were made. Despite the violence during and after CHAZ, Seattle's city council remained sympathetic to antifa. They never condemned the violence against police officers and police buildings.

"The energy behind these demonstrations and riots was something I've never experienced. I was shocked," said Mike Solan, president of the Seattle Police Officers Guild (SPOG), the union for Seattle police officers. He's been in law enforcement for twenty-one years but says the riots led to the lowest point in his profession and, in his opinion, all those serving in the department.[90]

The SPD used to pride itself on being one of the most progressive and well-trained police departments in the United States on nonlethal use of force. Since 2000, the department averages fewer than four police-involved fatal shootings a year.[91] The city has a population of over 700,000 people. But now, the SPD was tarred with the same brush applied to all law enforcement. "Almost one hundred SPD officers have been hurt in these riots. Not one politician elected in Seattle has approached me to inquire how those officers are doing," Solan said.

Most of the injuries to SPD officers by rioters are lacerations and burns. But there have also been broken bones, nerve damage, and hearing loss. "These IEDs are the weapons of choice and their impact has played a significant role in the officers' hearing issues," Solan explained. "These physical injuries will last a long time and some will be permanent. But more importantly is the mental toll on officers." He noted that some officers are showing symptoms of PTSD.

Two days after the antifa riot on July 23, 2020, antifa again gathered in Capitol Hill. This time it was in solidarity with their militant brethren in Portland, who had been rioting for weeks by this point. Carrying bats and sledgehammers, they smashed up cars and other property. They marched around the city in broad daylight and firebombed several construction trailers, causing large fires. A Starbucks was smashed, looted, and severely damaged. Police finally declared a riot, but when officers responded, antifa threw explosive fireworks at them.

The East Precinct was also targeted again. Antifa militants threw a bomb at the building, causing an explosion and structural damage. By the end of the day, fifty-nine officers were injured. They were not allowed to use tear gas to disperse the violent rioters. Photos released by SPD of the injuries showed gashes, burns, and welts. One officer even had an explosive mortar burn through his shorts.[92]

And again, the violence didn't end there. It continued week after week. On August 16, 2020, antifa black bloc marched to the Seattle Police Officer Guild building. They tried to break inside using an explosive. Officers responding to the riot were pelted with rocks, bottles, and IEDs. Eighteen were arrested and multiple officers were injured, including one who required hospitalization.[93] But antifa promised to continue their rampage, which they now referred to as an uprising. On August 24, 2020, they amassed outside the East Precinct again. Some rioters climbed over the fence protecting the building and sealed an exit with suspected quick-drying cement. They then set the side of the building on fire. Officers were inside the building during this time. The brazen attempt to kill officers inside their own precinct using a barricade and fire garnered the attention of ATF.[94] I asked Mike Solan why police appeared to be letting rioters return week after week, and sometimes day after day, to attack the same areas. His response was blunt: "Our commanders are now hesitant to engage with some of these groups roaming around the city. If we do use force to stop the impending property destruction, SPD will not have the support from our politicians to publicly back us."

At an antifa riot on September 23, 2020, in Capitol Hill, a masked militant bashed an officer on the head with a metal baseball bat. The officer's helmet was cracked from the impact, and he barely escaped the assault. A nineteen-year-old related to a former Democratic state lawmaker, was later arrested and charged with multiple felonies. His accused accomplice is a Seattle-area real estate agent. The King County charging documents say investigators uncovered encrypted communications between the two on a mobile device. The chats showed them allegedly planning to firebomb Seattle police.[95]

THOUGH CHAZ, OR CHOP, was relatively short-lived, I'm still haunted by my experience there. The "autonomous zone" provided some of the clearest glimpses into what an antifa-run territory becomes full of: chaos, violence, and death. "The entirety of CHOP's existence is the craziest part of the story when you think about it," Rantz, the radio host and journalist, says. "The city of Seattle literally abandoned six city blocks, a park, all the businesses and residents inside, and even a police precinct. If you were in the occupied zone, you were completely on your own." Indeed, I was on my own—and antifa eventually found out.

I would have stayed longer than the week I was there, but on my last afternoon, I was outed. And by whom? None other than Nicholas Armstrong, the transsexual antifa militant who had previously stalked and threatened me online. Though I was in full black bloc, she recognized me after analyzing my movement for days. While I was recording an altercation, Armstrong pointed me out to a group that had gathered. "That's Andy Ngo! He's a fascist," she shouted. My blood ran cold. Though I was in front of the East Precinct, it was abandoned, and I knew no authorities would be able to help here. I immediately walked out of CHAZ and rushed to the Lyft car I ordered.

To this day, I still find myself underestimating how committed and sophisticated antifa are to their political agenda of destroying opponents and the state. They're obsessive and compulsive— and they will use any means available to achieve their goals. That includes doxing, disinformation, or straight-up thuggish violence.

The terror they subjected Seattle residents to had long-lasting consequences beyond CHAZ. By August 2020, the SPD police chief announced she was resigning. Carmen Best had served as an officer in the city since 1992 and became Seattle's first black female police chief. But as she said in one of her final press conferences, "I'm done. Can't do it."[96] The day prior, city council voted to cut SPD's budget, including eliminating one hundred positions.

As I left Seattle, I mourned for the law-abiding people who had been terrorized into silence. They were completely failed by their elected leaders. And despite the organized violence playing out in the open, the media headlines still denied the existence of antifa. "How much more violence and chaos by antifa are politicians willing to accept?" I asked myself while on the train out of the city.

Unfortunately, a whole lot more.

A protestor holds a rifle at an antifa protest in Louisville, Kentucky. Photo: Ford Fischer/News2Share

Antifa flags at a Portland Timbers soccer game in 2019

Portland's Apple Store was looted on the first night of Black Lives Matter rioting on May 29, 2020. Photo: Andy Ngo

Pool noodles filled with nails were used to pop police car tires. Photo: Portland Police Bureau

Women were used as human shields in the riots in August 2020. Photo: Andy Ngo

PNW Youth Liberation Front
@PNWYLF

Livestreamers are doing the fed's surveillance and scouting work for them. Whether they like it or not, they are serving as a literal counterintelligence operation for fed forces.
Any with a conscience will shut down their streams, and if they don't, they should be forced out.

A tweet by the Pacific Northwest Youth Liberation Front.

CHAPTER 3

Portland

THE JUSTICE CENTER is a large multilevel building spanning an entire city block in downtown Portland, Oregon. It houses the Sheriff's Office, Portland Police Central Precinct, courtrooms, and hundreds of inmates in the county jail. To Portland's Black Lives Matter-antifa, it is a physical manifestation of the American rule of law that they despise.

As the sun set on Friday, May 29, 2020, a crowd trekked through downtown Portland toward the Justice Center. Their angry faces, shouting "ACAB" for "all cops are bastards," were illuminated by red flares being carried by antifa black bloc militants. They had been primed for violence through hours of radical speeches led by black separatists in Peninsula Park in north Portland. During their march, protesters surrounded a car and one of them fired a gunshot, injuring the vehicle's passenger.[97] Police could not or would not stop them, and they continued unchallenged to their destination, where their comrades had already been camping out.

By 11:00 p.m., the crowd surrounded the building and transformed into an angry mob. They smashed the windows on the ground floor and flooded in. Staff working inside had to flee for their lives. Dozens smashed computer equipment and furniture using bats and other melee weapons.[98] "Burn this shit down," they shouted as they started fires. The building was still occupied by hundreds of inmates during the attack. After about ten minutes, police responded and cleared the majority of rioters from the area. But they simply ran to the business corridor of downtown Portland. There, BLM and antifa demonstrated their symbiotic relationship seen in other cities affected by rioting earlier in the week. Antifa militants, who are mostly white, took the initiative to break into businesses to initiate a chain reaction.

The first businesses rioters descended upon were Portland's flagship Apple Store and Louis Vuitton. Marching together as a mob and shouting, "Expropriate!" they broke inside and looted the stores clean. Video recorded at Louis Vuitton showed black bloc militants standing guard at the door they broke while young people rushed in and out with designer bags and wallets.

Outside, rioters shut down traffic by starting large street fires using accelerants and whatever they could steal for tinder: wooden pallets, trash bins, newspapers, and so on. When police tried to respond to the chaos, they were attacked in their vehicles by people using electric scooters as melee weapons. The Apple Store's iconic glass windows were smashed and spray painted with antifa messages, "ACAB" and its numerical rendering, "1312." As the rioting continued for hours, they next targeted banks, clothing stores, and marijuana dispensaries. Rioters shattered windows using bats, bike locks, skateboards, and other impromptu riot tools. Once inside, they started more fires.

In another part of downtown, rioters used a car to ram inside a building.[99] Businesses continued to be looted well into the early hours of the next day. Portland Mayor Ted Wheeler declared a state of emergency, but it was of no use. Police and firefighters were completely overwhelmed and surrounded. One officer was injured when he was hit by a thrown incendiary device. A Portland Police criminalist responding to a scene was hit in the head with a rock.

By the end of the rampage, only sixteen people were arrested. One of them went on to be charged by the district attorney for arson and other felony crimes. Amelia Joan Shamrowicz, a 25-year-old transsexual, allegedly was busted after her roommates contacted law enforcement. The affidavit reads:

> When [her roommates] asked how Shamrowicz started the fires, Shamrowicz responded by saying that it is not a conversation for Facebook Messenger and that she will be home soon. A subsequent in-person conversation occurred and the roommates reported that Shamrowicz stated [she] started the fire using a Molotov cocktail, and she is part of *Antifa*. Shamrowicz was reported to be extremely excited about being labeled a terrorist and was very animated about her hopes that police officers would be killed and injured by the riots. She also stated that she would be going out on another mission and the goal would be to set another fire.[100]

Shamrowicz was charged with first-degree felony arson, felony criminal mischief, felony riot, and two counts of conspiracy to commit a class A felony. Her ties to antifa were never reported in the local and national press.

All that occurred on just the first night of rioting in Portland. It continued the next day, and the day after that, and the day after that. For weeks, rioters descended on the Justice Center every night as if it were a ritual. They'd surround the building, confront the police standing guard, and attack them with projectiles and mortar explosives. Many of them used powerful lasers against police that could burn eyes and cause permanent damage to vision. By the middle of the summer, these lasers became so numerous that the rioters who carried them organized into their own "unit," and the protests began to look like laser shows. "Light mages," as they were called, stood far behind lines of hundreds of protesters to blind police while their comrades closer up threw projectiles.

Mayor Wheeler announced an emergency curfew lasting three

days following the first night of violence, but again, it failed to have much effect. Police were unable to do anything beyond writing curfew citations, nearly all of which were later dropped by the district attorney.

At every step of the way, the Portland City Council demonized its police force, accusing them of racism and brutality. City council members Jo Ann Hardesty and Chloe Eudaly were at the forefront of that effort. They pushed for the Portland Police's Gun Violence Reduction Team to be dissolved after Floyd's death, claiming it targeted blacks. The mayor gave his support, and the unit was dismantled. In the following months, shootings and homicides in Portland spiked to the highest levels in decades. Compared to the year prior, shootings in July and August 2020 in Portland increased by almost 200 percent.[101]

Meanwhile, the daily violent antifa protests were becoming more organized and sophisticated. Media pundits inaccurately described what was happening as spontaneous and organic, but what I saw on antifa social media accounts was a deliberate, strategic, and organized plan to grow and entrench the riots. Through advertising on Reddit, Instagram, Snapchat, and Twitter, they were widely successful in getting support not just from antifa fans but also from the wider left.

In September 2020, Rutgers-affiliated researchers released a study that examined the use of social media by antifa (referred to in the paper as "anarcho-socialists") in instigating widespread violence during the months of unrest throughout the year. They found evidence of systematic online mobilization and radicalization using memes, "rage posts," and coded language.[102] These types of extreme anti-police content grew more than 1,000 percent on Twitter and 300 percent on Reddit.

The study identified that the Youth Liberation Front (YLF), the antifa group in Portland that took the lead in organizing riots, used "cyberswarming" to coordinate real-world direct action.[103] Cyberswarming is the act of calling online followers to a real-life location or event. Antifa traditionally use it to immediately mobilize a crowd against people they perceive to be ideological threats. But in 2020, they were using it to direct people to locations to riot. The YLF released daily meeting locations, tactical plans, and maps on Twitter and Telegram. When they put out a call to meet at the George Washington statue in northeast Portland on June 18, 2020, their followers obliged. That evening, dozens of people lit the 100-year-old bronze statue on fire and used rope to pull it down. At the base of the statue, they wrote "White fragility" and "BLM." On the toppled statue itself, they spray-painted "1619," referencing the *New York Times Magazine*'s 1619 Project. Instead of repairing the damage, the city removed the statue. By November 2020, far-left rioters in Portland toppled or destroy seven more statues including ones of Thomas Jefferson, Theodore Roosevelt, and Abraham Lincoln. They also set a downtown museum on fire.[104] No one was ever arrested over the vandalism.

Mutual Aid

To achieve their goals, antifa use violence. But sustained, effective violence takes organization, planning, and money, in addition to participants. To achieve this, a smorgasbord of ad hoc antifa groups popped up. Describing themselves as "mutual aid" groups, they supplied everything from food and bail money to riot gear and weapons.

The Witches was one mutual aid group that formed to give out water, food, and supplies to rioters.[105] Riot Ribs was a pop-up kitchen that cooked hot meals.[106] Free food is a mainstay of the riots for a few reasons. It draws in protesters and vagrants to inflate crowd numbers. Secondly, it is effective for propaganda as it generates favorable news stories and photographs showing the "peaceful" side of the radical protests.

The Equitable Workers Offering Kommunity Support, or EWOKS, provided volunteer "street medics" for comrades injured during rioting.[107] Similarly, a group calling itself "OHSU4BLM" claimed to be made of medical students affiliated with the Oregon Health and Science University.[108] (They later shut down after receiving notice that they weren't allowed to use the OHSU brand.) PDX Shield provided homemade shields, which were more frequently used as battering weapons.[109] PDX Hydration Station distributed sticks and umbrellas—tools used to fight police and block cameras, respectively.[110] PDX Community Jail Support aided arrested rioters immediately after their release from jail.[111] They set up a camp outside the central police precinct and offered arrestees food, phone access, legal support, and rides home. In short, they streamlined the riot catch-and-release process.

These and numerous other anonymous "mutual aid" groups were all established between May and August 2020 in Portland. Using payment applications Venmo and Cash App, the groups were able to raise hundreds of thousands of dollars from a large number of anonymous donors around the country (and even internationally).

Thousands around the United States support antifa and the far left. They are willing to donate to their fundraisers. Politicians and celebrities promote their causes, and local media provide favorable coverage. Riot Ribs was one of the most successful Portland antifa mutual aid groups during the summer. It raised more than $330,000 but suddenly dissolved overnight in July 2020 and disappeared, along with the money.[112]

Of course, as much money as these mutual aid groups received to provide supplies to rioters, they pale in comparison to how much the Portland General Defense Committee was able to raise on GoFundMe. Similar to the wildly successful Minnesota Freedom Fund, which bails out rioters and those charged with serious crimes like murder, the Portland group pulled in over $1.37 million.[113] The huge flow of cash is used to bail out every rioter arrested, cover their legal expenses, pay for housing and new mobile devices, give donations to other groups, and whatever else they feel like supporting. When the charges get dropped or dismissed, and the overwhelming majority of them do, the bail bond is returned and reinvested in other nefarious causes.

The Portland General Defense Committee publishes a financial accountability page on its website.[114] I can only assume the information reported is accurate. They say $20,000 was given to a bail fund in Eugene, Oregon. Bail bonds ranging from several hundred dollars up to $50,000 were paid for more than a hundred people. In effect, the group is using a GoFundMe campaign to channel money to causes that are otherwise not allowed on the platform. The site's Terms of Service prohibit raising legal funds for those accused of violent crimes. But the Portland General Defense Committee does exactly that as people they bail out are accused of felony assault and other serious crimes.

And what exactly is the General Defense Committee? It is a local chapter of the Industrial Workers of the World (IWW) Defense Committee. The IWW is an anarchist-socialist labor union. Like the other antifa mutual aid groups, those involved use pseudonyms and monikers. However, the Portland chapter is a registered nonprofit with the state of Oregon. Its filing with the Oregon secretary of state shows the registered agent behind the group is Katherine "Corbyn" Belyea.

Belyea is one of the people who I allege had assaulted me in June 2019 at the antifa riot according to a criminal complaint. Before I was punched in the head by the mob, Belyea threw a cup full of liquid in my face. A photographer captured the moment. It shows Belyea grinning widely.

DURING THE SUMMER OF 2020, the antifa organizing infrastructure was now in place. They had everything they needed to be on auto pilot: a plan, people, supplies, and money.

In June, the city put up a protective fence around the Justice Center and the adjacent federal courthouse. In response, rioters came with tools to cut the fence open. Every night, police guarding the facilities were hit by hundreds of projectiles. When rioters ran out of supplies or things to throw, they were continuously resupplied by well-stocked support vehicles.

On June 1, a woman was stopped by police after she was observed allegedly handing out supplies to rioters.[115] She sped off in response, hitting multiple vehicles in the escape. She was only stopped once her tires were slashed by spike strips laid by police. No charges were pursued.

In my time on the ground in Portland, I observed sophisticated communication strategies between different antifa units during the protests. As in CHAZ, they communicated via walkie-talkies and sometimes subtle hand signals. Each faction of antifa served a function they had been trained for. Drivers carried supplies like water bottles, some of which were frozen solid and later used as projectiles against police. "Scouts" on foot, bicycles, or motorcycles watched the perimeter and kept an eye on every person entering the area. Those who looked suspicious were flagged and closely followed or monitored. On several occasions, random people accused of being "right-wing" were chased out or assaulted by the mob.

As the days went on, the weapons became more sophisticated—and dangerous. In addition to rocks, concrete chunks, and bottles, they were adding in large commercial-grade fireworks. The explosive mortars were used to distract and confuse police while others hurled projectiles at them. In some cases, officers close to the explosions suffered burns and hearing problems.

What amazed me about the strategic choice of weapons—both purchased and homemade—was how innocuous they looked on camera and to bystanders. For example, one doesn't necessarily register a water bottle as a dangerous and potentially deadly weapon. However, black bloc rioters froze them to make them hard as rocks. Taking one to the head could lead to a serious brain injury or death. And intermixed with the plastic bottles were glass bottles and canned food.[116] Other popular weapons were slingshots. Rioters stood hundreds of feet back and fired off marbles and metal ball bearings. On camera, they looked deceptively like children's toys.

And the umbrellas rioters used to shield themselves from cameras? On at least one confirmed occasion and likely more, rioters attached blades to the tips of the umbrellas so they could double as weapons.[117]

Lawfare

One of the most effective ways we've seen law enforcement agencies brought to their knees is through frivolous lawsuits bankrolled by endless donors. "Lawfare" refers to the act of abusing the legal system to achieve goals.

There exist large networks of far-left attorneys and legal groups who bring endless lawsuits in an attempt to defund, cripple, and embarrass police. In early June 2020, far-left BLM-style group Don't Shoot Portland filed a class action lawsuit against the city to stop the use of tear gas. The group is headed by Portland mayoral write-in candidate Teressa Raiford. Raiford advocates for the literal abolishment of police and is one of the few political candidates who garner the support of some militant antifa.[118]

One of the attorneys on the case is Juan Chavez, a lawyer with the far-left Oregon Justice Resource Center. The group takes cases representing antifa and far-left clients. Chavez is also a prominent member of the National Lawyers Guild (NLG), a legal group with historical ties to the Communist Party. It has chapters across the United States. The organization formally declared its support for antifa and political violence in a statement on its website in 2017: "While many abhor tactics that involve violence, historical evidence shows that direct action has contributed to shutting down fascist movements before they gain too much power or influence."[119] In effect, the NLG is the legal arm of antifa. Its 2016 nonprofit tax form shows it pulled in over $711,000.[120] The NLG's executive director, Pooja Gehi, identifies as an anarchist. The organization provides green hat–wearing "legal observers" at left-wing riots and protests. Even before COVID-19, they frequently hid their identities by wearing masks. The volunteers appear to be neutral legal observers, but in fact they are only there to record out-of-context video to use in lawsuits against police or their political opponents. They do not film antifa.

By October 2020, in Portland alone there were twenty-one protest-related lawsuits filed against Portland Police.[121]

AS CHAOS OCCURRED NIGHT after night on the streets of Portland, the Portland Police Bureau (PPB) was convulsed by another high-level resignation. One week into June 2020, Portland Police chief Jami Resch resigned. She wasn't even six months into her position, which she took over from Danielle Outlaw. Outlaw, a black woman, was hired by Mayor Wheeler in 2017. Wheeler and the city's progressive left assumed she would prioritize her black and female identity. Instead, she performed the job of a police chief of a major American city—maintaining law and order. This earned her the ire and hatred of antifa, who frequently called her a "race traitor." The local left-wing press regularly demonized her as the overseer of a department that was too aggressive with left-wing protesters.

In November 2018, left-wing paper *Willamette Week* published a cover story on Outlaw that showed her as an ugly cartoon caricature with exaggerated facial features. The Portland Police Association released a statement calling the profile racist.[122] Outlaw resigned from the bureau at the end of December 2019 to become the new commissioner of the Philadelphia Police Department. Sources tell me Outlaw tried to restore order to Portland during mass street brawls throughout 2017 and 2018 involving antifa and right-wing groups, but she did not have the support of city council.

Politicians in the city are terrified of political and media backlash for holding antifa and far-left protesters accountable. The local and national media are staunchly on the side of antifa, regardless of their violence against police and property. Resch, Outlaw's replacement, resigned two weeks after George Floyd–inspired riots began in May 2020. Resch is white, and the rumor among beat cops is that Mayor Wheeler wanted a black person in charge of police. Resch's replacement, the third police chief in Portland within six months, was Charles "Chuck" Lovell, a black lieutenant in the PPB. Lovell's leadership has not been welcomed by the city's BLM-antifa brigade. They too view him as a race traitor. By September 2020, Wheeler publicly voiced his disapproval of Lovell after the PPB released a statement criticizing his draconian tear gas ban.[123]

Send In the Feds

Week after week in June 2020, the riots continued to escalate outside the Justice Center. The weak fence set up by the city was easily torn down and cut open by rioters. Eventually the city removed it altogether.

Lownsdale Square and Chapman Square, two adjacent parks in front of the Justice Center and the Mark O. Hatfield Federal Courthouse, became the operations center for antifa. There, the numerous antifa pop-up groups set up tents that supplied rioters with everything they needed. Though nearly 280 people were arrested throughout May and June, almost all of them were quickly released without bail or conditions, even when they violently resisted arrest and were found to be carrying weapons. COVID-19 policies for the county meant that only the most egregious suspects were held in jail, but even then, they were quickly bailed out by the bail fund. Rioters would simply return to riot again, sometimes within the same day, and face no consequence for subsequent arrests.

Within less than two weeks, there were nearly a hundred arson fires in and around downtown Portland.[124] Despite the violence and vandalism, a federal judge temporarily banned the PPB from using tear gas. The response from elected city officials was to deny the violence and praise the protests. After the first night of mass looting, arson, and violence, Mayor Wheeler tweeted: "We talked about agitation—yes even violent agitation and how it has historically occurred with purpose and resulted in change that has moved this country forward."[125]

Though most of the rioting focused on attacking the Justice Center and the central police station it houses, by late June, rioters were increasingly turning their violent attention to the neighboring federal courthouse. Rioters first tagged every inch of the building's front with extremist antifa slogans and anti-police messages. They smashed the windows on a few occasions, leading to the front glass doors and windows being boarded up with wooden planks. But for the most part, the Justice Center, a county property, was the focus of violence.

Then in July, the mob's attention fully switched to the federal courthouse with an intensity not previously seen. They first began launching commercial-grade aerial fireworks at the building in an attempt to set it on fire. On July 2, 2020, they shattered a front window and tried to gain entry inside the courthouse. They were repelled by officers from the Federal Protective Service (FPS), a law enforcement agency within the Department of Homeland Security (DHS). The following day, they forcibly tore off the protective wooden planks to firebomb the lobby of the courthouse. Federal officers were forced to extinguish the flames.

A 19-year-old affiliated with the Youth Liberation Front, tried to barricade officers inside to prevent them from responding to rioters who were setting the building on fire. The front door shattered. He was the only one arrested that night.

On the Fourth of July, the violence escalated to unprecedented levels. That day, around a thousand people surrounded the building, throwing rocks and explosives. They disabled the security cameras around the building using hammers, spray paint, and paint balls. Several in the mob openly carried rifles and handguns. One of the men arrested at the riot was antifa shooter Michael

Reinoehl.[126] He was carrying an illegal firearm and resisted arrest, requiring three Portland Police officers to be subdued. However, he was only cited and released because he claimed to be injured. His criminal charges were later dropped by the Multnomah County District Attorney. Reinoehl went on to kill a Trump supporter the following month in downtown Portland.

By now, a surge of federal officers from the FPS, U.S. Marshals Service, U.S. Border Patrol, and Immigration and Customs Enforcement (ICE) were on call to protect the federal courthouse. Under Mayor Wheeler's orders, local police were not allowed to aid in protecting federal property. On July 5, 2020, hundreds returned to again attack federal officers, and they tried to burn down the courthouse. They also assaulted construction crews who were working around the clock to replace wooden barriers that were torn down.

Christopher Fellini, 31, was arrested that night and charged with assaulting a federal officer. In his possession, officers found a knife, pepper spray, and a powerful laser. Fellini was previously arrested and charged at another Portland antifa riot in 2017. Another arrestee that night was Andrew Steven Faulkner, 24, who was also accused of assaulting a federal officer. During his arrest, he was found carrying pipe bomb components and a sheathed machete.[127]

For the next four weeks, antifa's plan of escalating attacks on federal property to provoke a federal response for the cameras produced the exact propaganda they wanted. On any given night, there were dozens who identified as press. At its peak there were probably more than one hundred journalists and livestreamers, most of whom were sympathetic to the rioters and protesters. Instinctively, and at the urging or demand of others, their cameras were trained solely on law enforcement to capture their every move.[128] Those who ran afoul of antifa's rules were forced out or assaulted and robbed. Left-wing livestreamer Tristan Taylor was beaten to the ground and had his recording equipment stolen.[129]

Every use of force by officers, whether it be tear gas, smoke, peppers balls, or arrests, was heavily scrutinized. Out-of-context video snippets were released on social media and published by news outlets, generating mass rage and universally negative press for law enforcement and the Trump administration. The officers were called "Trump's gestapo," "storm troopers," and "thugs" by Democratic politicians and the media.

Erin Smith, a conservative trans woman and writer who goes undercover at large antifa riots on the West Coast, says antifa use a "calibrated level of violence" to provoke reactions by law enforcement for propaganda purposes.

"Antifa seek to force law enforcement into a dilemma action, where there are simply no good responses from a public relations standpoint," Smith told me via email. "They either fail to respond to antifa harassment and look weak, or react in ways likely to be perceived by the casual observer as an overreaction. Both choices undermine the legitimacy of the state and its security forces."

As useful idiots for antifa, the press predictably published reports that helped provoke more hatred for law enforcement in Portland.

"Trump sent cops to Portland and they're 'kidnapping people off the streets,'" read a Vice News headline. "'It was like being preyed upon': Portland protesters say federal officers in unmarked vans are detaining them," read another from the *Washington Post*.

All these stories based on antifa talking points were meant to create an impression that Trump had literally sent secret police to disappear left-wing opposition. It was false. Using unmarked vehicles to make targeted arrests is neither illegal nor unusual. Every law enforcement agency around the world uses unmarked vehicles. When officers had attempted the usual route of moving in to physically arrest someone, they were mobbed by rioters who "de-arrested" their comrades by surrounding police and pulling them away.

Accusations of there being "secret police" and "unidentified federal agents" were false. Every officer wore official uniforms that displayed their agency via badges on the shoulders with clear

words on the front that read "POLICE." That politicians and journalists did not or pretended not to recognize the uniforms is not
an excuse. And no one was ever "disappeared." All those detained
were properly processed and read their Miranda rights. Most were
released within hours.

As bad as the riots already were, city council and local politicians actively worked to undermine the federal government's
attempts to protect federal property. In effect, they were cobellig-
erents with antifa in their uprising. When Acting Secretary Chad
Wolf of DHS flew to Portland from Washington, DC, in mid-July
to survey the extent of the violence and destruction, local officials
preemptively refused to meet with him.

"We're aware that [DHS leadership is] here. We wish they
weren't," tweeted Mayor Wheeler.[130] "We haven't been invited to
meet with them, and if we were, we would decline." Oregon Democratic senator Ron Wyden called federal officers an "occupying
army."[131] Oregon governor Kate Brown echoed and amplified the
false media headlines. "This is a democracy, not a dictatorship. We
cannot have secret police abducting people in unmarked vehicles,"
Governor Brown tweeted.[132] By mid-July, the Portland City Council officially banned Portland Police from cooperating in any way
with federal law enforcement.[133]

The anti-police and anti-Trump echo chamber involving antifa,
the media, and local politicians brought Portland into international
headlines. With that, protesters from the region and around the
country descended on the city. Gatherings in front of the federal
courthouse swelled from a couple hundred to more than five thousand. Antifa now had the perfect opportunity to carry out attacks
they planned using huge numbers of protesters as human shields.
It worked incredibly well. When I was undercover on the ground,
what I saw was a literal war zone with armed belligerents.

On the side of antifa were units of fighters with explosive fireworks, lasers, rocks, and loaded slingshots. They were joined by
street medics, resuppliers, tear gas leaf blowers, and human shields.

Many were dressed in riot gear and gas masks. Perhaps the most important faction was those labeled "peaceful protesters." They stood arm in arm in the front to shield everyone behind them.

The photographs of the "Wall of Moms," dads, and veterans against federal officers were propaganda. The "peaceful protesters" were used as human shields to deter or delay law enforcement from taking action. It was incredibly effective. When officers inevitably responded following hours of assaults and property damage, photographers were ready to capture "moms" being tear gassed. These were the photos published around the world. However, many of the so-called moms were young antifa women who simply put on yellow T-shirts. (Yellow became the color associated with the Wall of Moms.) I recognized some of them from their distinct glasses or hair colors as regular black bloc rioters from previous nights. And on many occasions, the "moms" were caught on camera participating in violent rioting, such as giving out concrete to throw or helping to tear down the fence.[134]

In mid-July, the federal government put up a strong reinforced barrier around the courthouse. Other barriers previously put up were quickly torn apart. This one was made of thick steel, and it was reinforced by concrete blocks on the other side. The fence withstood for many days, but on the fifty-ninth night of rioting, hundreds gathered with tools and equipment to bring down the barrier. They used electric saws to cut into the fence, but the holes they made were too small for people to fit through. Next, they tied rope around strategic points of the fence, and hundreds of rioters participated in pulling it down. "Heave! Ho!" they shouted. It eventually worked. One section on the south end buckled under the collective force of hundreds of rioters. Officers inside the courthouse rushed out to fire tear gas to prevent a mob from rushing the building.

THOSE ACCUSED OF COMMITTING serious crimes throughout the downtown riots included a 43-year-old convicted of possessing child pornography named Blake David Hampe. On July 25, 2020, he was filmed in a livestream video allegedly stabbing black conservative activist Andrew Duncomb with a knife near the federal courthouse. Originally from New Hampshire, Hampe has a prior conviction for possession of child sex abuse images.[135] I have seen him at various protests wearing bright children's-themed clothing, but he was far from childlike or innocent.[136] Hampe is extremely confrontational and threatens others he perceives as right wing. He was one of the people who confronted me before I was beaten in June 2019.[137]

Hampe was held on a $250,000 second-degree felony assault charge but was bailed out within days by a left-wing bail fund.[138] He pleaded not guilty to the assault. Another arrestee was a 23-year-old Texan who was filmed barricading the door of the federal courthouse with his body while prepping for an overhead strike using a hammer.[139] The officers broke his hold, and one U.S. Marshals Service deputy was struck three times with the hammer. Then there was an 18-year-old was caught on a livestream video throwing an object that exploded in a large blast in front of the courthouse. The explosion could be heard blocks away. He was outed by his Trump-loving grandmother who recognized him from viral video and photos.[140] He's been federally charged over the incident.

ONE NEW PHENOMENON that developed over the weeks of rioting was antifa activists masquerading as press in order to avoid being arrested by police or to get closer to them to throw projectiles. They simply printed out homemade media badges and wrote "press" on their clothing. On multiple occasions, they were seen participating in violence themselves, such as throwing rocks and fireworks at officers or blinding them with flashlights.[141] Sometimes they actively provoked the police into arresting them so their comrades could record video and send out tweets about police "targeting" media. This was effective, and the ACLU of Oregon sued Portland police and federal agents on behalf of left-wing legal observers and journalists in July.[142] A federal judge granted an emergency injunction exempting anyone who identified as a journalist from dispersal orders. The injunction immediately did exactly what one would expect it to: any rioter wanting to avoid arrest simply self-identified as press.

BY THE END OF JULY 2020, Deputy Secretary Ken Cuccinelli of DHS reported to Congress at a U.S. Senate hearing. He said that at least 277 injuries had been inflicted on about 140 federal agents in Portland alone.[143] Agents suffered concussions, burns, and other injuries from being hit with projectiles. The most common injuries were eyesight related from rioters using high-powered lasers. Rioters also suffered numerous injuries in their clashes with law enforcement. One of the most high-profile incidents caught on video involved a young man who was hit in the head with an impact munition after he threw a canister back at officers. Donavan La Bella suffered a skull fracture and required emergency surgery.

After four weeks of bloody battles involving nightly antifa attacks against federal property, Governor Brown announced she had finally agreed on a plan that would see federal officers withdrawn from the city. Under a limited deal negotiated with Oregon State Police, state troopers would take over policing duties in the three-block square of downtown at the center of the riots. "After my discussions with VP Pence and others, the federal government has agreed to withdraw federal officers from Portland. They have acted as an occupying force & brought violence," wrote Governor Brown on Twitter.[144]

The move was declared a victory by the media. Left-wing protesters and "anti-fascists" had successfully resisted the federal government and sent them packing. "Portland protests calm after federal officers leave the city," read a headline from the

Washington Post. "Violence subsides after feds exit Portland protests," read another from *Forbes.*

The "parachute" journalists coming to Portland from Washington, DC, and New York didn't have their finger on the pulse of the city or antifa. To them, police and Trump were always to blame, never those who actually organized and initiated violence. Not only did the rioting continue after federal officers withdrew from the courthouse, it became even more violent and bled into other areas of the city.

"Out of Your House, into the Streets"

On August 8, 2020, hundreds of BLM-antifa protesters shut down the streets of a residential area in north Portland as they marched to the Portland Police Association building. They shined bright lights into homes and apartments. "Out of your house, into the streets," the mob shouted to families in their homes. One person who looked disapprovingly out of his window had a large light shined into his home. "We're gonna burn your building down," a protester shouted to the man. "We know where you live!" another protester yelled.

Soon, the mob made it to the police union hall. They first erected a barricade on North Lombard, a busy north Portland street, using stolen dumpsters and fences from nearby businesses. They then set it on fire. As in downtown, they destroyed the security cameras around the police association building. Before midnight, they smashed their way into the front of the building and set the interior on fire.[145] Their goal, as they have always stated, was to burn down police and government facilities.

Responding officers from Portland Police and Oregon State Police were met with a barrage of hurled glass bottles and paint balloons. The violence that night capped off a week of daily BLM-antifa riots that were now becoming entrenched in residential areas on the east side of Portland, far from downtown. The previous night, hundreds of rioters surrounded the Penumbra Kelly Building in southeast Portland. They threw concrete chunks and explosives at police. Responding police cruisers had their tires slashed by rioters who dumped nail-filled pool noodles on the street.[146] On August 6, the night before, rioters tried to break into the Portland Police East Precinct. Two elderly women who lived nearby tried to stop the mob from setting fire to the building.[147] As one of them used an extinguisher to put out a fire, she was screamed at and harassed. The mob then hurled paint at them. One woman had it thrown in her face and eyes.

The two days of calm at the end of July and the beginning of August after federal officers scaled back their presence were merely the eye of the hurricane. In fact, those forty-eight hours were used by antifa to restrategize and plan their next moves. Without federal officers to fight, they took their riots elsewhere. From August onward, some of the most intense violence yet took place in residential areas of the city.

Day to day, BLM-antifa rioters met in parks around Portland where they would distribute riot gear, food, and extremist literature. They'd train in shield formation tactics to prepare them for the evening's riot. Locations targeted for arson and vandalism primarily rotated among Portland Police's North, East, and Southeast police stations. On several occasions, rioters also targeted Mayor Wheeler's condo in a posh part of northwest Portland. By early autumn, they began to regularly attack the local ICE facility.

For months, Portlanders had to suffer through a daily nightmare version of Groundhog Day. It was the same every evening: rioters gathered at a park, marched to a location to attack, were arrested, and were quickly released or bailed out. Rinse and repeat.

From May through August 2020, hundreds had been taken into custody by law enforcement. But the result was the same for almost everyone: the Multnomah County district attorney dropped the charges, even the serious felonies. Assarrah Butler, the accused riot supplier who, in June, sped off in her car, hitting other vehicles, was originally charged with felony riot, felony failure to perform duties of driver to injured person, felony criminal mischief, felony fleeing, reckless driving, and reckless endangering. Every single charge was dropped. Likewise, an accused arsonist who allegedly admitted to roommates she was part of antifa, had all her charges dismissed. The dropping and dismissal of their felony charges were the norm, not the exception.

In the United States, local criminal charges are pursued—or not—by the county's elected district attorney. They have complete discretion to act. Portland's left-wing political monoculture means that the Multnomah County District Attorney's office has to make politically calculated prosecutions that are favorable to the city's vocal woke populace. Justice is not blind in Portland. Antifa and BLM rioters are let go almost as quickly as they can be processed through jail.

From 2013 to 2020, Multnomah County elected and reelected Rod Underhill to be its district attorney. Underhill is a liberal, and it was reflected in his office's soft approach to crime in the seven years he was there. However, on August 1, 2020, Underhill stepped down early from office. This opened the way for Mike Schmidt to take the reins as the city convulsed through months of riots. Schmidt, 39, ran and won in a landslide election as a "progressive" candidate who promised criminal justice reform. Two weeks before he took office, Schmidt signaled his approach to riots in an interview with *Willamette Week*, saying:

> I think that when you look historically at this nation, it's during these protests when we've gotten some of the changes that we are proudest of in our nation's history. And sometimes it took some property damage. It took more than just peaceful protests to get the government's attention. I'm very mindful of that.[148]

Eleven days into office, Schmidt announced an official policy regarding riot and protest cases in the county. Under his policy, the Multnomah County District Attorney's Office preemptively declines to prosecute charges of interfering with an officer, disorderly conduct, criminal trespass, escape from law enforcement, and harassment. Felony riot charges are also automatically dropped unless coupled with a charge not already included on the list. What this means is that Multnomah County essentially decriminalized all crimes short of assault, arson, and property destruction at riots. Those who try to stop police from making arrests, ignore their lawful orders, and escape? They face no legal consequences even if they are arrested. Further, Schmidt's policy states that charges of resisting arrest and assaulting a public safety officer "must be subjected to the highest level of scrutiny by the deputy district attorney reviewing the arrest." That is a softer way of saying assault on police is conditionally allowed. And rioters charged with misdemeanors or felonies where there was "only financial harm" would be offered conditional dismissal.[149]

The announcement exacerbated the riots. Antifa already had practically free rein before, but now it was official policy. On September 1, 2020, BLM-antifa rioters gathered outside Mayor Wheeler's condo for a second time. As much as Wheeler tried to kowtow to protesters for months, it was never enough. They demanded he resign. That night, they threw explosive fireworks at his building, which houses dozens of other family units. By around 11:00 p.m., rioters smashed their way in the ground level of a large occupied apartment building. They started a fire inside and stole furniture to start another fire on the street.[150] A riot was declared, and police made nineteen arrests. All arrestees were released from jail within a few hours or bailed out. In response to the targeted violence, Mayor Wheeler announced he was moving.

Firebombs

On September 5, rioters marched to attack the East Precinct, as they had done many times before. But that night, they hurled lit firebombs for the first time. Over the previous months, Portland Police had confiscated unused Molotov cocktails, but none had actually been used at the riots.[151] However, that night, a masked rioter hurled a firebomb in the direction of a line of police. It fell short of its target and instead landed at the feet of a group of protesters. Two people were set on fire, including one who desperately flailed about and rolled around while his feet were engulfed in flames.[152] Police extinguished the fire and offered him help.

For the next four hours, rioters continued to light fires on the street and hurled more mortar fireworks at officers. One sergeant was directly hit by an explosive, which burned through his glove, injuring his hand. Officers were struck with rocks. In response to the violence, they used tear gas to disperse rioters. The street, filled with homes and families, was clouded with smoke from fires and tear gas. Over fifty people were arrested that night, including Kristina Narayan, the legislative director for Tina Kotek, the Democratic Speaker of the Oregon House.[153] Joseph Robert Sipe, 23, was arrested and charged with first-degree attempted murder, first-degree attempted assault, first-degree arson, and possession of a destructive device. Court documents say he admitted to lighting the wick of a Molotov cocktail and then launching it toward police officers. The district attorney later dropped three of the four most serious charges.[154] The following week, Mayor Wheeler announced a total ban on the use of tear gas for crowd control.[155]

THE RIOTS CONTINUED INTO OCTOBER. The city never put out a full estimate of the costs, but in early July, Portland Police deputy chief Chris Davis said there had been an estimated $23 million in damages and lost business.[156] He made the statement only five weeks into the protests. The riots continued for at least four more months.

Between May and October 2020, there were nearly a thousand protest- and riot-related cases in Portland referred to the district attorney's office. Many of the cases involved people who were arrested on numerous occasions. Tracy Lynn Molina, 47, was arrested by Portland Police seven times, for example. Her charges were dropped every time. Of the 978 arrests and citations, over 90 percent were rejected for prosecution.[157] The main reason given? Out of the "interest of justice"—whatever that means. Despite accusations of systemic racism and misogyny in the Portland Police Bureau, the majority of those arrested (77 percent) have been white and male (67 percent).[158]

Four weeks before the November mayoral election, a local poll found incumbent Ted Wheeler trailing by double digits to far-left candidate Sarah Iannarone. In 2019, Iannarone proudly wrote, "I am Antifa" on her Twitter.[159] Those words were later echoed by Willem van Spronsen, an antifa terrorist who firebombed a Tacoma, Washington, ICE facility, and Michael Reinoehl, the Portland antifa shooter. She has stood by her outspoken support for antifa and, in an August 2020 interview with KGW, declined to denounce the violent riots in her city.[160]

"Peaceful protests in my opinion might not necessarily be moving the conversation forward," Iannarone said. She ultimately lost to Wheeler by about six percentage points in the November 2020 election—but only because the write-in candidate to her left, Teressa Raiford, received more than 13 percent of the votes.[161]

A few months before the riots began, I offered to put my differences aside to meet off-the-record with Mayor Wheeler. I believe him to be a misguided but well-intentioned man whose ignorance about antifa leads him to make poor choices for the city. My request to meet was acknowledged—and ignored.

On the evening of October 4, 2020, BLM-antifa rioters marched to the brand-new Multnomah County Courthouse. The $324 million project was scheduled to open the following day. There, rioters proceeded to vandalize the building. Police pushed them out of the area, but they simply moved on to City Hall. Six people were arrested that night. One of them was 33-year-old Jeffrey Richard Singer. He was dressed in black bloc at the time of arrest and charged with felony assault of an officer, felony criminal mischief, interfering with a peace officer, and escape. Like the others, he was quickly released on his own recognizance without having to pay bail.

Though that night was no different than the other 120 violent protests that proceeded it in Portland, Singer's name stood out. He's been active in the Portland militant antifa scene going back years. In 2017 during a public meeting at City Hall, a masked Singer took to the microphone. His tirade was directed at Mayor Wheeler at that moment, but it could have just as easily been directed to every Democrat and every American.

"This is little Beirut, Mayor Wheeler. This is the City of Roses, and it has thorns. They're standing behind me," Singer said, pointing his finger at city council while a black bloc group held an anarchist banner behind him. "You are laying the fucking seeds for an insurrection....It is not a threat, it is a fact. You are building towards something that's gonna blow."[162]

They fulfilled their promise.

By autumn 2020, cold weather and rain severely affected the turnout of the riots. But that only made those who came more extreme. With smaller numbers, they were better able to carry out "hit and run" style attacks on businesses and property. On October 11, rioters shot out the window of the Heroes American Café in downtown Portland during a night that also saw the toppling of two statues and the severe vandalism of a nearby museum. Heroes American Café is owned by John Jackson, who is black. Three days before the attack, an antifa account on Twitter added the café to a list of businesses it said are "anti-BLM."[163] There are photographs of first responders in the business that they took offense to.

After the election, antifa stepped up their violence even though it appeared that Democrat presidential nominee Joe Biden had won over Donald Trump. On November 4, 2020, several hundred antifa gathered in downtown Portland. Wearing black uniforms and masks, they held a large banner that read: "WE DON'T WANT

BIDEN—WE WANT REVENGE!" After marching, they proceeded to smash up dozens of businesses and property on West Burnside Street using hammers and other tools.[164] One of the buildings targeted was Saint Andre Bessette Church.

In response to the riot, Oregon Gov. Kate Brown activated the National Guard—a first since riots began six months prior. Thirteen people were arrested. The majority had their charges immediately dropped. The damage to the Catholic church was so severe that it had to halt its charity work and outreach to the city's large homeless population.

The rioting continued.

The following day, a mob of antifa descended on the home of Portland city council member Dan Ryan and vandalized his house.[165] They were angry he was the swing vote against a city proposal to defund the Portland Police. Separately, an antifa activist set the front of City Hall on fire.

Democrats thought they could pacify antifa by refusing to condemn or even acknowledge them. But they were playing with fire. On November 8, 2020, several dozen antifa in black bloc marched to the headquarters of the Multnomah County Democrats office.[166] They destroyed the building by smashing most of the glass windows. On the building, they spray-painted: "FUCK BIDEN" and "No presidents." They drew a symbol of anarchism to make it perfectly clear who was responsible.

Antifa manuals and booklets given out at the Capitol Hill Autonomous Zone in Seattle. Photo: Andy Ngo

Antifa graffiti in downtown Portland. Photo: Andy Ngo

Graffiti in downtown Portland after a riot. Photo: Andy Ngo

CHAPTER 4

Rose City Antifa

BETWEEN 2017 AND 2019, there were around two and a half dozen violent protests and riots involving antifa in Portland. Before 2020, that was considered a lot. Most of the incidents were organized or coorganized by Rose City Antifa (RCA), the oldest antifa group in the United States. It takes its name from the "City of Roses," a nickname for Portland.

Antifa began accelerating their mass organizing in early 2017 as Donald Trump took office. Within a couple months, they had developed a sophisticated system that included propaganda, outreach, operation security, reconnaissance, and group fighting strategies. Despite the mantra claiming there is "no organization" to antifa, I could see their operations clearly took planning, coordination, money, and recruitment. From one riot to the next, their numbers grew and they became better at carrying out carnage on people and property. Still, without being inside RCA myself or speaking to someone who was, and they never willingly speak, the inner workings of the organization remained speculation. Then, in June 2020, the public finally received a rare glimpse into the workings of the group through a video release by Project Veritas, the independent investigative journalism site founded by James O'Keefe.

After being conditionally approved to join RCA on a probationary status, a journalist at Project Veritas who used the moniker "Lion" was sent the following welcome email on September 22, 2017, after spending time in Portland and befriending antifa. The email detailed the six-month vetting process that includes an intense radicalization process and training curriculum. Only upon completion of the program *and* the unanimous consent of members can one officially be welcomed in the organization.

Congratulations and welcome aboard! After deliberating as a group, we are excited to invite you to join us as a prospective member! Our orientation will be held at In Other Words (14 NE Killingsworth St, Portland, OR 97211) on Sunday November 5th at 10 am. It is really important that you come to this initial meeting so please save the date! Childcare will be provided. Please just let us know the number and ages of the children ahead of time.

The remaining classes will develop a baseline understanding of the strategy, tactics, and history of militant antifascism, dissect various strains of fascism and insurgent white supremacist formations; go over security topics; get training on various specific skill sets including militant direct action and research methods; and explore class, gender, and race issues as they relate to the struggle against fascism. In the next month it may be a good time to think about tightening up your personal security. You may want to adjust your social media accordingly, and read up on security culture. There are many excellent zines out there—and we will go over this subject in person as well—but you may want to look over this basic primer on the topic: http://www.crimethinc.com/texts/atoz/security.php.

We recommend installing Tor on your computer (a browser) and Signal on your phone (an encrypted text and call app) if you are able in the meantime. These are both really user friendly so should be relatively straight-forward to install. If you are having a hard time doing this, please let us know at the orientation. We have attached the full syllabus which includes a lot of resources for further study. Don't be overwhelmed by the length! This document is meant [to be] used as an ongoing reference guide if you are looking for information on specific topics at any point in the future. You are only expected to read the required materials. Those have been isolated and attached in a separate document as well to make it easier to find them. Feel free to get started on gathering those materials before classes start.

Remember you will have six months to get through them all and they are meant to line up with the specific class discussions on those topics so you don't need to power through everything at once. If you need an accommodation on the readings due for any reason, feel free to let us know. We have members for whom English is not their primary language, as well as members with disabilities that make doing these readings impossible. So don't hesitate to let us know if you are unable to do them for such a reason. We can see if there are other things we can do to substitute.

The main thing we are looking for is people that are dedicated and will follow through on tasks. So these assignments are as much about assessing that as about learning the material in them. Classes will be held on the 1st and 3rd Saturday of each month except the orientation at 10 am. The exceptions are the orientation, the guest lecture, and the optional firearms training. Here is the schedule:

Orientation—**Sunday** 11/5
Security—11/18
Intro to Antifascism—12/2
Guest Speakers (Alexander Reid Ross, Shane Burley)—12/16
    7pm
Typologies—1/6/18
Research—1/20
Group Project Presentations, Intro to Workgroups—2/3

Class Issues—2/17

Gender Issues—3/3

Black Bloc—3/17

Recon and Tactical—4/7

**Intro to Firearms—2nd Saturday 4/14 (optional unless DA)

Facilitation and Group—4/21

Final Individual Project Presentations—5/5

We are excited to work with y'all during this prospecting period and are more than happy to answer any questions that may arise before then. Feel free to reach out to us at any time and we will pass along updates, important news, and potential event opportunities as they arise.

In Solidarity, Rose City Antifa[167]

Since 2016, we have been told over and over by biased media and antifa apologists that antifa is not an organization. We've been lied to. While there is no single capital A "Antifa" organization with one leader, there are indeed localized cells and groups with formalized structures and memberships. Though officially leaderless, these are organizations by every definition.

The RCA curriculum is modeled on a university course. Yet it includes training on how to use guns and do reconnaissance against enemies. Unsurprisingly, one of the "guest speakers" is an academic: Portland State geography instructor and writer Alexander Reid Ross. (I contacted Ross for comment. He posted my contact information on his social media and did not respond to my inquiries.[168])

RCA was founded in 2007 and is the first-known formalized antifa group in the United States using "antifa" in its name. Those involved in its founding have been kept secret, but through Lion's time in RCA, he learned that it was started by a Portland woman, Caroline Victorin (née Gauld). She has been in a long-term relationship with a Swedish national.[169] Together, they worked to bring a tried-and-true European antifa model to the United States.

It worked.

The couple's social media accounts have all been wiped clean, but what still exists reveals that they were members of the Timbers Army soccer fan club, the organization involved in mainstreaming antifa symbols and ideology in Portland through soccer. The fan club is modeled after European football (soccer) fan organizations and their hooligan social culture. (A representative from the Timbers Army declined to confirm or deny her membership in the group.) She moved to Sweden sometime in 2016.

As a prospective member of RCA, one of Lion's first tasks was meeting with members at the Coffeehouse-Five café in North Portland for operation security training. There, he was instructed to install VeraCrypt on his laptop. The software is used to encrypt files and digital storage devices. Next, he had to install a list of programs and applications all centered around bypassing surveillance and maintaining anonymity: Tails (an operating system), Tor (for anonymous web browsing), Thunderbird (an email application), KeepassX (a password manager), and Exif (to strip all metadata from files).

The Syllabus

The fifteen-page RCA syllabus is broken into nine sections called "units." Each unit addresses a different aspect of militant antifa training and has a set of required readings and optional texts for "further study." Unit one introduces members to Rose City Antifa and its history, structure, and goals.

RCA is one cell within the Torch Network, a network of connected violent militant antifa groups across the United States. The radicals running the network are officially anonymous, but a search of the site's domain registrant shows the name Michael Novick. Novick is a former member of the Weather Underground terrorist group.[170] There are eight chapters in addition to Portland: Antifa

Sacramento, Western North Carolina Antifa, Rocky Mountain Antifa, Atlanta Antifascists, Pacific Northwest Antifascist Workers Collective, Antifa Seven Hills (Richmond, Virginia), Central Texas Anti-Racist Action (Austin, Texas), and Northern California Anti-Racist Action.

"We are born out of, and pay our respects to, the Anti-Racist Action Network. We are dedicated to confronting fascism and other elements of oppression. We believe in direct action," states the Torch Network on its website.[171] "Direct action" is a dog whistle for protest activity that includes violence. To join the network, one's group "must be vouched for by at least two network chapters, and delegates [need] two individual vouches."

The "Points of Unity" RCA members have to pledge to state they must agree to disrupt "fascist" activity, refuse cooperation with law enforcement and courts, oppose oppression, hold themselves accountable, and, most importantly, support not only those within the network but also those "outside the network who we believe have similar aims or principles."[172] This is the phantom cell structure of antifa that makes them analogous to global jihadism. A unifying ideology and political agenda ties together individuals, cells, and groups.

RCA's website further reaffirms the group's commitment to violent direct action in the name of "anti-racism." It regularly publishes reports and doxes on individuals and groups for their members to target in real life and online. I myself was targeted in an article shortly before being beaten in 2019.

RCA's second unit in the curriculum centers around in-depth training on operations security, known as "OPSEC." Security is drilled into the heads of all antifa members and their allies. They're trained to not trust those around them, including friends and family. They know they are participating in criminal conspiracies and are hypervigilant about hiding their tracks from law enforcement and anyone who might report them. The curriculum reads:

UNIT TWO: SECURITY

What are the primary security vulnerabilities online?

What are the most important programs for me to use?

What are the best available technological safety measures to put in place to do this work?

What are some security vulnerabilities in my life and how can I amend them?

Who can I talk to about RCA and what can I share?

How is communication about sensitive info best handled? What about in an emergency?

What is "security culture"?

KEY COMPETENCIES:

Have a grasp on technological weaknesses and the best measures currently available to address these.

Grasp of basic, crucial internet security.

Get comfortable using Tor, Signal, Keypass, and PGP.

Be able to STFU [shut the fuck up]: no bragging, no loud talking in bars, no Facebook updates, no discussion of sensitive matters with close friends, partners, etc.

Know your rights when you are dealing with the cops.

Understand that your actions impact the entire group, and that your comrades are depending on you.

REQUIRED:

An Activist's Guide to Information Security by Sprout Distro[173]

What Is Security Culture? by CrimethInc[174]

Complete tech security training

The two required readings, "An Activist's Guide to Information Security" by Sprout Distro and "What Is Security Culture?" by CrimethInc, are among the most popular instruction manuals on how to anonymize oneself online. They are available for free and are regularly printed and disseminated at anarchist and antifa events. In CHAZ and throughout the 2020 Portland riots, these manuals were also given out to riot attendees. The second unit's recommended readings for further study include a doxing guide by antifa blog and news site It's Going Down.[175] It's Going Down has almost 100,000 followers on Twitter.[176] The extreme site had its Facebook page deleted in August 2020 following a crackdown on far-left and far-right extremist accounts.

UNIT THREE: ANTIFA BASICS

What is militant antifascism?

What is "antifa"?

KEY COMPETENCIES:

Be able to articulate why militant antifascism is important and how it differs from liberal anti-racism.

Start familiarizing yourself with militant anti-racist and antifascist history, here in Portland, in the U.S., and abroad.

Get some responses down to common criticisms, i.e. "free speech," being the "real fascists," etc.

REQUIRED:

"Confronting Fascism: Discussion Documents for a Militant Movement" by Don Hammerquist, J. Sakai, ARA Chicago, & Mark Salotte[177]

"Portland History in Review" by M. Treloar[178]

"Claim No Easy Victories: Anarchist Analysis of ARA" by Common Struggle[179]

"The Divorce of Thought from Deed: A Compilation of Writings on Social Conflict, White Supremacy, and the Mythology of Free Speech at UNC " by the North Carolina Piece Corps[180]

Confronting Fascism is published by the extreme anarchist publishing house AK Press. It publishes and sells many of the books and booklets promoted by antifa. One text for further study in the unit is Mark Bray's *Antifa: The Anti-Fascist Handbook*. M. Testa's popular *Militant Antifascism* is another recommended reading on the list. This unit is all about theory. It is akin to Muslim Brotherhood radicalization, which involves having members read texts that intellectualize religious extremism and romanticize Islamic law.[181] Likewise, the readings in the RCA antifa unit brainwash members on the failures of liberalism and capitalism and the need to create a new utopian society.

Websites the RCA curriculum recommends members become acquainted with include the aforementioned It's Going Down, the Southern Poverty Law Center (SPLC), and Idavox. The SPLC has establishment liberal and media legitimacy as an arbiter of "hate groups," but too often it actually serves to launder antifa's ideology into the mainstream. For example, groups that hold traditional Christian views meet the threshold for being an SPLC "hate group."

Idavox is an antifa blog site dedicated to publishing information about accused white racists and "fascists." It is a project of the American nonprofit One People's Project (OPP), founded and run by Daryle Lamont Jenkins. Its motto is "Hate has consequences." I knew of Jenkins from when he organized a protest of my speaking lecture at Heritage Foundation in Washington, DC, in late 2019. Think tank Capital Research Center describes the One People's Project as a nonprofit "arm of antifa" that curates lists of enemies where personal information is published. They wrote this about Jenkins and his organization in a March 2020 report:

> In a now-deleted interview from 2005 with an anarchist website, Jenkins explained that OPP doesn't go after just white supremacists and fascists, but also targets mainstream conservatives, such as Sean Hannity. Jenkins told the interviewer that the organization is "rather aggressive and controversial in some areas, such as when we publish the home addresses of neo-Nazis and even mainstream

conservatives, like Sean Hannity, who lives at [address redacted by CRC]."[182]

Unit four, "White Supremacy and Fascism Defined," is where readers will see some critical race theory manifest in the curriculum. These are recent additions in the evolution of antifa ideology, particularly in its English-speaking groups.

UNIT FOUR: WHITE SUPREMACY & FASCISM DEFINED

What is white skin privilege?

What is White Nationalism?

What are key features of structural white supremacy?

How about insurgent white supremacist movements?

How do these things relate? Where do they collude? Where do they come into conflict?

How is fascism different than just right-wing politics in general?

What are the appropriate uses of these words: Fascist, White Supremacist, Alt-Right, Nativist, White Nationalist, National Socialist, Islamophobia, Anti-Semite?

KEY COMPETENCIES:

Be able to articulate why it is important to fight insurgent WP [White power] groups.

Be able to define and talk about Third Positionism.[183]

Be able to point out fascism's key traits.

Be able to explain the idea of contested space: ideological, cultural, political, and physical.

Start familiarizing yourself with various strains of insurgent racist & fascist groups.

REQUIRED:

"Fascism: A Very Short Introduction" by Kevin Passmore

RCA's definition of fascism
"Blood in the Face" by James Ridgeway
"A Hundred Little Hitlers" by Elinor Langer
Typologies training

To my surprise, this part of the curriculum shows members are educated on the nuances of right-wing and far-right ideologies. For whatever reason, that nuance is not reflected in their public statements, propaganda, and chosen targets. Since Trump's 2016 election win, antifa in Portland and around the country has militantly and violently confronted both mainstream conservative activists and the radical far-right with equal hatred and violence.

The required "typologies" training by RCA was conducted secretly at the In Other Words Feminist Community Center in February 2018. RCA member "Bryne" gave a lecture on neo-Nazi groups in the United States. One of the senior RCA members at the training, Adam Carpinelli, told members to get a concealed carry license—not because they actually respect laws but rather to avoid being criminally charged should they get arrested. Carpinelli, originally from Virginia, is a Portland-based musician who majored in black studies at Portland State University in the McNair Scholars Program.[184] The scholarship program is funded by the U.S. Department of Education.

RCA trainers include radical left-wing activists.[185] Medical students from the Oregon Health and Science University are also alleged to be high-level activists, one of whom is now a medical doctor who started the splinter RCA group Popular Mobilization to provide a moderate facade of militant antifa to the press and wider left.

Unit five indoctrinates prospective members with Marxist ideas on economics and class warfare. This is the communist part of antifa's anarchist-communist ideology. The unit trains members that white supremacy and capitalism are linked through the history of American chattel slavery and can never be divorced from one another.

UNIT FIVE: CLASS STRUGGLE & WHITE SUPREMACY

What is the relationship between class and white supremacy?

What lessons can we learn from militant liberatory movements in the past?

How does our work fit into the broader struggle for a classless free society?

KEY COMPETENCIES:

Be able to discuss how whiteness was invented to break working class solidarity.

Familiarize yourself with different perspectives and strategies on how to oppose white supremacy, hetero-patriarchy and capitalism.

Look at the ways that various anti-racist, anti-capitalist movements organized historically, the unique conditions that created them, their weaknesses and strengths, the ways in which they advanced or derailed radical social change. Think about how these lessons can augment your own antifascist work.

We strongly encourage members to familiarize themselves with a wide range of Left perspectives on these issues, including those they do not agree with. We encourage critical thinking!

Be able to articulate how and why our work is an important component in the struggle for a classless free society.

REQUIRED:

"Between Infoshops and Insurrection: U.S. Anarchism, Movement Building, and the Racial Order" by Joel Olson[186]

"With Allies Like These: Reflections on Privilege Reductionism" by Common Cause Ottawa[187]

"Clenched Fists, Empty Pockets" by Fredric Carlsson-
    Andersson & Atilla Pişkin
"Accomplices Not Allies" by Indigenous Action[188]

Unit six further explores ideas of critical race theory introduced earlier in the training—in particular, the vogue academic theory of intersectionality.

UNIT SIX: INTERSECTIONS WITH GENDER
What is intersectionality of oppression?
Why and how are you a feminist?
Why and how do you fight patriarchal oppression?

KEY COMPETENCIES:
Be able to challenge internalized, patriarchal behaviors and
    beliefs to foster a healthy group dynamic.
Begin to identify ways that sexism, homophobia, and
    transphobia relate to other systems of oppression.
Understand how fascist ideologies rely on misogyny, rigid
    gender roles, and virulent homophobia.
Familiarize yourself with feminism's historical weakness,
    including racism, classism, and transphobia.
Understand how intersectionality of oppression translates
    into real world violence and trauma.

REQUIRED:
"Why Misogynists Make Great Informants: How Gender
    Violence on the Left Enables State Violence in Radical
    Movements" by Courtney Desiree Morris[189]
RCA's Manarchist Questionnaire[190]
"Against Patriarchy: Tools for Men to Further Feminist
    Revolution" by Chris Crass[191]

Unit six's readings and indoctrination "competencies" are no different than what are taught in American universities and colleges. Courses on women's, black, gender, and queer studies all teach students the heuristics of understanding the world and people through a grievance lens. Antifa traditionally did not include critical race theory and intersectionality in its base ideology, but the current manifestation of the movement has been infected, like most institutions in the United States (e.g., academe, government, media, Big Tech, etc.).

Unit seven, innocently titled "Research," actually trains RCA recruits on how to dox their opponents and do reconnaissance and surveillance.

UNIT SEVEN: RESEARCH

Where do I go to get information?
How do I keep track of my information effectively?

KEY COMPETENCIES:

Start to navigate and search for information online.
Develop familiarity with key online places to get information.
Learn how to organize research so it is easy to retrieve.
Begin to discern urgent vs. non-urgent information, how to
    prioritize and look for what you need.
Begin to think creatively about how to get information.
Start experimenting with fake personas in WP [white power]
    forums.

REQUIRED:

Attend our research training workshop.
"Intelligence Gathering, Dissemination, & Internet Security"
    by ARA
Learn how to strip data from photos.
Create a "sock puppet" account on Stormfront and/or New
    Saxon.
Set up Google alerts.

In September 2020, I received a security alert that someone had approached the front door of my parents' home. In reviewing the security footage, I saw two masked females. One with magenta-pink hair approached the front door and tried to open it. Another stood further back on the street to keep watch.[192]

Before walking on the property, they circled the front of the home. After trying to open the door, the pink-haired woman looked around the property and saw a package. She examined it, carefully looking at the name on the label. She then shouted to Padilla: "Confirmed. He has a package at the front door." Both quickly left on foot. This incident, which was immediately reported to police, is an example of antifa's "creative" recognizance. They were looking to confirm if that was my parents' home. Two weeks later, they released their findings and the address online, leading to people driving into my parents' property and stalking the front of the house again.[193] Portland Police took a report per policy but did nothing else.

The point of releasing a target's personal information into the ether with claims of the person being a Nazi or fascist is so antifa vigilantes will do something. It's already happened. Michael Reinoehl, the Portland antifa shooter, killed a man based on a whisper campaign of there being fascists in downtown Portland in August 2020.

The final two units in the curriculum train RCA recruits on how to put the ideology and skills they acquired throughout the program into (violent) action.

UNIT EIGHT: ADVANCED STRATEGY AND TACTICS

How do I create a strategic plan?

How do I give and receive critical feedback in a productive and honest way?

How do I assess risks and plan accordingly?

What distinguishes oppositional organizing from other types
of organizing?

How do I leverage the weaknesses of my opponents?

KEY COMPETENCIES:

Be able to create strategic plans: how to think through
alternate scenarios, anticipate possible outcomes, identify
potential threats and vulnerabilities, choose allies wisely,
and select tactics that best meet goals and objectives.

Be able to give and receive thoughtful critiques on ideas,
plans, and actions.

Have at minimum basic self-defense abilities.

Be prepared to deal with a variety of scenarios.

REQUIRED:

Black bloc training.

Advanced recon topics training.

Active participation in ongoing martial arts trainings.

UNIT NINE: GROUP PROCESS

How do I assess when a meeting is going well?

How can I keep things on track and not waste time rehashing
worn territory?

How can I intervene in unhealthy or damaging dynamics?

How can I help make sure we are hearing from quieter
people, POC [people of color], women, and others that
may not take up as much space in meetings?

KEY COMPETENCIES:

Be able to effectively facilitate meetings.

Be able to assess unhealthy or time-burglary dynamics and
have some skills handy to address them.

RCA's previously secret curriculum forces transparency on a group and movement that is secretive and designed to deny it even exists. But it's not only RCA that has a formalized structure. The other cells in the Torch Network follow a similar plan. Antifa groups outside the network still operate similarly based on the sharing of the same extremist literature and training materials. Unfortunately a full exposé on RCA and all its members was cut short. Project Veritas's undercover journalist lasted in the group from late 2017 to mid-2018. When it came time for him to proceed further, he was voted out. They didn't suspect he was an infiltrator but instead questioned his commitment to antifa due to his reluctance to engage in criminal activities during planned direct action events.

Nowhere else in America has antifa managed to radicalize and train so many than Portland. The consequences were felt in real time during 2016 to 2019 through various riots and street brawls, but in 2020 it was taken to an unimaginable level for an American city.

A 1932 Antifaschistische Aktion poster. Photo: Stadtgeschichtliches Museum Leipzig

The 'Unity Congress' event organized by the Communist Party of Germany (KPD) at the Philharmonic Opera House in Berlin in 1932. Photo: Bundesarchiv

The headquarters of the Communist Party of Germany (KPD) in Berlin in 1932. The text on the building reads: "Join the Antifascist Action against war, hunger and fascism. Elect communists. Vote KPD." Photo: Bundesarchiv

CHAPTER 5

Origin Story

I N LATE OCTOBER 2016, a magazine called *The Week* published an issue that predicted how supporters of Donald Trump would react when he inevitably lost the presidential election to Hillary Clinton. Titled "After the Election," the cover artwork showed angry Trump supporters with ugly, contorted faces carrying guns, weapons, and torches.

On November 8, 2016, the day of the election, Sally Kohn, a left-wing CNN commentator at the time, tweeted: "My sense is that if Trump wins, Hillary supporters will be sad. If Hillary wins, Trump supporters will be angry. Important difference."[194] The tweet received thousands of shares and likes. *The Week*'s cover illustration and Kohn's tweet ended up being prescient, but both misidentified the would-be rioters.

Hillary Clinton lost, and those who took to the streets in Portland were not wearing red "Make America Great Again" hats but rather black uniforms. They were antifa. Carrying bats and other melee weapons, antifa militants smashed property in downtown

Portland and started fires on the streets. They caused over a million dollars in damage in one night. The rioting lasted for days, leading to more than a hundred arrests. In Austin, Texas, around two hundred people gathered at the State Capitol to protest the election results. Many of them were masked. A group began to attack the few Trump supporters who showed up to counterdemonstrate. Police made six arrests, identifying them as members of the Red Guards Austin, an antifa group.[195]

Similar carnage was repeated a few months later during the day of the presidential inauguration in January 2017. In Washington, DC, marauding gangs of antifa overwhelmed police by breaking windows and hurling projectiles. They set a limousine owned by a Muslim immigrant on fire. The rioting caused more than $100,000 in damages. Less than two weeks later, more antifa violence was repeated on the West Coast—this time at the University of California, Berkeley, home of the Free Speech Movement. On February 1, 2017, around 1,500 left-wing protesters amassed on campus to shut down the scheduled speaking event featuring right-wing provocateur Milo Yiannopoulos. Masked antifa extremists started fires on campus, destroyed property, threw incendiary devices, hurled rocks at police, and assaulted event attendees who lined up outside Sproul Hall. Violent riots continued in Berkeley throughout the summer of 2017, as they did in Portland.

Over and over, street violence against individuals, property, and law enforcement was repeated in major U.S. cities, forcing Americans to become quickly acquainted with the antifa phenomenon. The meteoric rise of the movement virtually unknown to Americans only a few years ago has led some to believe that antifa is new. This is wrong. The militant far-left movement and ideology have existed for over half a century in Europe. It has had decades to develop a coherent ideology and both violent and nonviolent strategies to undermine liberal democracy under the guise of fighting fascism.

The Weimar Republic

The defeat of the Germans in World War I led to a period of intense political instability. The signing of the Treaty of Versailles in June 1919 was meant as a peace settlement, but the conditions it gave rise to eventually paved the ground for Adolf Hitler's ascension to power.

Under the peace treaty, Germany was punished with crippling reparation payments to the Allied powers for its role in the war, in addition to a massive reduction of its territory and restrictions on its military. Emperor Wilhelm II's sudden abdication of the throne further threw the new nation-state into confusion. Between 1919 and 1920, the Weimar Republic faced uprisings from both the left and right. In January 1919, around 50,000 communists, known as the Spartacists, led a failed armed rebellion in Berlin.

By August that year, a constitution was written and adopted in the city of Weimar. But Germany did not have a democratic history or tradition, and the Weimar government was deeply unpopular.

The country's monetary hyperinflation, caused by reparation payments it couldn't pay, was further exacerbated by the global Great Depression. By 1923, German cash was practically worthless, adding to the political instability of the country that already existed since its founding. Historical photographs taken during the time show citizens burning cash to warm their homes. And throughout the 1920s, political paramilitaries became the norm as groups and parties prepped their members to try to seize power— or crush an opposing party's uprising.

The paramilitaries were used as security for political gatherings and to violently shut down the meetings of opposing groups. The republic was marred with wave after wave of tit-for-tat political violence. The paramilitaries, both left and right wing, are notorious for carrying out assassinations and committing brutal acts of violence. Efforts throughout the 1920s by the government to ban some of the paramilitaries failed. They simply regrouped and reorganized under new names.

Nearly every political group or party had a paramilitary: the communists, the centrists, and, of course, the fascists. For good reason, the most remembered of German paramilitaries is the Sturmabteilung, the original paramilitary of the National Socialist German Workers' Party, also known as the Nazi Party. Called "Brownshirts," based on the color of their uniforms, these paramilitary men were Hitler's violent street thugs. The unfathomable evils of the Sturmabteilung, and later the Schutzstaffel (also known as the SS), are well documented by historians and survivors of WWII. The SS, which originally started as a bodyguard-type paramilitary for Nazi Party leaders, later came to replace the Sturmabteilung and was used to carry out Hitler's "final solution" plan.

While the Brownshirts are well remembered in contemporary Western society, the history of far-left paramilitaries in the German interwar years has faded to memory. Like the Nazis, the Communist Party of Germany (German: Kommunistische Partei Deutschlands, or KPD) had its own paramilitaries. The party was Stalinist in orientation and was closely aligned with the Soviet Union.[196] At the national conference of the German Communist Party in 1924, they formed a new paramilitary: the Red Front Fighters' League (German: Roter Frontkämpfer-Bund). The league's paramilitary members had their own uniforms, and the group adopted the clenched fist as its symbol. Leftist groups today from Black Lives Matter to antifa have adopted that communist symbol.

Throughout the 1920s, the Red Front Fighters' League was extremely violent, engaging in clashes with the paramilitaries of liberal parties. Come again? You read that right: the communist paramilitary was mostly preoccupied with fighting liberals and socialists rather than the Nazi paramilitary. Under the leadership of Ernst Thälmann, the German Communist Party and its various offshoots viewed social democrats and liberals as "social fascists" no different from Nazis. In fact, Communist International, the Vladimir Lenin–founded group that promoted communism around the world, believed that social democracy would inevitably lead to fascism.[197]

Scholars estimate the communist Red Front Fighters' League had upward of 130,000 members before it was banned in 1929 following days of deadly rioting. Despite claiming to be Germany's "only anti-fascist party," the German Communist Party sometimes worked with the Nazis to undermine the governing Social Democrats.[198] They wanted to seize power by any means necessary. For example, in 1931 they supported the Nazis and other right-wing groups who had initiated a (failed) popular referendum meant to bring down the Prussian Social Democrat government.

Antifascist Action

In May 1932, the German Communist Party announced the formation of the Antifaschistische Aktion (Antifascist Action, commonly referred to as "Antifa"), a new paramilitary communist group. This is the original "Antifa" and the group that contemporary antifa around the world take inspiration from. The paramilitary was created to bring together a coalition of communists at the community level to oppose and fight political opponents.

Though calling itself the Antifascist Action, those who served as decision makers on its executive boards consisted of members of the German Communist Party and other allied communist groups.[199] Simply put, the Antifascist Action was a communist organization under a thinly veiled new name. It held rallies and developed its own propaganda. The two-flag logo used by today's antifa groups is based on the original red flags logo of the Antifascist Action. The two red flags symbolized the union of communism and socialism. Like the other communist paramilitaries before it, the Antifascist Action was involved in political street brawls. They also acted as security and self-defense for communists who lived together in select neighborhoods and apartment buildings.

While the communists were occupied with fighting the social democrats and liberals, the appeal and power of the Nazi Party continued to grow. By July 1932, the Nazis became the largest party in parliament, with 230 seats. The Social Democrats were behind at 133 seats, and the German Communist Party had 89 seats. The campaign season was marred by exceptional levels of political violence between fascist, social democratic, and communist members.

By January 1933, President Paul von Hindenburg appointed Hitler as chancellor. Two months later, the Reichstag, or parliament, passed the Enabling Act, which gave Hitler's government the legal authority to be a dictatorship. The communist efforts to take control of the state failed. The German Communist and Social Democrat Parties were both banned, leaving the Nazis with no political opposition as they implemented their expansionist and genocidal agenda.

Antifa State Building

Historians of WWII have documented how German communists aided the Nazis in their rise to power. For one, their preoccupation with fighting the social democrats and liberals, who they called "social fascists," weakened a united opposition to the Nazis and further undermined the legitimacy of liberal democracy in the republic.[200] And at times throughout the 1930s, the German Community Party even collaborated with the Nazis to oppose a mutual enemy.

While the Antifascist Action and all opposing groups were banned after Hitler became head of state, the antifa communist ideology never went away. From the ashes of WWII, it was absorbed and institutionalized in the official state ideology of what would become the German Democratic Republic, also known as East Germany. From 1949 to 1990, East Germany existed as a communist state carved out of the Weimar Republic by the Soviet Union, one of WWII's victorious Allied leaders. For over forty years, the extremely repressive conditions in East Germany exemplified what "antifa" state-building actually looks like.

Through the East German Ministry for State Security, better known as the Stasi, citizens were monitored and spied on through a vast apparatus of informants who infiltrated all aspects of life and civil society. The secret police agency was originally modeled to be similar to the Soviet Union's secret police, the KGB. The Stasi's mandate by the state was to weed out political dissenters and to terrorize the masses into compliance, in addition to conducting espionage. Antifa groups today do something similar on a community level.

Secret police form a pillar of communism. Under Maoist China, a similar system was deployed to spy on its citizens.[201] One could never know if their friend, family member, or spouse was an informant. In East Germany, the mass persecution and psychological warfare against its own citizens suspected of political wrongthink were justified by the communist state in the name of fighting fascism. But to them, "fascism" referred to the West and its governing system of liberal democracy.

Following the end of WWII, Walter Ulbricht, a key architect of the Weimar-era German Communist Party, returned from exile in the Soviet Union to reestablish a communist party along Stalinist lines in the Soviet-occupied part of the country. Under his leadership, the Socialist Unity Party of Germany (German: Sozialistische Einheitspartei Deutschlands) was founded. This remained the one party in control of East Germany from the state's founding in 1949 to its end after the fall of the Berlin Wall. Under Ulbricht's leadership, East Germany ruled over its citizens with an iron fist. The East German uprising in June 1953, in which more than a million people revolted against the communist government, resulted in the Soviet Union using its military to violently suppress demonstrators.[202] The death toll has never been officially determined, but historians estimate that hundreds were killed.[203] The early years of East Germany demonstrated that political dissent would not be tolerated, much like how antifa treat their critics today.

Political scientist Helmut Müller-Enbergs estimates that up to 620,000 people worked as secret informers for East Germany's secret police. Formally called "unofficial collaborators," the informants numbered in the tens of thousands at any one point. The level of state infiltration into every aspect of daily life cannot be understated. From apartment buildings to factories, schools, universities, and more—no activity or space was free of spies.[204] Citizens deemed worthy of additional surveillance had their homes secretly bugged with cameras and microphones.

The documentation of East Germany's four-decade reign of communist oppression in the name of "anti-fascism" is extensive. In fact, one of its most important tools in addition to the Stasi was the Berlin Wall—known by its name in the East as the anti-fascist defense wall (German: Antifaschistischer Schutzwall).

EAST GERMANY'S "ANTI-FASCIST" repression against its own people was not its only sin. Like antifa idealogues today who call for terrorist attacks against the state and its institutions, East Germany supported terrorism. Of note was the Stasi's logistical and financial support to West German far-left terrorist group the Red Army Faction (German: Rote Armee Fraktion), also known as the Baader-Meinhof Gang, which was formed in 1968. Throughout the 1970s, they killed dozens of people in West Germany through assassinations, bombings, robberies, arson attacks, and shootings. The goal was to undermine the West German government, which they viewed as fascistic, as well as to oppose American "imperialism." In 1967, future Baader-Meinhof Gang founder Gudrun Ennslin declared: "This fascist state means to kill us all.... Violence is the only way to answer violence."[205]

The rhetoric used by Baader-Meinhof Gang members is nearly indistinguishable from language used by antifa extremists today. The same goes for their violent tactics, although contemporary antifa groups currently lack the high-level support needed to carry out mass deadly attacks (but that doesn't stop them from trying).

The misnomer of "anti-fascism" holds steady today for contemporary antifa groups—they advocate for the overthrow of liberal democracies and the abolishment of capitalism. And the legacy of a pervasive surveillance culture provides one of the pillars for antifa activities. East Germany, or CHAZ for that matter, demonstrates how the antifa ideology functions in practice when it is institutionalized across a population.

Europe

Today, the largest, most organized and violent antifa groups remain in Germany, even though the ideology has spread all over the West. One reason for this is the history of the Holocaust and Nazism for the Germans, making any movement calling itself "anti-fascist" palatable to a portion of the public ignorant of the past. Another is the presence of true neo-Nazi organizing, ironically most concentrated in the eastern region of the country that formerly belonged to the "anti-fascist" East Germany. Further, the development of left-wing, anti-government movements (with origins in 1960s West German student protests) has allowed far-left subcultures to take root and grow in many cities.

Despite now having a strong, stable, and prosperous liberal democracy (Germany has the leading GDP in the European Union), the culture of polarized politics remains. The Federal Office for the Protection of the Constitution (German: Bundesamt für Verfassungsschutz), Germany's domestic intelligence agency, released data showing left-wing extremists have become more violent in recent years. Between 2012 and 2017, the number of "violence-oriented" left-wing extremists identified by authorities increased by 27 percent. That's an increase from 7,100 to 9,000 individuals.[206] The number of violent incidents by left-wing extremists also increased by 88 percent during that time period.[207] The agency also monitors sympathizers of violent left-wing extremism. From 2017 to 2018, there was about an 8.5 percent increase, from 29,500 to 32,000 individuals.[208]

Italy and Spain

To a lesser degree, contemporary antifa groups take inspiration from the historical anti-fascist efforts in Italy against fascist dictator Benito Mussolini. Originally a member of the Italian Socialist Party, Mussolini later founded the Italian Fasci of Combat (Italian: Fasci Italiani di Combattimento) in 1919. Members were organized in paramilitary squads known as the "Blackshirts" for the color of their uniform. They are analogous to the Nazi Brownshirts that came later in Germany.

Argo Secondari, an anarchist, founded a militant anti-fascist organization in Rome in 1921 called the People's Daring Ones (Italian: Arditi del Popolo). The group included communists, socialists, anarchists, and anti-monarchists. They led fights against the Blackshirts in various towns in the Italian countryside. These historical fights form part of the borrowed mythos used by contemporary antifa groups today. By fighting people on the streets of Portland, Berkeley, and elsewhere, they claim to be engaging in the same anti-fascist tradition. By 1922, Mussolini, who now headed the Fascist Party, was invited to form a government by King Victor Emmanuel. After chipping away at the liberal institutions of the state, he declared himself Il Duce, meaning "the leader," in 1925. Under his leadership, Italy was one of the Axis powers with Germany and Japan in WWII.

Antifa groups today also borrow mythos based on the history of Spanish anarchists and communists who opposed the nationalists led by Francisco Franco during the Spanish Civil War. Dolores Ibárruri Gómez, a member of the Communist Party of Spain (Spanish: Partido Comunista de España), popularized the slogan "No pasarán," or "They shall not pass," in a speech in 1936. No pasarán is still used today at antifa rallies and in graffiti messages. While Franco, a Catholic traditionalist, was not a fascist, he received significant military support from fascist Italy and Nazi Germany. Franco won the civil war in 1939 and established a dictatorship over Spain that lasted until his death in 1975.

Antifa in Europe Today

Like the Antifa Action of the interwar years that claimed certain buildings, neighborhoods, and districts in the Weimar Republic, contemporary antifa groups do the same. Of particular note are parts of the Kreuzberg-Friedrichshain and Neukölln neighborhoods in Berlin. Here, radical far-left squatters occupy abandoned property and land. The "blind-eye" approach by local governments allowed squatting communities to fester for decades, resulting in the development of their own parallel societies where the authority of the state and the rule of law are challenged.[209] Antifa in CHAZ attempted to turn Seattle's Capitol Hill neighborhood into a variant of this.

Every year on May 1, also known as May Day, the inhabitants and supporters of these antifa-friendly neighborhoods turn violent. In July 2016, thousands of masked militants attacked police in Friedrichshain to protest redevelopment efforts in the area. They hurled projectiles at police, destroyed shops, and damaged police cruisers. Over 120 police officers were injured. It took about 1,800 officers to bring the rioting under control.[210]

Then in July 2017, hundreds of antifa black bloc extremists embedded themselves within crowds of thousands of anti-capitalist protesters who demonstrated against the Hamburg G20 summit. The G20 summit is an annual gathering of heads of states and finance ministers who discuss global monetary policies. At the 2017 summit, antifa militants hurled rocks and lit mortar fireworks at police. Over days, they looted businesses and set cars on fire.

The deployment of twenty thousand officers wasn't enough to contain the violence. Nearly five hundred officers ended up injured.[211]

Sven Mewes, the command leader of the Saxony branch of the German state police, had this to say on television at the time: "Such violence I've never experienced, and I've been a police officer for over 30 years."[212]

In November 2019, nineteen police officers were injured again in Friedrichshain, Berlin, after violent antifa militants attacked them during an eviction attempt of a building illegally occupied by squatters. The rioters also attacked a construction trailer occupied by two security guards. The violence was so bad that police retreated.[213]

Antifa violence is also prevalent in pockets of the east of the country. On New Year's Eve 2019 in the Connewitz district of Leipzig, police say a group of violent left-wing extremists threw rocks, bottles, and fireworks at them. One officer was so badly injured he lost consciousness and required surgery at hospital. Leipzig police investigated the attack as an attempted murder.[214]

SUFFICE IT TO SAY, the examples of left-wing violent extremism against the state, individuals, and property are numerous and frequent in Germany, the home of the original Antifascist Action and the largest antifa movement today. Defenders of the left and far left often decry these observations, stating they create a "false equivalence" with the far right. They point to the far right's higher body count to justify their own excesses. However important the observation may be in directing counterterrorism strategies and resources, it is ultimately irrelevant to the argument at hand.

In 2017, Bernd Palenda, the former head of the Berlin branch of the German domestic intelligence agency, stated astutely in an interview with the *Berliner Morgenpost* that the "extreme left would kill if necessary."[215] That they have been less effective than the far right is not an excuse. Both the extreme left and right seek to undermine liberal democracy and the rule of law, whether through the use of violence or other means. They have differing political visions and goals, but both would result in the destruction of the liberties we value.

At the moment, the threat of the far right is understood by the American public and actively countered by government, academia, media, and civil society. No comparable resolve or mass organization exists to counter the far left. Why? One explanation is the cultural dominance of the left. The political homogeneity in popular culture, academe, and urban centers of influence (e.g., New York, Washington, DC, Los Angeles, etc.) has produced a populace with severe blind spots.

This chapter chronicled antifa's communist origins in the Weimar Republic, an origin reflected in contemporary antifa groups' propaganda, symbols, and mythos. The next chapter will explore the evolution of the movement's ideology as it eventually established roots in North America. Over the last fifty years, the movement has syncretized with aspects of anarchism, autonomism, and punk culture, producing a more virulent and violent ideology than the original Antifa Action of the 1920s.[216]

Antifa rioters try to break the fence protecting the Mark O. Hatfield U.S. Courthouse. Photo: Andy Ngo

Rioters try to tear down the fence protecting the Justice Center in June 2020. Photo: Andy Ngo

Students at Western Oregon University tried and failed to cancel a College Republicans event in June 2019. Photo: Andy Ngo

CHAPTER 6

American Mutation

S ATURDAY, JUNE 30, 2018, was a warm day in Portland. Patriot Prayer, a conservative group headed by an evangelical preacher named Joey Gibson, organized a permitted march in downtown Portland. The right-wing gathering was met by hundreds of left-wing protesters. Ahead of the rally, Rose City Antifa created a Facebook event page titled "Defend PDX: Patriot Prayer's Violence Must End." "PDX" is a moniker for Portland, taken from the airport code for Portland International Airport.

The Facebook page accused Gibson of bringing in "alt-right bullies, Nazis, homophobes, and unsavory characters" to brutalize vulnerable people.

"We are united in our opposition to the rise of fascism in this country and we sure as hell will not let it take our streets. No pasarán!" continued the post, ending with the antifa Spanish-language rallying cry.

As the right-wingers began their march, they were confronted by dozens in the antifa black bloc. The two sides stared each other down. Suddenly, someone hurled a flash-bang grenade at the right-wingers. Its explosion acted as the cue to brawl. Both sides rushed toward each other with fists, sticks, and batons swinging. Those knocked to the ground were pummeled and stomped on. Antifa militants wearing helmets hurled rocks and bottles. No police were around as people beat each other bloody.

After both sides regrouped, more fighting broke out on a nearby street. Then the punch happened. A masked black-clad militant with a collapsible baton was joined by his comrades. He took a swing at a right-winger and knocked him to the ground. Then he made eye contact with 28-year-old Ethan Nordean, a Proud Boy member from Washington state. He swung twice and hit Nordean with the baton. Nordean didn't flinch and punched the antifa militant in the face, knocking him unconscious and sending his sunglasses off into the distance. He collapsed to the ground and was dragged away by his comrades.

The punch was captured on video, and the footage became an internet sensation to Donald Trump fans across America. To many conservative Americans who don't follow the esoteric politics of antifa, the footage was simple to understand: antifa started a fight with a Trump supporter and lost.

That violent summer in Portland, I was traveling the United Kingdom and Europe to work on stories for an unrelated beat. But the videos and photos out of my hometown made their way to the international press, giving me an opportunity to ask locals what they thought of this new American phenomenon. They weren't surprised.

"You're just seeing this now there? We've had hooligan street fights for decades," said one Englishman. He pointed out the shaved heads and punk-style clothing of some of the antifa militants.

Before antifa made its way to the United States, it spread to Britain first from continental Europe. There, it cross-pollinated with the punk subculture, creating a uniquely English-language form of antifa.

British Antifa

Before developing an American offshoot, antifa found footing in Britain in the 1970s punk rock music scene, particularly through the "Oi!" subculture, which brought together punks and skinheads from the London working class. Though skinheads are now commonly thought of as being associated with neo-Nazis, skinhead subculture can be left-wing, right-wing, or apolitical. Its origin in London in the late 1960s was particularly multiracial, taking strong influence from Jamaican street culture and music. But by the mid-1970s, a strain of it was influenced by far-right racist ideology.

Mark Bray, the antifa historian and author, says this was caused by economic stagnation during the time and strong recruitment efforts by the National Front, a British party founded in 1967.[217] In response to the development of far-right skinhead subculture in the 1970s and 1980s, a countermovement of anti-racist skinheads formed. On the surface, they looked visually similar. They sported very short or shaved heads, bomber jackets, Fred Perry polo shirts, and steel-toed Doc Martens boots. But more subtle cues, such as bootlace colors, tattoos, and patches, would signal which ideological faction one belonged to. At punk shows, they often fought each other. The fighting became ritualized and an act to show up for in and of itself. As Britain struggled with instances of organized far-right violence targeting South Asian immigrant and black communities, a plethora of militant left-wing groups formed to oppose them.

In 1985, the Anti-Fascist Action was formed in London. It was made up of members who belonged to numerous other far-left groups, like Red Action and the Direct Action Movement.[218] The Anti-Fascist Action took inspiration from the original German Antifa paramilitary and made it a primary goal to fight far-right groups like the National Front and the British National Party. In many ways, it was a small-scale repeat of the far-left versus far-right street battles that plagued the Weimar Republic in the interwar years.

The militant antifa organizing in Britain during the 1980s could be argued as legitimate, or at least more legitimate, than the American manifestation that has become popular since 2016. First, the war against the fascist Axis powers took place on European soil, and the Nazi Luftwaffe bombing campaigns in Britain were still in living memory. But even before that, actual fascist party organizing was part of the mainstream British political landscape in the twentieth century.

The British Union of Fascists (BUF), led by Oswald Mosley, had up to fifty thousand members at its peak in 1934.[219] The BUF organized rallies that were protected by its own paramilitary, the Fascist Defence Force. They wore black uniforms. They were involved in a number of notoriously violent clashes against protesters. The most notorious riot of all is known as the "Battle of Cable Street," named after the large-scale fighting that occurred on Cable Street in East London in October 1936. Upward of twenty thousand counterprotesters (some estimates put this number much higher) organized to fight the two thousand to three thousand BUF members, who were escorted by police.[220] Mosley eventually had his black shirts retreat from the march, while rioters moved on to fighting cops.

The Battle of Cable Street remains one of the most important mythos for contemporary antifa groups in establishing and legitimizing a physical force tradition. This is a trait of extremist groups. An analogy to antifa is the Irish Republican Army, who also romanticize violent heroism. Its ideologues use the 1916 Irish uprising against the British as justification for the deadly terrorist acts it carried out on UK soil in the second half of the twentieth century.

Antifa literature and propaganda cite the Battle of Cable Street (and later, other clashes against the National Front and British National Party) as a prime example of how mass violent direct action can stop fascist organizing. But this is wrong. What stopped the far-right parties from organizing was their falling out of favor with voters due to their extremism. Mosley's British Union of Fascists lost significant popular support for its open embrace of anti-Semitism. During World War II the group's members were interned, and Mosley later exiled himself to France, where he eventually died. The National Front had its best electoral performance at some local elections in the mid-1970s, though it never managed to get even 1 percent of the national vote at its peak. Membership of the party rapidly declined by the late 1970s, and the party is obsolete today.

This history of fascism in Britain over the course of a century was accompanied by a long history of mainstream anti-fascism as well. But today, communists, socialists, and anarchists claim a monopoly on "anti-fascism" and define it to mean something entirely else.

As for antifa's cross-pollination with British punk music and punk culture, it was a lasting influence that aligned the ideology toward anti-authoritarianism and anarchism.[221] This form of antifa, different from its German communist origin, eventually was exported to the United States.

American Antifa

Though American antifa groups today are associated with left-wing West Coast cities like Portland and Seattle, the first antifa groups to emerge in the United States actually came out of the American Midwest. In the late 1980s, a group of far-left skinheads known as the "Baldies" began meeting in Minneapolis to strategize how to oppose the far-right skinhead movement that was growing in the American neo-Nazi scene.[222]

The Baldies believed violence was the appropriate way to respond. They were influenced by British extremist anarchist papers like *Black Flag* and *Class War*, publications that encouraged violence and insurrectionist behavior.[223] Together with other left-wing skinheads from across the Midwest, they formed one of the first known American antifa networks. Made up of numerous groups, such as the Anti-Racist Action, they named the network the "Syndicate."

The Anti-Racist Action had a model of organizing violence to oppose or disrupt what they say are far-right groups and individuals. It is the immediate precursor to contemporary American antifa groups. Their tactics and ideology were taken directly from the UK Anti-Fascist Action, who in turn took inspiration from the German Communist Party's Antifaschistische Aktion. According to Mark Bray, who interviewed an early Anti-Racist Action member, the group decided to name itself the Anti-*Racist* Action rather than the Anti-Fascist Action because fascism "sounded like a dogmatic leftist term" in an American context.[224] A simpler explanation is that until recently, the word "racism" had much more political resonance in the United States than "fascism." America's history is marred by state-sanctioned and state-enforced racism, and its war against actual fascism was never fought on U.S. soil.

Throughout the late 1980s and into the 1990s and 2000s, militant antifa organizing remained on the margins of society, as did neo-Nazi and KKK organizing. While traditional fascism has not been part of modern American political culture, unlike countries in Europe, there have been many far-right white identity groups and inspired "lone wolves" operating outside the American mainstream. Their involvement in violence and intimidation of minority groups have been extensively covered by government agencies, news media, pop culture, and cinema. From 1997 to 2006, the FBI tracked an average of 7,900 hate incidents a year, of which 46 percent were intimidation-related and 31.9 percent were simple assaults.[225] Thousands of reported hate incidents a year may sound like a lot, but the United States has a steadily growing population of more than 320 million people. Calculated as an incident rate, it is less than 2.5 incidents per 100,000 people. Additionally, looking closer at the data reveals nuance. Whites are underrepresented as offenders at less than 60 percent. They make up more than 76 percent of the U.S. population. Blacks are overrepresented as more than 20 percent of offenders, compared to being around 13 percent of the overall population. Further, the number of FBI-tracked hate incidents have declined since 2006, even though more agencies are reporting data.[226]

Although hate crimes are relatively rare in the United States, each and every anecdote has the potential to create social trauma and panic. For example, the murder of nine black parishioners in Charleston, South Carolina, by far-right shooter Dylann Roof in 2015 has more lasting salience than the murder of fourteen people by a jihadist husband and wife in San Bernardino, California, the same year. People remember the homicide of Heather Heyer in Charlottesville, Virginia, in 2017, but few know the name of the victim killed by an antifa shooter in Portland in 2020. Stories of violent white racism, though exceptionally rare, are impactful to the American public because they remind us of American history. Antifa exploit this sensitivity to justify their own violent extremism.

Antifa and Academe

In February 2017, Milo Yiannopoulos was scheduled to speak at the University of California, Berkeley. By then, the right-wing provocateur had already completed a number of speaking gigs across the United States as part of his Breitbart News–sponsored tour. He and his entourage of cameramen and assistants were transported in a rock star–style tour bus with the name of the show printed across its side: "The Dangerous Faggot Tour." The text was accompanied by a large cartoon of a regal-looking Yiannopoulos being carried by four muscular men.

"Why do lesbians fake so many hate crimes?" was the title of his speech in September 2016 at Texas Tech University. At Louisiana State University: "Fat shaming works." The speeches continued across the United States in the autumn and winter of 2016 and into 2017. One by one, the speeches defiled the sacred cows of the left: "10 things I hate about Islam." "Trannies are gay." "Why ugly people hate me." "No more dead babies."

As the tour moved westward, it attracted larger protests and angrier people. Soon, outside left-wing groups organized to join their comrades on campus. Among them were antifa.

While early protests produced comical footage primed for viral memes, such as scenes of screaming and crying students, the antifa came equipped with weapons. Yiannopoulos, an editor at Breitbart at the time, was protected by professional security. However, his fans had none and bore the brunt of violence from rioters while waiting in line outside auditoriums.

On January 20, 2017, at the University of Washington (UW) in Seattle, it was nearly deadly. In the coincidentally named Red Square, hundreds of anarchists and left-wingers confronted Trump supporters. Many of them were in black bloc. In addition to their hatred of Yiannopoulos, tensions had reached a peak because it was also Inauguration Day. Left-wing militants hurled bricks and other projectiles at law enforcement, who tried to keep the two sides separated. Just as Yiannopoulos was about to speak inside Kane Hall, a shooting occurred outside. Joshua Phelan Dukes, a 35-year-old antifa militant also known as "Hex," was shot in the abdomen by Elizabeth Hokoana. She claimed that Dukes had rushed toward her husband, a conservative Asian American man, with a knife. (At trial in August 2019, Dukes refused to testify, and the jury failed to reach a consensus. The judge declared a mistrial.[227])

Nevertheless, the Dangerous Faggot Tour continued. Yiannopoulos headed to northern California next. Only a week and a half after the UW shooting, he was scheduled to speak at UC Berkeley on invitation by the Berkeley College Republicans. Though hundreds of tickets were sold and the venue was booked, Yiannopoulos never got to speak.

On the evening of February 1, 2017, an estimated 1,500 protesters amassed outside Sproul Hall to shut down the event. Around

150 of them were masked in the black bloc carrying communist and anarchist flags.[228] Many of the militants belonged to By Any Means Necessary (BAMN), a Bay Area militant antifa group previously involved in organizing violent Black Lives Matter protests.[229] In 2002, BAMN was investigated by the FBI for suspected "terrorist activities," though the group was never charged.[230]

Only months after Donald Trump's election and days after his inauguration, left-wing activists and militants across the country joined causes to stop what they say was American fascism. Yiannopoulos was one of Trump's loudest cheerleaders, and he dared to trespass in progressive coastal cities viewed as safe spaces to the left. Going to UC Berkeley, one of America's most left-wing universities, was not just a poke at a hornet's nest but the kicking of several nests. Nearby cities include the progressive bastions of Oakland and San Francisco. Protesters and militant leftists from across the region converged on the campus to violently shut down the event.

Despite lines of police on duty near the Berkeley Student Union, officers were unable to stop or contain the violence. As at UW, antifa militants pepper sprayed and attacked those standing in line outside. They used sticks to hit people and threw rocks and fireworks at law enforcement.[231] Stolen MAGA hats were set on fire, leading to cheers from the mob. UC Berkeley police chief Margo Bennett said Molotov cocktails were also thrown.[232] Antifa stole metal barricades originally set up to separate attendees and protesters. They used the barriers as impromptu weapons to smash the Student Union's windows.

Large mobile lights set up to illuminate the plaza were knocked over and set on fire. The crowd cheered and celebrated the sight of the destruction. Even after Yiannopoulos's speech was canceled, the militants continued to riot. Police stood by and watched. The rioters slowly made their way to downtown Berkeley, where they smashed business windows and ransacked the interiors. Yvette Felarca, a leader in BAMN who was at the riot (and participated in the summer 2016 protest at the State Capitol that had become violent), told local media the protest was a success.[233]

"I think shutting down and forcing the cancellation of a white supremacist like Milo Yiannopoulos was a stunning achievement," she told *Berkeleyside* news that night. "This is about our right to be free of intimidation."[234] Given free rein by sympathetic elected officials, antifa's violence continued in the city. On April 15, 2017, Eric Clanton, who was an adjunct professor of at a local college, allegedly assaulted several people with a heavy bike lock.[235] Viral video footage of one incident allegedly showed a masked Clanton using the bike lock to smash the head of a Trump supporter in Berkeley.[236] Clanton was arrested and ultimately pleaded no contest to one misdemeanor charge, but his felony assault charges were dismissed. He was sentenced to only probation in a sweetheart deal.[237] Clanton is not the only academic to be involved in antifa: there's also Mark Bray, the author of *Antifa: The Anti-Fascist Handbook*. And during the 2020 Portland riots, those arrested included professors and instructors from various academic institutions in the Portland area.

THE CAMPUS FAR-LEFT VIOLENCE and rioting involving students and academics in early 2017 were only the beginning. On the other side of the country, around two hundred students at Middlebury College in Vermont shut down a scheduled speaking lecture featuring American Enterprise Institute scholar Charles Murray in March 2017. They accused the political scientist of racism and fascism for his 1994 book *The Bell Curve*, which in one chapter compared psychometric disparities across population groups.

An online profile by the Southern Poverty Law Center declaring Murray a white nationalist was also shared among activists to rally them to shut down the event.[238] Unable to speak on stage due to the shouting and chants, Murray was ushered to another room where he spoke to a camera that livestreamed the footage. By that point, students outside the hall were joined by antifa militants in the parking lot, many dressed in black bloc. Campus security attempted to escort Murray and Alice Stanger, a professor at Middlebury, to a vehicle that was supposed to whisk them away from campus. But they were confronted by violent left-wing militants and antifa who prevented them from getting to the car. Stanger said that during the attack she was shoved and had her hair forcefully yanked, leading to a neck injury that required hospitalization.

"We intercepted them between the door and the car and surrounded them with signs and chanting and clapping," said one of the antifa to *Politico* at the time.[239] "And really, just like letting Charles Murray know that you can't come to this campus and expect to leave without repercussions."

Once Murray and the professor made it inside the car, antifa surrounded the vehicle and prevented it from leaving. Security desperately pushed rioters out of the path of the car, but they kept regrouping. Once the car nearly made it out of the parking lot, one of the antifa jumped on its hood.[240] The driver drove down the block with the militant still on top before slamming on the brakes, causing the attacker to fall off. The antifa promptly took off running before Middlebury Police arrived at the scene. As witnessed in other cities, swarming cars and attacking those inside is a riot method of choice for antifa.

Antifa violence on American university campuses continued month after month in 2017. In May, dozens of radical left-wing students at the Evergreen State College in Olympia, Washington, shut down a biology class taught by Professor Bret Weinstein. They took issue with his emails expressing concern over the university's planned "Day of Absence" event where whites were asked to stay away from campus.

Protests continued the following day leading to several hundred rioters barricading doors and windows so that the university president and administrators could not leave. They demanded radical changes and the firing of Weinstein. The following month, the university canceled classes for two days following a violent threat that was phoned in. During this time, rioters roamed the campus with sticks and baseball bats, causing $10,000 in property damage.[241]

On June 15, 2017, the Evergreen Anti-Fascist Community Defense Network organized a mass gathering on campus to confront a small rally by Patriot Prayer, the Portland-area conservative group. Violent skirmishes initiated by antifa militants in the Red Square led to Patriot Prayer leader Joey Gibson being left bloodied in the face. Law enforcement were there in large numbers but responded only after violence reached a high threshold. There were over one hundred left-wing protesters, many of them in black bloc and ready for battle. They held signs that read, "Black Lives Matter" and "America Was Never Great." After being separated from the other side by police, who had set up metal barriers, they used whatever they could gather to hurl as projectiles.

Although most protesters at the event were politically polarized, a dozen people observed from the sideline. Alex Pearson, a junior at Evergreen State at the time, told me he supported racial justice but didn't agree with all of the militant tactics.

"If you're not to the level of where they are, you have the risk of being put with the complete opposite people," he told me.[242] On the Day of Absence, Pearson—who is white—said he accidently attended class, a mistake his peers made sure he knew.

In 2017, I was unknown to most people as a no-name student journalist. The anonymity allowed me to more easily ask antifa militants for interviews. All declined that day except for one young woman. "People frame antifa very poorly and call them terrorists," she said. "Theoretically, I haven't heard of antifa beating up any minorities ever."

After the rally, several of the right-wingers' cars were found vandalized. The tires were completely slashed. I didn't witness who committed the vandalism, but earlier in the day I observed a group of masked people monitoring cars as drivers pulled into the campus parking lot. Some of the masked people took photos of the vehicle license plates. This information, I would later learn, is used in antifa-compiled dossiers on their opponents. Known as doxing, they release addresses, car details, and employment information to the public so that their victims can be hounded en masse.

The campus violence and far-left radicalism continued through 2017 and into 2020. Each year appeared to show students' willingness to be more extreme than the previous one. On Halloween 2020, around 150 students from Northwestern University joined forces with outside agitators to riot in Evanston, Illinois, at an anti-police protest.[243] They smashed windows, threw bricks, and hurled explosive mortar fireworks at Evanston police officers. They also used high-powered lasers to blind police. Northwestern University is one of the world's most prestigious private research institutions. And yet a faction of its student body organized and behaved exactly as the antifa who riot in Portland and other cities. How did American institutions of higher learning become breeding grounds for far-left violent extremism?

Critical Theory

Antifa do not view their premeditated and preemptive acts of violence as "violence." It is part of the strategy of remaking words to have completely new meanings. But it also pulls from a left-wing philosophical tradition established by twentieth-century German philosopher and sociologist Herbert Marcuse. Marcuse is one of the most important philosophers and social theorists to the modern left. His theories and ideas form the ideological pillars for many so-called social-justice and antifa movements today, even without its adherents realizing so.

Born in Berlin in 1898, Marcuse was a committed leftist all his life. As a young adult, he studied the writings of Karl Marx and voted for the German Communist Party.[244] In 1933, he joined the Institute for Social Research, a think tank at Frankfurt University. It is more commonly known as the "Frankfurt School." With the rise of fascism in Europe, many of the intellectuals at the Frankfurt School escaped to the United States, where they became faculty and influential thinkers.

Columbia University in New York City took in a number of Frankfurt academics. One of the Frankfurt School's lasting legacies is the development of critical theory—the Marxist-inspired theory that undergirds all the various "studies" disciplines in academe today. In short, critical theorists develop ways to "criticize" perceived structures and systems of oppression in order to bring about radical change. It offers a heuristic for understanding all human interaction through power dynamics between groups. When applied to race, concepts like white privilege, whiteness, and intersectionality purport to explain why there are disparities in outcomes among racial groups. Colloquially, critical theory is sometimes referred to as "cultural Marxism," an application of Marxist theory to groups of people based on identity rather than class.

Many dogmas of critical theory have become so mainstream in American academe and society that people don't even know the origins of those truth claims. Have you heard it argued that there is no such thing as objective reality and truth? Social-justice ideologues use this dogma to "deconstruct" science, e.g., biological sex, for example. That's from critical theory.[245] What about "words are violence"?" Antifa militants cite this to justify their violent behavior against opposing views. This is also from critical theory.[246]

Marcuse became known as the "father of the New Left" for his ideological influence on left-wing student protest movements in the 1960s and 1970s, particularly through establishing the now far-left foundational belief that tolerance means actively suppressing "intolerant," usually right-wing, ideas.[247] In 1965, Marcuse coauthored a book with sociologist Robert Paul Wolff and philosopher Barrington Moore Jr. titled *A Critique of Pure Tolerance*.

Marcuse's essay in the book, "Repressive Tolerance," laid the foundation for redefining "tolerance" to mean militant intolerance toward "prevailing policies, attitudes, opinions" and the extension of tolerance to "policies, attitudes, and opinions which are outlawed or suppressed." In other words, we should not allow perceived intolerant ideas the space to be expressed and should be more accepting of extreme beliefs on the left.

For decades, American academe has been marinating in Marcuse's ideas, spreading it to students who then form the next generation of politicians, leaders, and activists.

Even stalwart civil liberty organizations like the ACLU, now filled with members educated in this worldview, have been retreating quietly from their principle of defending free speech. In a 2018 document sent to members titled "ACLU Case Selection Guidelines: Conflicts between Competing Values or Priorities," the organization responded to the onslaught of resignations and criticisms it received after defending the right of the alt-right to march in Charlottesville.

In August 2017, the ACLU supported Unite the Right organizer Jason Kessler in his lawsuit against the city when it forced him to relocate his permitted rally. However, the 2018 guidelines in response to left-wing criticism stated that "a decision by the ACLU to represent a white supremacist group may...directly further an agenda that is antithetical to our mission and values and that may inflict harm on listeners."[248]

The mainstream left's retreat from liberal values of free speech has worked to the benefit of antifa in every way imaginable. Now, not only are large factions of the left sympathetic to antifa violence, some are actively working to suppress their opponents through getting corporate businesses and Big Tech to ban them.

One small sample analysis of public figures banned or suspended on Twitter from 2005 to 2019 published on *Quillette* showed that with only one exception, all are right-wing.[249] On the surface, that doesn't necessarily show evidence of political bias since different groups have different behaviors and thus different outcomes. But given the left's documented abuse anti-white of Twitter's policies through doxing and calls to violence and racism, it's fair to question the disparate treatment.

The consequences of legitimizing left-wing extremism don't stay within the realm of academe, corporations, or Big Tech. It spills out onto the street through what antifa does best: violent hooliganism and street thuggery. That type of urban violence is nothing new, but we're beginning to witness a growing tolerance and support for it from factions of mainstream society.

In 2020, the recurring theme from the left in response to mass BLM and antifa violence in the streets is "People over property." Indeed, an author named Vicky Osterweil, who uses the Twitter username "@Vicky_ACAB," was championed by the mainstream press for her book *In Defense of Looting*, published in August 2020. NPR interviewed Osterweil, who argued that looting is moral.[250]

"The very basis of property in the U.S. is derived through whiteness and through black oppression, through the history of slavery and settler domination of the country," she said in the interview with reporter Natalie Escobar. "Looting strikes at the heart of property, of whiteness, and of the police. It gets to the very root of the way those three things are interconnected. And also it provides people with an imaginative sense of freedom and pleasure and helps them imagine a world that could be." This is verbatim what antifa say when they are asked to justify why they try to burn down businesses and homes. What the journalists, pundits, and intelligentsia don't understand is that at antifa riots, there is really no line between property destruction and assault. One bleeds into the other as they all serve the same purpose of chaos and violence.

HOW DID ANTIFA DEVELOP such a close relationship with radical students on American campuses? Over and over, we witness students and outside antifa militant groups working hand in hand to carry out violence, threats, disruption, or harassment against targets at institutions that are supposed to uphold free speech and open inquiry. This close relationship is a unique development of antifa in the North American context. Although contemporary European antifa groups grew out of the tradition of radical left-wing student protests in West Germany in the 1960s, what is happening in the United States and Canada more recently demonstrates a unique cross-pollination of several radical ideologies: Marxism, anarchism, and critical theory.

American antifa has the communist and anarchist origins of European antifa, but it has evolved to include contemporary social-justice politics from critical theory. Intersectionality flows through American antifa. The revolution they are fighting for will not be led by workers but rather trans, black, and indigenous "folx" of color.[251]

The radical influence travels in both directions. Campus social-justice politics are now much more tolerant, if not encouraging, of extremism. Few students who have engaged in the violent shut-down of events or people have ever been held accountable by the university administrations. In some cases, like the students who mobbed and harassed a Yale professor over a nonissue Halloween costume controversy in 2015, were actually awarded by the university administration for "enhancing race relations."[252]

The mutation of antifa in America didn't end with its embrace of academic critical race theory and campus riots. The rise of antifa coincides with the rise of BLM. Both movements share an ideology that seeks to upend American liberal democracy and the rule of law. They have important differences from one another, but their mutual hatred of the United States has brought them together to form a powerful, dangerous union.

Antifa mutual aid groups set up their base of operations in Chapman Square and Lownsdale Square in downtown Portland. Photo: Andy Ngo

Antifa and far-left protesters in downtown Portland in May 2020. Photo: Andy Ngo

CHAPTER 7

Black Lives Matter

AFTER DONALD TRUMP was sworn into office, Black Lives Matter (BLM) cofounder Patrisse Cullors was interviewed in the *Los Angeles Times*. In August 2017, she was asked if BLM would be open to a conversation with the president. She responded: "We wouldn't as a movement take a seat at the table with Trump, because we wouldn't have done that with Hitler. Trump is literally the epitome of evil, all the evils of this country—be it racism, capitalism, sexism, homophobia."[253]

In her own words, one of the founders of BLM demonstrates how closely the organization's ideology aligns with antifa. Central to both is the goal of abolishing law enforcement, American jurisprudence, national borders, and free markets in the name of anti-racism and anti-fascism. BLM also seeks to undermine free speech.

In October 2017, students affiliated with BLM at the College of William and Mary in Virginia prevented the executive director of the Virginia chapter of the ACLU from speaking. Livestreaming the shutdown on a student BLM page, students shouted: "The revolution will not uphold the Constitution" and "Liberalism is white supremacy."[254] They were angry the ACLU had given a principled First Amendment defense of far-right ideologues. Earlier that year, Cullors was interviewed by Katy Tur on MSNBC, where she stated, "Hate speech, which is what we're seeing coming out of white nationalists groups, is not protected under the First Amendment rights."[255]

Foundation of Lies

On August 9, 2014, an 18-year-old black male named Michael Brown committed a strong-arm robbery at a neighborhood convenience store in Ferguson, a suburb of St. Louis, Missouri. Shortly after, police officer Darren Wilson, who is white, questioned Brown. Brown matched the description of the robbery suspect reported to police. According to Wilson, Brown assaulted him during the questioning and attempted to grab his pistol, causing it to fire inside the car.

Wilson says he chased after Brown, who turned around and charged at him. Wilson fired upon the six-foot-four man, who died at the scene. The killing of Brown set off days of rioting and looting in Ferguson, as well as other protests across the United States. With the aid of social media and wall-to-wall broadcast coverage featuring rumors that Brown had surrendered with his hands up and was "executed," the BLM narrative was born. From coast to coast, "Hands up, don't shoot" became the mantra that drove tens of thousands to the street to protest or riot against what they say is institutional racism in policing and the American legal system.

In November 2014, a St. Louis County grand jury declined to bring criminal charges against Wilson, finding that he was justified in the shooting. In the hours after the announcement of the decision, more rioting, fires, and looting occurred in St. Louis County. Protests broke out across the country in 170 cities. The evidence that emerged in the hearing that corroborated Wilson's account didn't matter. Many pinned their hopes on President Barack Obama's Department of Justice (DOJ) to prosecute Wilson. Eric Holder, the left-wing attorney general, made statements openly sympathetic to Brown and BLM. But to the disappointment of many, the report produced by the DOJ in 2015 further exonerated Wilson.[256] How? Physical evidence, ballistics, DNA, and vetted witness statements.

"Hands up, don't shoot" was a myth perpetuated by Brown's friend Dorian Johnson, who was found to be unreliable by investigators. Other witnesses who claimed they saw Brown "surrender" admitted they had just repeated rumors they heard from the media or others.

That so few Americans are aware of the true story behind the death that made BLM a household name and top political issue demonstrates the power of storytelling. It wasn't just Brown who benefited from false narratives but also other deceased or injured figures posthumously adopted as martyr figures in BLM, for example, Trayvon Martin, and Sandra Bland.

The most devastating consequence of BLM is that it provided the outlet for radical Marxist views to enter mainstream American media, politics, and society under the guise of "racial justice."

Marxist Ideology

BLM is usually presented as an anti-racist uprising and movement focused on countering anti-black police brutality and "systemic racism." This effective branding strategy in the name has masked BLM's true radical ideology.

"[The slogan is] very difficult for anyone to disagree with," says Carol Swain, a retired political scientist who taught at Vanderbilt University. [257] Swain, who is black, is a scholar of American politics and law. She has spoken critically about BLM and its laundering of radical Marxist ideas into the mainstream. For her outspokenness, she was protested by students at Vanderbilt and subjected to demands she be fired.[258]

Swain ended up taking early retirement from Vanderbilt in August 2017. She tells her detractors and critics to simply read the material BLM and its leaders have published to see the truth. Indeed, on-record statements and writings made by the group's three founders, Alicia Garza, Patrisse Cullors, and Opal Tometi, demonstrate their agenda to mainstream hatred of law enforcement, capitalism, free speech, and the United States itself. If this sounds familiar, it is because these are also core ideological components of antifa—with one notable exception being that BLM is not necessarily opposed to the concept of a nation-state *if* they are at the helm.

BLM was founded in 2013 shortly after George Zimmerman was acquitted in the shooting death of black teen Trayvon Martin in Florida. Zimmerman, who is Latino, was found by a jury to be defending himself from Martin, who was beating him on the ground.

Since its founding, BLM's leaders have not hidden its radical Marxist orientation. BLM draws from the legacy of the militant black power movement of the 1960s and 1970s, seen in figures it reveres like convicted cop killer and fugitive Assata Shakur (formerly known as JoAnne Byron). In July 2015 at the BlogHer media conference in New York, two of the three BLM cofounders led the conference in reciting part of a letter authored by Shakur:

> It is our duty to fight for our freedom
> It is our duty to win.
> We must love each other and support each other.
> We have nothing to lose but our chains.[259]

This chant is part of a manifesto written by Shakur in 1973 while she was imprisoned for being an accomplice in the murder of New Jersey state trooper Werner Foerster. In the letter, she calls herself a "Black revolutionary" who has "declared war on the rich... and all the mindless, heart-less robots who protect them and their property." The line about losing chains is lifted directly out of the Communist manifesto.[260]

At protests, Shakur is honored through the recitation of this chant as well as through clothing worn by BLM supporters.[261] That Shakur is treated as such a revered figure in BLM is no small detail. Shakur was a member of the far-left violent extremist group Black Liberation Army (BLA). The BLA declared war on the United States and carried out a series of bombings, robberies, and cop killings in the 1970s. Its actions mirrored those of the Baader-Meinhof Gang.

Shakur escaped prison in 1979 with the help of BLA members who took correctional officers hostage. She later fled to Cuba, where she was granted asylum and treated as a hero by the communist Fidel Castro regime. She is believed to be there to this day.

BLM's adoration of communism is not just indirect through its honoring of Shakur. An essay authored by the group on its official *Medium* blog, titled "Lessons from Fidel: Black Lives Matter and the Transition of El Comandante," mourned the death of the communist despot in 2016.

"As a Black network committed to transformation, we are particularly grateful to Fidel for holding Mama Assata Shakur, who continues to inspire us," the essay reads. "We are thankful that he provided a home for Brother Michael Finney, Ralph Goodwin, and Charles Hill, asylum to Brother Huey P. Newton, and sanctuary for so many other Black revolutionaries who were being persecuted by the American government during the Black Power era."[262]

Finney, Goodwin, and Hill were members of the Republic of New Africa, a militant Marxist group that sought to create a black ethno-state in the American South.[263] They killed a New Mexico state trooper named Robert Rosenbloom in 1971 and hijacked an airplane at Albuquerque International Airport. Africa was their preferred destination, but there wasn't enough fuel, so they instead flew to Cuba, where they were given asylum. Huey Newton was a cofounder of the Black Panther Party and a convict with a violent history. He was involved in the shooting-related death of an

Oakland police officer in 1968 and was accused of shooting a teen sex worker in 1974.[264]

BLM is also a member of the Movement for Black Lives (M4BL), a collective of radical left organizations that share the "BLM" agenda of overturning capitalism and destabilizing the United States.

On its now-deleted page listing various demands, the M4BL had stated:

> The interlinked systems of white supremacy, imperialism, capitalism, and patriarchy shape the violence we face. As oppressed people living in the U.S., the belly of global empire, we are in a critical position to build the necessary connections for a global liberation movement. Until we are able to overturn U.S. imperialism, capitalism, and white supremacy, our brothers and sisters around the world will continue to live in chains.[265]

The usage of "chains" in this context is again a reference to classic communist literature. Additionally, accusations of American "imperialism" harken explicitly to the Cold War–era propaganda of the Soviet Union, which viewed U.S. imperialism not necessarily as an expansion of territory but the spreading of liberal politics, capitalism, and culture.

The anti-capitalism agenda of BLM naturally filters down to its local chapters. Whenever there have been BLM riots, looting follows. During the summer of rioting in 2020, mass looting broke out in downtown Chicago in August after false rumors spread on social media that Chicago Police had shot and killed a black child. Among the thousands of people who amplified the lie? The Chicago chapter of BLM.

"If your rules include you shooting our youth, you can't expect people to play by your rules," tweeted BLM Chicago in the middle of the looting spree on Michigan Avenue. Videos livestreamed from the area showed police completely overwhelmed as thousands of looters ransacked luxury stores, including Gucci, Louis Vuitton,

Apple, and Tesla. Some rioters even used a stolen car to smash through storefronts.

By the end of the night, more than a dozen officers were injured and around a hundred people were arrested. Chicago Police and the city's mayor confirmed that rumors of a police-involving killing of a child were false.[266] Police say 20-year-old convicted felon Latrell Allen was armed with a handgun at a park where children were playing. When police responded, he allegedly took off running and fired at police. The police shot back and injured but did not kill him. Allen's handgun retrieved at the scene matches photographs of him posing with a gun posted on his own social media.

After the night's mass looting in Chicago, the response from BLM Chicago was to hold a protest in support of looters who were arrested at the scene. They held a rally outside the South Loop police station and displayed a banner that read in all caps, "LOOT BACK." In addition, the group released a statement saying that downtown businesses were the ones that had " 'looted" from black communities.[267] Ariel Atkins, a local BLM organizer, told NBC Chicago: "I don't care if someone decides to loot a Gucci or a Macy's or a Nike store, because that makes sure that person eats."[268]

BLM's contempt for property rights is demonstrated over and over in the actions and thoughts of leaders in the group. But those still unconvinced of BLM's greater revolutionary Marxist agenda need only look to the words of Alicia Garza, Opal Tometi, and Patrisse Cullors.

"How do we stop 'black on black crime'?" asked Garza in a January 2015 tweet. "First stop: by understanding the root. It's not black pathology. It's capitalism."[269] In July 2016 she followed up on the subject by tweeting, "White supremacy and capitalism are the underlying causes of state-sanctioned police orchestrated violence."[270]

Opal Tometi echoed similar sentiments. In August 2015 she wrote on Twitter: "I'm anti-capitalism & I'm for the dismantling of a 2-party system that is doing nothing 4 us."[271] In July 2016, she tweeted: "I shared 3 core challenges we face: 1) global capitalism 2) white supremacy 3) suppressing dissent/ access to democracy."[272]

The third BLM cofounder, Patrisse Cullors, has been the most transparent and outspoken in her radical Marxist views. The 36-year-old was trained and mentored by Eric Mann, a former leader of the Weather Underground Organization, a far-left domestic terrorist group active in the 1960s and 1970s.[273] Mann was convicted in 1969 in an incident where live rounds were fired into the Cambridge Police headquarters in Massachusetts.[274] He served two years in prison.

In April 2019, Cullors, who is an associate professor in the Social Justice and Community Organizing master's degree program at Prescott College in Arizona, penned an article for the *Harvard Law Review*.

"Our task is not only to abolish prisons, policing, and militarization, which are wielded in the name of 'public safety' and 'national security,'" she wrote, "We must also demand reparations and incorporate reparative justice into our vision for society and community building in the twenty-first century."[275] Cullors goes on to describe the United States as "the most extensive purveyor of human rights atrocities at home and abroad." She called for no less than the dismantling of the United States: "Abolition means no borders. Abolition means no Border Patrol. Abolition means no Immigration and Customs Enforcement."

And if that's not convincing enough of BLM's Marxist extremism, a resurfaced video of a 2015 interview featuring Cullors went viral in June 2020. "The first thing, I think, is that we actually do have an ideological frame. Myself and Alicia [Garza] in particular are trained organizers," she said in an interview with Jared Ball of the Real News Network.[276] "We are trained Marxists. We are super-versed on sort of ideological theories. And I think that what we really tried to do is build a movement that could be utilized by many, many black folk."

Retired professor Carol Swain, who called out BLM for its radicalism years ago, isn't surprised by the video. "We see them making progress because you see how easily and quickly police have become the enemy, as opposed to people who are trying to harm others."[277] She points to the deadly effect on black American communities when law enforcement pull back from policing and are reluctant to arrest suspects out of fear. Observers have called this documented and studied phenomenon the "Ferguson effect."[278] A 2016 study released by the U.S. Department of Justice and conducted by Richard Rosenfeld, a University of Missouri–St. Louis criminologist, found murder spiking in urban areas after the riots in Ferguson, Missouri.[279]

Convergence

James Lindsay, coauthor of *Cynical Theories: How Activist Scholarship Made Everything about Race, Gender, and Identity—and Why This Harms Everybody*, pinpoints BLM as the vector that allowed social-justice activism on campuses to metastasize into a violent, virulent movement in the rest of American society.

"Black lives matter was enormously visible," Lindsay says. "It was everywhere, and presented as a matter of life and death."[280] Indeed, the urgency surrounding BLM pressured sympathetic liberals to tolerate and even excuse even the most illiberal excesses of the movement. From street protesters carrying signs and chanting slogans urging for police to be killed to even instances of mass murder, BLM's legitimacy was protected by liberals.[281]

And while the murder of Heather Heyer at Charlottesville continues to be a rallying cry for the left, few seem to remember that in July 2016, a 25-year-old black man killed five police officers with a sniper rifle at a BLM protest in Dallas. According to the Dallas Police chief, the shooter, Micah Xavier Johnson, verbalized a grievance related to BLM and said he wanted to kill white people, particularly white police officers.[282] A failed negotiation resulted in police sending in a bomb attached to a robot to kill Johnson. Ten days later, 29-year-old black separatist Gavin Eugene Long (who went by Cosmo Ausar Setepenra) shot six police officers, killing three, in Baton Rouge, Louisiana. He left behind a letter expressing grievances against the police similar to BLM's ideology.[283]

Despite the BLM-inspired violence in 2016 and riots in 2020, the group and movement are still protected by the mainstream media.

"There is absolutely zero, none, zero evidence that Black Lives Matter has ever pushed for anything violent, pushed for anything violent to happen to police," said MSNBC host Joy Reid in October 2020.[284] Her comment echoed the denial of antifa violence repeated throughout the year by journalists.

Through BLM, antifa ideologues saw an opportunity to be mainstreamed. Taking advantage of the urgency and panic, antifa were able to say that their militant actions were needed to address white supremacy and fascism.

As the Republican Party base began to consolidate behind candidate Trump in 2016, BLM took to the streets to protest. It was during this time that an informal alliance developed between BLM and antifa. Trained in fighting and ready for battle, antifa militants acted as volunteer "security" at BLM-style protests.

In July 2016 in downtown Portland at a BLM protest organized by Don't Shoot Portland, I witnessed this relationship developing in real time. White people in antifa were asked by an organizer to stand on the edges of the rally in order to physically shield people of color in case a "white supremacist" carried out an attack.

The speeches that day were extreme. "You pull your pistol out and you fucking bust them [the cops]," said one speaker at the center of Pioneer Courthouse Square. "At the end of the day, it's going to be you against them." The crowd clapped and cheered in response.[285] Another speaker, a young woman, railed against the "capitalist system." Halfway into the protest, a group of antifa black bloc militants pushed Michael Strickland, a conservative videographer, out of the public rally. They pursued him with sticks.

Strickland brandished a legal handgun in response and told the mob to get back before holstering the weapon. He was promptly arrested by police and ultimately convicted on numerous felonies for unlawful use of a firearm. Those who chased and threatened to hurt him that day faced no consequences.

As antifa in Portland solidified their relationship with BLM, the convergence was also witnessed at the national level. Jeffrey Shaun King, better known as Shaun King, a celebrity left-wing activist, became BLM's most powerful social media influencer. With over a million followers on Twitter, King has made videos, allegations, and stories go viral—usually capturing the attention of powerful politicians. But his overzealous sharing of unverified content has also blown up in his face.

On more than one occasion, King amplified an accusation that turned out to be untrue, misattributed, or a complete hoax. For example, in late 2018, King set off a media and political frenzy when he repeated a Houston family's claim that a white male with blue eyes had shot and killed 7-year-old Jazmine Barnes. King helped raise over $100,000 as a bounty and even shared the photo of a possible suspect. But he was entirely wrong. Police arrested two suspects, both of whom are black. The family of the man falsely blamed by King for killing Jazmine received violent death threats.[286] But despite King's reckless social-media activism, he still has significant influence and is sought after by journalists as a voice for BLM.

Following the BLM-antifa convergence, King leveraged his huge following to promote antifa and present them as true first responders. In August 2017, he tweeted: "I support ANTIFA. In fact, I'm grateful for them. Several people told me ANTIFA activists saved their lives in Charlottesville."[287] In the same thread, he continued: "I support the communists & socialists standing against Trump and against bigotry & white supremacy."[288]

In March 2018, he wrote on Twitter: "I've said it before & I will say it again, I'm thankful for all of the #Antifa counter protestors [sic] standing against bigotry from coast to coast. You don't get the love you deserve."[289] King's support for antifa's "direct action" veered into supporting terrorism. Two days after antifa militant Willem van Spronsen launched the armed attack on a Tacoma, Washington, ICE facility in July 2019, King called the man a "martyr." Sharing van Spronsen's manifesto on Twitter, King said the text was a "beautiful, painful, devastating letter."[290]

Sometimes the BLM-antifa relationship is more explicit at the organizational level. In September 2017, the official verified Washington, DC, chapter of BLM promoted an antifa gathering on its Twitter page: "Antifa to meet up at 6 p.m. at Franklin square to protest fascists coming into the city.[291] Then in July 2019, the same BLM chapter defended antifa after the violent rioting in Portland where I was beaten. "STOP SPREADING THE DANGEROUS FALSE RIGHT-WING NARRATIVE ABOUT PORTLAND ANTIFA AND ANTIFA IN GENERAL!!!" the account tweeted, providing a link to antifa blog site It's Going Down.[292]

THOUGH BLM HAS SOME differing goals from antifa (e.g., the more explicit promotion of communism rather than anarchist-communism), both ideologies now cross-pollinate and influence one another to the point that they are linked entities. In Portland and Seattle, they are one and the same, with the same people showing up to each other's events.

Their convergence has been immensely mutually beneficial. Antifa get mainstream legitimacy on the back of American racial divisions while BLM gets a volunteer militia at helm.

A flyer for the June 2019 antifa protest-turned-riot. Photo: Popular Mobilization

Antifa rioters threw feces-filled water balloons and condoms at police protecting the north precinct. Photo: PPB

Portland Police asked for the public's help in identifying a masked individual who assaulted me with a blinding chemical spray in May 2019. Photo: Twitter

CHAPTER 8

Violence

"I JUST GOT BEAT UP by the crowd. No police at all."

These were my first words as I recorded a livestream video on Twitter on June 29, 2019, outside the Multnomah County Courthouse. Sitting on the ground because I was losing balance, I saw my bloodied face and swollen eyes on my phone's screen. Beside me was BuzzFeed News reporter Joseph Bernstein. I asked him to call the police because he'd witnessed my beating.

I was dazed and confused. "Did this really just happen?" I thought to myself. I was also angry. "Where were the police?" Before the beating, I'd already reported two instances of assault by antifa to law enforcement. While recording the demonstration earlier at Lownsdale Square, a masked male had run up behind me and slammed a cup filled with a viscous white liquid on my head.

One of the rally's organizers that day was Popular Mobilization (or PopMob), a new antifa group. PopMob gave out what they said were vegan milkshakes. I saw their volunteers pouring the drinks into paper cups from industrial buckets. The paper cup used to hit my head had the Iron Front's three arrows logo printed on it.

I reported the assault to a nearby Portland Police officer who stood watch on the periphery. A stringer and friend for the *Federalist* news site who witnessed the incident photographed the suspect and pointed him out to police. The officer let me know that he could take a report but would not approach or question the masked person.

The first minor assault was meant as a warning by antifa that I needed to leave. I thought about the implications for following their demand. Local television crews have been attacked by antifa militants before and now only record footage from a far distance away with security. If I left, it would cede the public space to antifa and set a precedent that I could be threatened to leave. I stayed.

A group black bloc militants began following me and preventing me from working by physically blocking my path. I ignored them and walked around as needed. They followed, whispering to one another and appearing to take orders from someone else. Nearby, police approached a masked individual who came armed with a metal bat. He initially refused to turn it over but eventually discarded the bat under a car. He was not arrested.

Worried about the potential for violence, I had earlier asked Bill Bradley, the owner of a local martial arts gym, to be my security in a worst-case scenario. The long-time Democratic Socialists of America (DSA) member had standing with left-wing activists in the city. He disagreed with some of my views but supported my right to document public events unimpeded.

I'd never sought out security before, but following incidents of antifa violence against me in the month prior, I needed to take additional steps to protect myself. On May 1, 2019, also known as May Day, antifa and left-wing protesters rioted outside Cider Riot, an antifa pub, in northeast Portland. While recording the incident on my phone and standing behind a nearby van for cover, a masked woman in black sprinted and maced me directly in the face.[293] I was blinded and retreated from the riot. My skin burned for days from the chemical spray. The assault was caught on camera, and I reported the attack to police, but no suspect was ever identified.[294]

I NAIVELY THOUGHT I WAS prepared by bringing along one plainclothes security escort. It was a bonus that he was known as a leftist. But Bill Bradley's relationship with many of the people there proved to be a critical vulnerability. They screamed and yelled at him, accusing him of "protecting a fascist" and betraying the community. One of the people who shouted at him was an ex-girlfriend. The goal to isolate me worked. Bradley got cold feet, pulled back, and withdrew. I didn't see him again after he left Lownsdale Square. Soon, another person walked up to me and threw another cup of liquid at my face. The white substance splashed under my goggles and went into one of my eyes. I reported the assault to the same police officer. His response did not change.

The protesters began marching, and I followed them. If all they were going to do was throw drinks at me, I could handle that, at least that's what I thought. The protesters cycled through banal chants against police, fascism, racism, President Trump, and the Proud Boys. The day's protest was organized by Rose City Antifa and PopMob to counter a flag-waving event by right-wing pro-Trump fraternity the Proud Boys held on the other side of downtown. The DSA Portland chapter showed up with red banners to march alongside their comrades. The Youth Liberation Front also came with a large banner.

I continued livestreaming the antifa march on my phone in one hand while holding a GoPro attached to a stick in the other. Police kept so far back I couldn't see them. Some of the masked antifa militants grabbed traffic cones and ran off. This was a sign of trouble.

I continued walking and narrating what I saw to my Twitter followers. A Rose City Antifa member and an unofficial media representative for the group, walked near and stared at me. I tried to avoid eye contact. He has been arrested at numerous violent antifa demonstrations in Portland since 2017. At the time, he had an upcoming trial for alleged criminal harassment of a Portland city employee he claimed was a fascist.

I pressed onward. The protesters made a turn and marched in front of the Multnomah County Justice Center. This was the same area where, in 2016, I witnessed a man being pursued by an antifa mob. He was prosecuted and convicted for brandishing his handgun to stop the mob from chasing him.

After I was kicked, punched repeatedly on the head, and robbed of my camera equipment, I stumbled away to sit on the ground outside a nearby courthouse. "Where the hell were you?" I asked the police medic team who arrived. I raised my voice. They informed me that I needed to walk back to the Justice Center, where an ambulance would pick me up in front of the Central Precinct. Traffic was shut down by rioters, and the police medic team needed to rush to another part of downtown to aid officers.

Bernstein, the BuzzFeed reporter, agreed to escort me to the police station. He had flown all the way from New York to work on a story about journalists who write about hate crime hoaxes. I knew of his left-wing bias but remained hopeful he would see that I wasn't the far-right caricature my detractors accused me of being.

The morning of, we spoke at length over breakfast in a downtown café. I knew his catalog of reports included hit pieces on right-wing people. But I admired Bernstein's professionalism and friendliness. He wore a bulletproof vest and brought along a Kevlar helmet. I thought it was excessive. I told him antifa generally harass and shove journalists, not try to kill them. I would regret my naivete a few hours later.

The seven minutes it took to walk to the police station felt interminable. My face was burning from the substances seeping into my facial abrasions. Bernstein recalled this moment in his BuzzFeed feature that was published three weeks later. The focus of the story was no longer on journalists who write about hate crime hoaxes but rather the events of the day:

At the police station two paramedics put Ngo on a stretcher. As they loaded him into the back of the ambulance, I noticed he was using Twitter. Ngo asked that the paramedics let me ride along—I realized now, with the GoPro gone and the Federalist stringer nowhere to be found, that I was the crucial media witness to his victimization. I climbed up front and we rode up into the hills of Southwest Portland to the Oregon Health & Science University Hospital.[295]

Indeed, I was on Twitter to see if any witnesses had captured video or photographs of my assailants. I wanted justice.

At the hospital, I was moved on a stretcher into a room in the emergency department. Bernstein came with me. I naively viewed him as a guardian of sorts. He was the only person near me during the beating who wasn't laughing or cheering. But he was there only to gather information for his reporting. Before he left, he asked me if all this was worth it. "No," I responded. He, along with my detractors, took the cynical view that I secretly wanted the beating for fame.

Quick Drying Cement?

The emergency room was busy that afternoon. I later found out that other people injured by the ongoing riot were treated there. One patient in the room nearest to where I was waiting began shouting. The woman with him yelled for help. A team of nurses and doctors rushed in. I don't know what happened, but I could see blood and other bodily fluids on the ground.

By now, several hours had passed without a doctor examining me. I mistook this to mean that I must have been okay. All I could think about was wanting to shower. The liquids on my face and hair had long ago dried and hardened. My vision was slightly blurry. I began to think about how much all this medical care was going to cost. Unknown to me at the time, conservative activist Michelle Malkin started a GoFundMe campaign on my behalf.

I was eventually wheeled into another room where I was given a CAT scan of my head.

By now, some of the local reporting on the day's riot was published. The Portland Police also released numerous updates throughout the day. Their press release read:

> During today's events, there were multiple assaults reported, as well as projectiles thrown at demonstrators and officers. There were also reports of pepper spray and bear spray being used by people in the crowd. Officers deployed pepper spray during the incident.
>
> There were reports of individuals throwing "milkshakes" with a substance mixed in that was similar to a quick drying cement.[296]

Most people became fixated on the claim from police that some of the shakes used to assault people may have had some form of quick-drying cement mixed in. This led to an intense back-and-forth between the police and journalists sympathetic to antifa who sought to disprove the claim. A police report written that day by Lt. Richard Stainbrook stated that during the riot, a woman who was covered in a thick liquid told him the shake was filled with Quikrete, a concrete mix. Cement has a high pH level and can cause burns on the skin.

"I looked at the female and she was covered [above] her head and shoulders with a gray-colored substance that was starting to dry. I have worked with concrete periodically and specifically 'QUIKRETE,' which is pre-mixed concrete, specifically many times," Stainbrook wrote. "The substance on the female smelled like 'QUIKRETE.' I also noticed as the substance was drying it was turning into a chalky consistency which from my experience is consistent with drying concrete."[297]

Left-wing journalists, like Katie Shepherd formerly of *Willamette Week*, authored a lighthearted story where a team at the paper photographed themselves throwing restaurant-purchased milkshakes mixed with Quikrete on a mannequin.[298] The mayor's senior advisor on public safety stood by police and said that it was reported to him that a person hit with a shake reported having skin and eye irritation.[299] However, the Portland Police ultimately said they did not retrieve a sample to test.

Other than the field observation by the lieutenant and a threatening anonymous email to police that included a "recipe" for cement shakes, there was no conclusive evidence for the claim.[300] The focus on this particular aspect after the riot was a red herring. I don't know what substances I was hit with that day. My face felt like it was burning, but I was also covered in cuts and abrasions. In past antifa riots in Portland, some black bloc militants have filled balloons with urine, feces, and chemicals before launching them at targets using slingshots.[301]

Milkshaking

PopMob was not subtle about the group's goal in distributing free milkshakes.[302] Its leader is a member of the Industrial Workers of the World, a revolutionary Marxist and anarchist labor union.[303]

PopMob named their event "Shake Back the Streets." The event was promoted with posters and a video ad showing a white liquid being thrown in the air. Hundreds of flyers distributed at a Timbers soccer game at Providence Park stadium called for "antifascists" to come out to oppose "fascist violence." All of this was a left-wing dog whistle for the act of "milkshaking," where protesters throw and dump drinks on others to mark and humiliate them.

Milkshaking first became a phenomenon in the United Kingdom during the European Parliament election in 2019 when Nigel Farage and others were assaulted in public. On social media, the assaults were nearly universally praised and celebrated by Labour Party voters, anti-Brexit campaigners, and the wider left who viewed it as a new take on tomato throwing. The act was quickly appropriated by the American left. Eater, a popular food and dining website owned by Vox, described milkshaking as a nonviolent "form of dissent."[304]

Journalists who have defended or excused milkshaking have unsurprisingly never experienced being on the receiving end. On the surface, it looks relatively innocent. A dairy drink, or something approximating it, is thrown at someone to humiliate him or her and to ruin their clothing. However, journalists forget that thick, dense liquids are blinding when they land directly in your eyes. On top of that, milkshaking performs the function of marking you as a target for everyone else to attack.

And one can never know what exactly he or she is being doused with by a masked mob. Considering that the United Kingdom has some of the highest reported per capita cases of acid attacks in the world, it is disturbing the British left has been so willing to praise assaulting people with liquids.[305] In my case, I suspect that many people who threw drinks and objects at me as I was stumbling away didn't actually know who I was. By that point, my face was already obscured by all the substances. The milkshakes served the function of signaling to others that it was okay to hurt me.

Subarachnoid Hemorrhage

After hours of sitting and waiting on the stretcher in the emergency room, a doctor finally met me to explain the results of the X-ray. He said I had a "subarachnoid hemorrhage." I was unfamiliar with that medical term. "You have a bleed on the top of your brain," he explained. Having no experience with brain or head injuries, I didn't comprehend the seriousness of the diagnosis. "So what happens next?" I asked. I assumed I would be discharged right away and told to take it easy. No. I was held in the hospital for an additional twenty-four hours under supervision.

I had the hubris of most young people: I thought I was invincible. That night, I was moved to my own room. All I wanted was to sleep. The events of the day felt like they would never end. But the nurse told me I would be woken up every hour for cognitive and physical movement tests if I fell asleep. The hourly tests involved answering basic questions, tracking eye movement, and responding to physical commands.

Hour by hour, I laid in bed thinking about what could motivate those who say they are defending people of color to brutally beat a person of color. The laughs of the mob as it happened kept playing in my mind. I cursed at myself for not holding on to my camera equipment more tightly when it was being yanked away. That video footage could have been key evidence in identifying my attackers. Even when I wanted to think about something else, or nothing else, the burning sensation on my swollen face and scalp kept bringing me back to the moment of the attack.

In the time since the beating, I've been receiving ongoing treatment. The most challenging time was in the early weeks of recovery. In my first televised interviews on CNN and Fox News after the attack, my speech was slow, and I stuttered and slurred words.[306] I still feel emotional when I catch glimpses or screenshots of those interviews from *New Day* and *Tucker Carlson Tonight*, respectively. My face was bruised and cut, and I was shaking.

I later learned that Bill Bradley, the leftist martial arts instructor who had bailed on me, was threatened for even being there with me at all. An anonymous antifa account sent him a disturbing email.

"I understand that you felt that at the time you were doing the right thing by thinking you were protecting an innocent reporter [Ngo] from the possibility of violence. However, you need to admit that taking this action last weekend was a mistake based on a lack of information," the email read. It proceeded to lay out options the Portland antifa community were willing to give him:

> One solution you're considering right now is publicly denouncing anti-fascism and the actions of those people on July 29th. Let's go over how this would play out. This week, you issue a statement about standing for nonviolence and say the actions of several people on Saturday were unjustified and wrong. You say that everyone deserves to feel safe in this city and you therefore cannot support

the actions of antifa attacking an innocent reporter. This alienates you from the majority of the community out here who understand the context of the situation, as they themselves know from experience what it feels like to have hate speech directed at them, who have to constantly look over their shoulder, who have had friends hospitalized thanks in part the lies spread by Andy Ngo. Many people here will withdraw their memberships and leave your gym, leaving bad reviews. Some people may even become angry at you for defending the legitimacy of fascist views and seek retribution on the reputation of the business itself.[307]

The second choice was to turn his gym into an antifa training base:

Another option is to publicly endorse anti-fascist actions as a legitimate form of community self-defense....This will bring you plenty of community support, but on the other hand will make your business a target for [right-wing] extremists, who may even come to attack your business in person like they did recently with Cider Riot on May 1st. I can understand why you might be scared to take this stance, and worried about the repercussions on your business. However, you will have the support of the community here to help pay for damages, as well as the opportunity to hold these people legally accountable if they do come with the intent to harm your members or damage your property.

The email closed with the following statement: "You can learn a lot about someone based on the enemies they make over time, and right now you have the opportunity to take a stand against hatred in our community. Please consider who you want to publicly denounce and make your decision wisely." Bradley rejected the choices in the email and also refused to denounce me. In the time since, antifa activists in Portland have tried to ruin his business's reputation with lies.

Behind the Violence

My recovery path, which is ongoing, involved physical, speech, cognitive, and occupational therapies. I had vision issues and deficiencies in memory and balance. And most challenging of all, I had a debilitating and paradoxical fear of both being around people and being alone. While walking to a grocery store or back to my car, I kept having flashbacks, fearful that someone could run up from behind to strike my head again.

I didn't want to leave my home anymore. But antifa knew where I lived. In describing these fears to my cognitive therapist, she responded, "It sounds like PTSD." Post-traumatic stress disorder? I thought that condition was reserved for people who experienced war, rape, and other horrors. She referred me to a specialist.

The violence myself and others experienced at the hands of antifa is not confined to that day or even their riots in general. Their lust for violence is so extreme that they've even beaten their own on accident. On August 4, 2018, antifa black bloc militants beat a leftist ally at one of their protests using a spring-loaded club. Why? Paul Welch made the mistake of carrying an American flag. They thought he was a conservative and beat him on the head. He was left laying in a pool of blood dripping from his head.

"I hit the ground and was dazed. I realized within a few seconds that some of these people were kicking me as well. I was trying to protect my head," Welch says.[308]

Indeed, both the Department of Homeland Security and the Federal Bureau of Investigation began warning state and local law enforcement in early 2016 that left-wing extremists associated with antifa are increasingly engaging in "domestic terrorist violence."[309] And though violence is one of the defining features of their organizing tactics, it is second to their ideology. Antifa tactics will adapt and change over time in different contexts, but their extremism is constant.

In an August 2019 on-camera interview with Rose City Antifa, NBC reporter Dasha Burns directly asked a masked member about the group's violent street actions.

"We see fascism as an inherently violent ideology, so when we disrupt its organizing, we see that as self-defense," the man answered.[310] He was wearing sunglasses and a black hoodie printed with a professionally designed Rose City Antifa emblem.

"So you're saying that when far-right groups come here and throw demonstrations and rallies, they don't necessarily have to throw the first punch in order for you to react violently," Burns asked. He doesn't answer yes or no. "The purpose of these groups coming to Portland is to attack people." The implication in his answer is that preemptive violence is warranted.

The short interview was a rare opportunity to hear from the camera-shy militants who otherwise have a hostile and sometimes violent relationship with reporters. Rose City Antifa stands out as one of the few militant antifa groups in the United States willing to engage with media in prearranged sit-down interviews. Their unofficial spokespeople dress in black bloc and speak eloquently. They're experienced at dodging questions that bring attention to their violent extremism.

In that NBC interview, the masked interviewee never referred to their militant actions as "violence." He was careful to label them "self-defense"—even when the reporter asked him about antifa assaulting people with weapons and projectiles. This line has been carefully toed by Rose City Antifa since scrutiny was brought to bear on their actions following high-profile riots in 2017.

"We are unapologetic about the reality that fighting fascism at points requires physical militancy," Rose City Antifa posted in a statement on its Facebook in 2017.[311] "Anti-fascism is, by nature, a form of self-defense: the goal of fascism is to exterminate the vast majority of human beings."

Street Violence and Project Veritas

From 2016 to 2019, Americans were given a preview into what organized street violence by antifa looks like. Every few months, mass brawls broke out, usually in a downtown area of a few cities on the West and East Coasts. Most of these incidents occurred in Portland, which by 2017 gained a reputation for being the epicenter of American antifa street violence. Through those years, I got to see up close with my own eyes some of the tactics they use to carry out mass violence. The plan was simple: announce a gathering to oppose some alleged right-wing event, come in black bloc, and use weapons like pepper spray, batons, bats, sticks, and brass knuckles. You'll notice that firearms are not on that list. This does not mean that some individuals don't come armed. They most definitely do, but antifa's goal generally does not include carrying out mass casualties—at least not for now. They recognize that they are working at a disadvantage against the state. Their comrades who kill others will be prosecuted and their whole networks jeopardized in the process.

The U.S. government has a good track record of identifying, prosecuting, and jailing far-left terrorists. So much so that young people today aren't even aware of the history of far-left terrorism in the United States during the 1960s and 1970s. And the left-wing bias of the media certainly tries to hide that history by focusing only on far-right extremism.

The FBI, in conjunction with local police departments, was able to arrest members of terrorist communist groups like the Black Panther Party, Weather Underground, and the May 19th Communist Organization, among others. By the 1980s, these groups' organizational activities were severely disrupted. Antifa valorize these past extremists and share many of the same goals of overthrowing the government, but they also learned not to repeat the mistakes that led to their arrests.

The plan now is to create a decentralized system of cells and affinity groups who share in the same ideology through disseminated propaganda and literature. They recognize that accelerationist tactics like mass killings of police or political opponents are too high risk. The goal is to inflict maximum damage without death and to maintain the momentum of riots to drain government resources and law enforcement morale.

It costs little money to buy bear mace, brass knuckles, or batons. They can deploy a whole army to carry out smaller-scale assaults and vandalism at riots, making it difficult for police to make arrests and to maintain the illusion that "antifa has killed no one." This is meant to mislead the public into thinking antifa aren't dangerous.

Few seem aware antifa specifically train for street violence. The media coverage on antifa almost always focuses on how they're "not organized" or "not a group." It is not a coincidence that a large group of militants dressed in the same uniform know how to coordinate mass attacks on people and property. Project Veritas, the investigative media organization, did what I thought was impossible: they successfully managed to infiltrate Rose City Antifa. From 2017 to 2018, Project Veritas sent an undercover journalist into the shadowy organization. He got in for a time. His written reports and videos—which, to date, are the only content leaked from a formal antifa group—provide some of the first glimpses into how prospective antifa members are recruited, radicalized, and trained.

In June 2020, Project Veritas released the first video in its series called *#ExposeANTIFA*. The video exposé is narrated by a masked journalist going by the moniker "Lion." His face and identity were withheld for safety reasons. Besides cooperating with law enforcement, antifa see betrayal as the second mortal sin. In the narrated video, Lion wears a branded black RCA hoodie. Since 2017, Rose City Antifa members sometimes wear their branded merchandise at riots and protests and also during media interviews. Part of it is for propaganda purposes. It increases recognition for the group within Portland and also helps establish camaraderie among members. They're a gang. The design features the antifa two-flags logo within a cutout of the state of Oregon, with the words "Fighting fascism since 2007" next to a red rose.

In the Project Veritas video, Lion opens up by saying: "I've been undercover with Rose City Antifa since July of [censored audio]. Depending on the setting, if I were to be caught, or found out, it could escalate to violence against me." That's quite an understatement. The video shows clips from secret trainings conducted at the In Other Words Feminist Community Center, a now-defunct radical feminist bookstore and community space. Founded in 1993 by a Portland State University sociologist and two women's health activists, the store gained notoriety as a filming location for the IFC comedy show *Portlandia*. On the show, Fred Armisen and Carrie Brownstein played two humorless feminist bookstore staffers. The gag proved far too accurate, and the store publicly banned the show from filming in 2016, accusing it of being racist, contributing to gentrification, and being "trans-misogynistic." Though In Other Words had a reputation as a beloved quirky Portland establishment, it lent its space to extremist causes behind doors. The Project Veritas investigation exposed this for the first time.

During a 2017 training session at the bookstore, a Portland bartender instructed prospective Rose City Antifa members to hide their weapons from police. "Don't be that fucking guy with the goddamn spike brass knuckles getting photos taken of you," he said. "Police are going to be like, 'Perfect, we can prosecute these fuckers, look how violent they are,' and not that we aren't, but we need to fucking hide that shit." At another point, Cifuni told members to "practice things like an eye gouge" because "it takes very little pressure to injure someone's eyes."

The shocking words from the secret recordings told me what I suspected based on my observations of antifa's militaristic formations and fighting tactics: they are trained to hurt and maim.

"RCA and groups like them either attract or create violent offenders out of people. Most if not all carry a concealed weapon with

them at times," wrote Lion at the time in internal documents provided exclusively to me." Lion was required to attend "self-defense"
training to be part of antifa's direct action street confrontations.
That's where he and others were instructed to "destroy" the enemy.
"Consider destroying your enemy, not like delivering a really awe-
some right hand, right eye, left eye blow you know," he said in
another secret recording to antifa members at the bookstore. "It's
not boxing, it's not kickboxing, it's like destroying your enemy."

Bookstores

Using a radical bookstore as a front for extremist antifa training
isn't unique to Portland. In fact, a whole network of bookstores
and "community centers" exist for this purpose. The most well-
known one is the Slingshot Collective. On its website, visitors can
view all affinity spaces broken down by continent. I recommend
readers check out the website to see which extremist spaces may be
in operation in their state or city.[312]

In Other Words was part of this network before it shut down.
While it's not surprising that radical far-left "bookstores" exist on
the liberal coasts of the United States, red states aren't immune.
In fact, one of the most important regional antifa hubs is in the
American South.

Firestorm Cafe and Books, a "worker-owned" far-left bookstore and meeting space in Asheville, North Carolina, is the Southeast's
mecca for anarchists. Some of the books they proudly display in the front
of the shop include Mark Bray's *Antifa: The Anti-Fascist Handbook*
and also the *Antifa Comic Book* by Gord Hill. And like In Other
Words, it does not have a sustainable business model. But that's by
design. Selling books does not seem to be the primary purpose of the
bookstore. It is a space for comrades to meet one another and to be
introduced to extremist ideologies. Firestorm has a "Sustainers Program" whereby people commit to giving donations each month. In
Other Words sustained itself for years through large donation drives

but ultimately ran out of fuel once it lost its sweetheart deal with Portland State, which for many years gave the store a monopoly on selling feminist textbooks to students.

Asheville stands out in the Southeast for its leftist politics, hippy character, and arts scene. That type of political climate allows Firestorm to operate with public support, but some residents have been trying to raise the alarm about the bookstore's alleged role in a growing crime wave.

In November 2019, concerned residents spoke at a meeting for the Council of Independent Business Owners in west Asheville. The residents accused Firestorm of using its needle exchange program to bring in criminality and vagrancy in an effort to "reverse" gentrification.

"It's no accident, in my opinion, that you've got a bookstore fronting for an act of anarchy executed through the needle exchange program," said John Miall, a city employee, at the meeting.[313] Antifa's glorification of crimes and chaos is part of its ideology. They believe in destabilizing communities in order to delegitimize the authority of the local government. In turn, they set up their own "mutual aid" programs as alternatives to fool the public into believing the state is ineffective in meeting their basic needs.

Beyond the Southeast, another prominent bookstore in the Slingshot Collective is Wooden Shoe Books in Philadelphia, Pennsylvania. Inside the shop, it has a large mural on the ceiling showing black people in chattel slavery being abused by whites. The shop operates as a 501(c)(3) charity and heavily promotes donation links on its website. A friend who visited the shop was recommended Bray's Antifa handbook by staff.

The second #ExposeANTIFA video released by Project Veritas shows clips from inside The Base, an "anarchist political center" in Brooklyn, New York. By day it ostensibly operates as a bookstore, but the space is popular for running a program to write fan letters to jailed antifa "comrades," who they call "political prisoners."

Another "political prisoner" supported by that antifa prison network is David Campbell, an antifa black bloc militant convicted for his role in stalking and choking a 56-year-old Jewish Trump supporter outside a conservative event in Manhattan.[314] The victim was injured so badly that he wasn't breathing when first responders arrived. He later regained consciousness. Campbell was also accused of assaulting an NYPD officer during the arrest. He pleaded guilty to two counts of felony assault and was sentenced to eighteen months in prison in October 2019. A source with knowledge within the NYPD says Campbell refused to cooperate with investigators, per the antifa rule that they can never speak to cops.

Campbell's violent cause is championed by antifa around the country. A benefit concert was held to support him in January 2020, and a "Free David Campbell" website currently takes donations on his behalf.[315]

Other antifa sympathizing bookstores don't just act as a library for extremist literature and propaganda. Some also host antifa training sessions, including trainings on how to injure people in street fights.

"If you get a good liver or kidney shot, it's pretty much crippling to them," said an antifa fight instructor named Chris at The Base in the Project Veritas video.[316] "If you break one of the floating ribs," he points to the spot on the abdomen, "those are also very painful, it's hard to move after that, it's hard to catch a breath." In the background, exercise training equipment like weights and mats can be seen. What does one need those for in a bookstore?

The trainer continues: "One good body shot could potentially give you all the time in the world to run away while they're doubled over in pain, or really put a beating on them after that if you really don't like the person." Chris makes the criminal intent of the training clear in another clip: "We want to, in this space, reframe the idea of self-defense."

Of note beyond where the training is taking place is also who is participating. One of the men practicing punches in the undercover video is Andrew Gittlitz, a New York–based writer and producer of *The Antifada* anarchist-communist podcast. He writes under the name A. M. Gittlitz. Gittlitz has written for the *New York*

Times opinion section, Salon, VICE, and other publications. In 2017, the *New York Times* published an essay by Gittlitz for its "Red Century" series, which honored the legacy of the Russian Revolution.[317] I reached Gittlitz for comment on Twitter, but he did not respond.

To be fair, teaching others how to incapacitate someone isn't out of place in a self-defense class. Even comments about making a target kneel over in pain can be fitting in the right self-defense training context. But when this is coupled with an ideology that teaches adherents to "destroy" political opponents by "any means necessary," it becomes a combination for violent criminality and terrorism. It never ends with just fist fighting or street brawls.

Guns

According to Lion's reports on Rose City Antifa, prospective members were also told to train in handling and firing firearms. They trained at The Place to Shoot gun range in north Portland. (The gun range did not respond to a request for comment.) Further, in the third *#ExposeANTIFA* video released by Project Veritas, a female infiltrator details how she went undercover in 2018 in the Shelby, North Carolina, chapter of Redneck Revolt.

Redneck Revolt is an antifa militia-style group that is closely linked with its Pacific Northwest offshoot, the John Brown Gun Club. Redneck Revolt was founded in 2009 and gained national media prominence starting around 2017 when it was present at antifa events and protests in a support role. Its members wear military-style gear and open-carry pistols and semiautomatic rifles. They're unapologetic about intimidating opponents. They call themselves anti-fascist, anti-capitalist, anti-nation-state, and pro-gun.[318] They see themselves as revolutionaries. In other words, they are armed antifa who have the training to kill.

Clips in the video show a Redneck Revolt member named Matt interviewing the undercover woman as part of the initiation process.

"If an officer of the state came to the door and asked you questions about your political ideology and people you associate with, how would you respond?" he asks, testing to see if the woman is able to hide her extremist beliefs and connections to the militia. "If you were tabling at a gun show and someone loudly accused you of being a terrorist or part of antifa, how would you handle it?" he asked her next.

The Shelby Redneck Revolt chapter eventually announced on Facebook it was splitting off from the national group because the organization adopted "an internal culture that espouses capitalist characteristics."

> From this day forward, we will be known as Carolina Workers'
> Collective. We hereby re-commit ourselves to building communi-
> ties of mutual aid and defense among the poor and working class
> in our larger community. We stand against the state. We stand
> against white supremacy. We stand against patriarchy. We will
> actively work to dismantle the harmful capitalist and hierarchical
> system that exists in our culture.[319]

Shortly after, the Project Veritas infiltrator was kicked out after raising "security" suspicions among other members. They confronted the woman on Signal, an encrypted peer-to-peer messaging app used by antifa. She was asked to not return to their meetings.

I asked the woman in an interview if the people she got to know in the group were willing to kill for their cause. Her answer was unequivocal: "Yes, this is the reason they train with firearms." She continued: "They view themselves as armed protectors of minorities and the disenfranchised. This was borne out in reality when they acted as security for CHAZ in Seattle."

The woman showed me documents and literature she acquired during her time in the group. One booklet she was given was titled *Coloring Book for Revolutionaries*. The booklet features sketches of communist activist Angela Davis, a black power fist, Rafael Sebastián Guillén Vicente—the Mexican anarchist-communist insurgent—and other left-wing idols. The childlike presentation of the radical literature mirrors one of antifa's strategies: they hide their extremism behind a mask of banality or innocence. This extends to their violence as well.

IF YOU FOLLOW ANTIFA as a subject on social media, you've probably seen the right-wing meme that portrays them as weak and effeminate. This meme bothered me long before my own experience of being assaulted by them. It falsely portrays all antifa as harmless paper tigers. This is wrong. Some antifa are athletic and train in street fighting, as documented in the undercover videos. Those who are less athletic can use the weapons described above. And anyone can be trained to use a firearm. It is a catastrophic mistake to assume antifa aren't capable of mass carnage. This is not a movement that follows the rules of engagement. They go for the eyes, the genitals—whatever it takes to "bash the fash." If that means mobbing an individual in a twenty-on-one scenario, they'll do it. And if it involves killing for their cause, they're willing to do it as well.

Bullet holes at the Tacoma, Washington Immigration and Customs Enforcement facility. Photo: Andy Ngo

A border checkpoint at the Capitol Hill Autonomous Zone in Seattle. Photo: Andy Ngo

Outside the author's home. Photo: Andy Ngo

An office in the Justice Center in Portland was destroyed by rioters on May 29, 2020. Photo: U.S. Attorney's Office

CHAPTER 9

Deadly Violence

Willem van Spronsen

The Northwest Detention Center in Tacoma, Washington, is fully gated off and located on the outskirts of the city. The detention center is privately operated by GEO Group on behalf of Immigration and Customs Enforcement (ICE), making it the frequent target of left-wing activists from Seattle who oppose the Trump administration's position on border security. By driving there from out of town, I was retracing some of the final steps that Willem van Spronsen took when he launched a fatal attack on the facility in 2019.

On the early hours of July 13, 2019, the 69-year-old carpenter drove to the facility armed with a rifle and a stash of incendiary devices. At around 4:00 a.m., van Spronsen hurled firebombs at the property and cars parked on the street. One vehicle blew up and was completely engulfed in flames. Four officers from the Tacoma Police Department responded to the attack after GEO staff called 911. When they got there, van Spronsen allegedly tried to ignite a

500-gallon propane tank that was attached to one of the facility's buildings. "Shots fired" was reported, and police shot van Spronsen dead.[320] No one else suffered injuries in the terrorist attack.

The firebombing of the ICE facility came during years of heightened hostility from the American left in response to Trump's promises to crack down on illegal migration. In summer 2018, antifa and far-left extremists in Portland besieged the local ICE facility for more than a week. After the facility was retaken by federal officers from the Department of Homeland Security, antifa created an adjacent autonomous zone on city property.

In August 2019, two ICE buildings in San Antonio, Texas, were hit with bullets in a drive-by shooting.[321]

"Had the bullets gone two inches in another direction, we could be here today talking about the murder of a federal official," said Christopher Combs, special agent in charge of the FBI's San Antonio division, at the time. The same month, protesters threatened employees of GEO Group in Florida, where they are headquartered.

"We know where all your children live throughout the country," one protester shouted in video published by Breitbart News.[322] "We know everything about you and you won't just be seeing us here." Another person screamed: "We know where you sleep at night."

With the escalating rhetoric used by left-wing protesters against immigration and border protection officers, I feared it would only be a matter of time before someone would try to kill them. The graffiti I saw at the "Occupy ICE" Portland autonomous zone used dehumanizing language against ICE staff. Some plainly called for ICE agents to be killed.

When I first saw van Spronsen's photo online in a news article, I recognized him, but I couldn't recall how. Having been to so many protests and riots over the years, I picked my brain to remember. It finally came to me: Seattle City Hall in late 2018. On December 1, 2018, I had traveled to Seattle to cover the far-left protest against the Washington Three Percenters, a conservative group that promotes limited government. Antifa and other left-wing activists wrongly branded the group "fascists" because its name is similar to another group that was at Unite the Right in Charlottesville, Virginia. When I attempted to record the left-wing protesters that day, I was accosted and surrounded. They backed me up against a barrier and screamed at me and shoved signs in my face. Two people who confronted me were openly carrying semiautomatic rifles. I later learned they were members of the Puget Sound John Brown Gun Club, a regional affiliate of Redneck Revolt. One man confronted me inches from my face.

With bloodshot eyes, he leaned into me and calmly said, "I'm known to do this shit for real. Some of us didn't really come to talk. Some of us came to die, dude. Are you willing to die for YouTube shit? Death is going to come. Death is coming for you, dude.... You spying and doing this punk shit? It's going to get you hurt."[323] I didn't know who he was at the time, but perhaps he recognized me. I later learned he was an ardent supporter of antifa in both Seattle and Portland. He has photographs of himself with Rose City Antifa members on his Facebook page.[324] I reported the threat to Seattle police, but nothing ever happened.

Besides heated screams and yells from left-wing protesters, police kept the rallies peaceful. Before I left, one elderly man walked up and stood by me for a moment. He looked to be in his 60s or 70s, much older than the average protester there. He was wearing a hat with the abbreviation JBGC—for the John Brown Gun Club.

That man was Willem van Spronsen.

"I never had any concerns about his mental health," Yassine, a 34-year-old Seattle-area defense attorney and former friend of van Spronsen, tells me. Yassine, not his real name, knew van Spronsen from their time together in the Puget Sound John Brown Gun Club. Yassine had a prominent role in the group. "I think it's fair to say [the group] is militant," he says. "I was excited to see a left-wing organization that supported gun rights." Yassine describes his politics as "libertarian anarchist." He also used to be a member of the National Lawyers Guild, the far-left legal organization that provides legal aid to extreme left-wing individuals and causes.

Outside of their social activities, the Puget Sound John Brown Gun Club members volunteered as security for left-wing events. Many of those gatherings involved antifa black bloc militants engaging in criminal direct action. But Yassine says the gun club's members were never involved in those activities. He says their philosophy on left-wing criminal activity was simple: "If we don't see it, it doesn't exist." That view echoes a chant by antifa black bloc when their comrades engage in arson or vandalism: "We didn't see shit."

In December 2018, Yassine, van Spronsen, and other members of the Puget Sound John Brown Gun Club provided security for the protest outside Seattle City Hall. Yassine didn't know who I was, but he saw the way I was treated by some of his club's comembers who were armed. He says my political views are irrelevant. "Anyone has a right to be on the public street and record what they witness." He raised his concerns internally with the club's members. They disagreed with him and didn't want to be seen as "critiquing a member of their own community." Frustrated with their decision, he resigned from the organization.

I asked Yassine about van Spronsen. I wanted to know who he really was behind all the antifa propaganda that branded him a brave martyr. Yassine simply describes van Spronsen as a calm old man who suffered from chronic pain and was dealing with child custody issues from his ex-wife, Shelley. She accused him of domestic abuse and was granted protective orders by a court.[325] Beyond his personal issues, van Spronsen was deeply committed to left-wing causes and had been active in far-left protests for many years.

Van Spronsen was a naturalized immigrant from Holland who lived in Vashon, an island in the Puget Sound west of Seattle. He was well known in the anarchist and antifa community. Toward the end of his life, he turned to militant, violent direct action. The year before his deadly attack, he was arrested at the same Tacoma detention center when he assaulted an officer at a protest for open borders. Court documents say van Spronsen jumped on an officer and wrapped his arms around his neck, as if in an attempt to choke him. Van Spronsen was eventually subdued, arrested, and found to be carrying a knife and baton.[326] During one of his court appearances, he gave a black power fist salute to his comrades in the gallery. He ultimately pleaded guilty to a lesser charge of obstructing police.

Before his deadly attack, van Spronsen sent a printed manifesto to his friends. In it, he wrote the iconic words "I am antifa" and referred to ICE facilities as "concentration camps." The latter was popularized by New York congresswoman Alexandria Ocasio-Cortez the month prior to the attack. He also made a reference to "Bella Ciao," an Italian song from WWII often sung by antifa and other left-wing protesters today.

Van Spronsen's manifesto read in part:

> I am antifa. I stand with comrades around the world who act from the love of life in every permutation. Comrades who understand that freedom means real freedom for all and a life worth living.
>
> Keep the faith!
> All power to the people!
> Bella ciao...
>
> The semi-automatic weapon I used was a cheap, home-built unregistered "ghost" AR-15, it had six magazines. I strongly encourage comrades and incoming comrades to arm themselves. We are now responsible for defending people from the predatory state. Ignore the law in arming yourself if you have the luxury, I did.[327]

Van Spronsen's friends did not report his manifesto to the police.

In response to news of his death, antifa groups around the world issued eulogies.

"When our good friend and comrade Willem van Spronsen took a stand against the fascist detention center in Tacoma, he became a martyr who gave his life to the struggle against fascism. He was kind and deeply loved by many communities; we cannot let his death go unanswered," the Seattle Antifascist Action wrote on Facebook. Antifa in Washington state and Oregon organized memorials, including one near the scene of the attack. They held banners that read, "Rest in power" and "Fire to the prisons." In Exarchia, a neighborhood in Athens, Greece, home to many antifa and left-wing radicals, a mural of van Spronsen was painted along with a quote from José Buenaventura Durruti Dumange, the Spanish Civil War–era anarchist insurrectionist.[328]

Van Spronsen's failed attack on the Tacoma ICE facility remains one of the higher-profile incidents of antifa violence, even though apologists say it doesn't count because he was the only one killed. To that, I say the failure of a terrorist attack doesn't exonerate the perpetrator.

During my visit to the Northwest Detention Center, I walked around outside and found multiple bullet holes from the shooting. Investigators marked off the evidence with measurements. A staff member guided me around and showed me where van Spronsen's body was found. There was a stain there; I don't know if it was related to the attack. Nearby, the windows of one of the buildings he firebombed were still broken. Next to it stood an empty spot on the building's exterior that looked recently tampered with. The staff person said that's where the propane tank was.

We may never know if van Spronsen's goal was to commit suicide by cop or if he wanted to take others out with him. Yassine takes pity on his late friend. "He seemed like Don Quixote. He was fighting windmills."

I view van Spronsen not as a "martyr" but rather the victim of a hateful ideology that consumed him. Antifa's worldview taken to its logical conclusion results in the death of not just its adherents but sometimes also those unfortunate enough to be around them.

It's most effective at exploiting those who have grievances. Van Spronsen appeared to blame the state for siding with his ex-wife's domestic violence allegations.

A year after his attack, I still occasionally see van Spronsen's name, face, or manifesto evoked at events where antifa or the far-left are present. The Puget Sound John Brown Gun Club has refused to disassociate from its late member. In fact, the group relishes in the association and has been disseminating his manifesto in print when they table at events.[329] In November 2019, a member of the group was part of an antifa protest of a Dinesh D'Souza event in Portland where I was a guest speaker. When I came outside the venue to see what was happening, a man I recognized as being one of the group's members approached me and handed me van Spronsen's printed manifesto. I'm not sure if I should have interpreted the act as threatening. The booklet had an illustration of a burning ICE van. Nick Vasiliy, another member of the gun club, wears a rifle round that belonged to van Spronsen as a necklace.[330] They're proud of what he did.

Charlie Landeros

Many remember van Spronsen's firebombing because it was the first known time an attacker left behind a manifesto explicitly stating his ties to antifa. But he wasn't actually the first—or unfortunately the last—to carry out deadly violence inspired by antifa. In fact, six months earlier, an antifa extremist in Eugene, Oregon, carried out a failed shooting on resource officers at a middle school.

"He was a smart, loving, intelligent person who turned into a monster," Shayla Landeros tells me. She's the ex-wife of Charles Landeros, 30, who went by Charlie. They divorced years before his fatal armed attack on January 11, 2019, at Cascade Middle School but remained in close contact because of their two daughters.

Charlie didn't start out like a lot of the other antifa. He was born in Hong Kong to a Mexican American Christian missionary father and a Filipino mother. Shayla met him when they were in high school in Eugene, a college town in central Oregon. When he was 17, he enlisted in the Army. He was stationed for a time in Fort Drum, New York, and served deployments in Iraq and Afghanistan.

In 2007, they married. The following year, Shayla gave birth to their second daughter. For a few years, they lived as a family unit, even though he frequently spent long trips abroad working in helicopter transport services. Shayla says they separated when she learned Charles was having a romantic relationship with another man in the military. Their relationship ended in divorce in 2013. Both of them later relocated back to Eugene from Jacksonville, Florida.

In 2014, Charles began a pre-med program at the University of Oregon (UO). He wanted a career change and was interested in becoming a pediatrician. But Shayla says it was during his time at UO that he was introduced to an ideology that twisted him and set him on the path to death.

While at UO, Charles began taking an interest in leftist politics and social justice, as many students do. For a time, he worked as a sex educator at UO's Sexual Wellness Advocacy Team where he was introduced to more radical political ideas. He began to advocate for migrant causes in response to then candidate Trump's statements on illegal migration.

"He started telling people he was a 'Dreamer,'" Shayla says, using a term popularized by the DREAM Act, which was a legislative proposal to give permanent residency to those who illegally entered the United States as minors. "He started fighting for [Deferred Action for Childhood Arrivals] under the false pretense he immigrated here. This is not something he would have lied about before. He used to be proud that he was an American."

In October 2017, Charles was one of the students who led the stage storming and shutdown of the annual State of the University address by UO's president.[331] On stage, the protesters shouted and screamed about fascism on campus and complained about tuition increases. By that time, Charles was fully indoctrinated in extreme far-left views. Part of that transformation involved changing his gender pronouns. He identified as non-binary and used they/them pronouns.

He developed a deep hatred of law enforcement and the military. He cofounded the Community Armed Self-Defense group, a far-left anti-government organization that teaches "oppressed peoples" how to use guns. Its Facebook page description echoes a core tenet of antifa ideology: "The police are not here to protect us."[332] Shayla says Charles used the group to radicalize others in the belief that there needed to be an armed violent revolution.

Charles's radicalization continued and accelerated in the final two years of his life. By then, he was a full-time activist and was not paying child support. Shayla largely ignored discussing politics with her ex-husband. But his views concerned her when it became clear he was trying to radicalize their two children. She says they were becoming hyper-focused on race and had developed a sudden hatred of police. He was also teaching them how to shoot. "We have had several conversations where he proceeds to tell me I wouldn't understand because I'm white, and that I have 'white privilege.'"

Quietly, she was most disturbed about his involvement in the "self-defense" group. She says he was stockpiling guns. In May 2018, special agents with the FBI stopped by her home to interview her. According to the twenty-five pages of the FBI investigation into Charles, they received a tip in February 2018 from someone who knew Charles from the Army that he had "legitimate plans to cause riots and uprisings with the goal of destabilizing local governments."[333] The investigation failed to find that a federal crime had been committed. But for Charles, that was enough for him to shut out most of the people in his life over fears he or they were being monitored. He got rid of his mobile device and stopped visiting his children. He pulled in closer to his group of "comrades."

Shayla says he was involved in the Eugene antifa scene and that in one of their few conversations about the FBI investigation, Charles said they were targeting him "because he was in antifa."

By late 2018, crisis hit the family. In response, Charles finally returned to see his children. He was no longer driving at this point because he was afraid of registering with the DMV. He got around town with the help of a far-left activist woman he was dating from his "self-defense" gun group.

At the beginning of 2019, Shayla caught her younger daughter sneaking out of the house. After an argument, the daughter called her father and said she wanted to live with him instead. When Charles picked her up, he took down Shayla's American flag that flew in front of the home and burned it.

When winter break was over and it was time to take their daughter to the charter military academy where she was enrolled, he refused. He hated the school's military affiliation and unilaterally withdrew her from attendance to enroll her at a different school. Even though Charles had joint custody of the children, his final divorce decree stated that Shayla has final decision-making authority involving the education of their children.

On January 11, 2019, Shayla brought her custody paperwork to Cascade Middle School. She intended to bring their daughter back to the military academy, where she had already been a student. Charles was called to the school to meet with Shayla and an administrator. Per the school district's policy on custody disputes, a school resource officer was also called. About an hour before Charles arrived with his new partner by car, he wrote, "Death to all pigs" on the Facebook page of the Springfield Police Department. Two days before that, he wrote in another post, "Time to start killing pigs."[334] When Charles returned to the middle school, he was armed with a concealed pistol, a loaded magazine on a gun belt, and additional ammunition in his backpack. He wore a shirt that read, "Smash the patriarchy."

School resource officer Steve Timm met with Shayla and reviewed her custody paperwork. He and another school resource officer, Eugene Police officer Aaron Johns, informed Charles that he could not be present when Shayla removes their child from the school. Charles refused to leave the property. He stood in the lobby and became belligerent. When Johns tried to escort Charles out of the school and inform him he was under arrest, he resisted and fought the officer. He then took out his handgun and fired twice in the direction of the second officer, narrowly missing him. His daughter was nearby in the lobby and was almost shot during the fight.

Charles came prepared and willing to kill police, but he was overcome. Timm fired one round at Charles, striking him in the head and killing him instantly.

Within hours, news of Charles's death spread within the antifa networks in the Pacific Northwest. The Eugene-based Civil Liberties Defense Center, an antifa legal group that describes itself as an "anti-racist social justice organization," immediately took up a case on behalf of Charles. The group released a statement suggesting racism was to blame for the shooting.

"While people of color comprise 38.5 percent of the U.S. population, they make up 51.5 percent of those killed by police," the Civil Liberties Defense Center wrote.[335] "The experience of dealing with police in America is different for whites and nonwhites. Charlie was of mixed Filipino and Mexican descent." The group asked for donations to fund their "investigation."

Despite there being no evidence race had anything to do with Charles's death, antifa networks amplified the copy-paste narrative set by the Civil Liberties Defense Center. They used the hashtag "#LoveandRage4Charlie" to help promote the campaign. It was lifted from a radical poem authored by Charles titled "Love and Rage":

Do not let anyone quench your fire. Do not let them dismiss your love nor pacify your rage. My love, do not water yourself down.

The poem was authored sometime after he had been radicalized and repeats a theme found in antifa literature and art: never moderate. In fact, Charles's extremism is what made him respected in the antifa community in the Pacific Northwest.

Portland antifa group PopMob tweeted on January 13, 2019: "Charlie Landeros, beloved comrade and street medic, was murdered by Eugene police 2 days ago. They were a non-binary activist of color who did amazing work in their community and were gunned down in front of their children's school. Pls support the [Civil Liberties Defense Center] investigation if you can."[336] American antifa blog site It's Going Down also posted in support of him and expressed doubt that he even had a gun.

Much of what Shayla learned about antifa came after her ex-husband's death. It was hard for her to recognize the person mentioned in the antifa groups' eulogies and memorials. But in the last years of his life, he was no longer the man she knew. "There are two sides of him," she says. "There's the Charlie I married and then there is the antifa Charlie." And being at the school during Charles's attack, she says it was absolutely false that he was killed because of police racism. Still, leftist groups and organizers fundraised on behalf of his family based on that accusation. Shayla says none of that money went to his two children. She paid for his funeral and had little contact with his side of the family.

Based on the evidence, the investigation conducted by Lane County District Attorney Patricia Perlow failed to find wrongdoing on the part of the school resource officers. Charles came with a gun and fired it at police before he was killed. And against Shayla's wishes, she says the Civil Liberties Defense Center attempted to interview her younger daughter without her present. Their independently funded investigation also failed to produce anything.

District Attorney Perlow wrote in her findings released to the media:

Eugene Police Officers Timm and Johns are trainers in active shooter scenarios. Their specialized training as school resource officers allowed them to recognize the potential risks in a custody dispute taking place in a school. They both were appropriate in their determination that Charles Landeros was creating a disturbance at Cascade Middle School and needed to be removed from the premises. When Charles Landeros refused to cooperate, they were justified in making an arrest. Upon making the arrest, their lives, and the lives of others, were placed in danger by Mr. Landeros physically resisting that arrest, brandishing a firearm and firing it twice. It is unknown why Charles Landeros chose to use deadly force in this circumstance, but he clearly had no regard for the lives of the police officers or the students or staff present, including his child. Officer Timm saved the life of Officer Johns, himself and perhaps many others given the number of rounds Charles Landeros had loaded in his weapon. There is no clearer circumstance that the use of deadly force is justified than this.[337]

Officer Timm's bodycam footage was released to the public. Despite the video exonerating the school resource officers, antifa have continued to repeat the lie that he was executed by racist cops. Four days after the district attorney's announcement that she wouldn't bring charges, explosives were left outside Eugene Police headquarters. They were discovered before they detonated, and a bomb squad was called in to defuse the devices. The attempted bombing remains under investigation, and law enforcement have not released any information since January 2019. Shayla believes the bombing was an act of revenge by antifa. She has good reason to think so. Charles was connected to a network of militant antifa who believed in and trained for armed conflict with the state. "This is somebody I cared about and loved. But the way he was going and the way he was headed—he was going to end up this way."

Connor Betts

As important as it is to study who revered political martyrs are—their beliefs, writings, biographies—it is just as important to examine who is doing the revering. One man in Ohio who joined the chorus of antifa in calling Willem van Spronsen a "martyr" was 24-year-old

Connor Stephen Betts. He went on to carry out his own deadly shooting in a packed commercial Dayton neighborhood on August 4, 2019. He killed nine people, including his sister, and injured twenty-seven others. Responding police shot him dead within less than a minute.

Bett's shooting came within twenty-four hours of another mass shooting in El Paso, Texas, that shocked the nation. Patrick Crusius killed twenty-three people, mostly Latinos, at a Walmart. Another twenty-three suffered injuries. The 21-year-old allegedly left behind a 2,300-word manifesto on internet forum 8chan espousing racist and white nationalist beliefs. The entire punditry class picked apart Crusius's manifesto word by word to blame the shooting not merely on him but on President Trump, white people, and every American who supported border security.

And before details were known about Betts's political beliefs, his mass shooting was also assumed to be related to white supremacy because he was white. For a few hours, we heard about both El Paso and Dayton and the crisis of white racism. But once it became known that Betts actually espoused militant antifa views, the Dayton shooting went down the memory hole.

Connor Stephen Betts did not leave behind a manifesto as far as we know. But he was an active Twitter user under name "@iamthespookster." Before that account was taken down after the shooting, it provided as clear a view into his beliefs as any manifesto could. Betts was antifa.

In his Twitter biography, a short section for users to describe themselves, he wrote "leftist" and listed his pronouns. Going through his posts week by week and month by month reveals someone who wasn't just a casual supporter of "anti-fascism" but someone who espoused the same language and ideology of antifa militants.

In August 2018, he wrote, "Kill every fascist." This echoes verbatim the graffiti and messaging of antifa. His tweets throughout 2018 and 2019 became increasingly violent. "Hey, if you're nazi-friendly or adjacent, fucking unfollow me cuz nazis deserve death and nothing else," he tweeted in October 2018. Betts frequently flung the label "Nazi" at those with whom he disagreed online and adopted the black and white antifa view that if you're not "anti-fascist," you are "pro-fascist."

By December 2018, he wrote to the Socialist Rifle Association (SRA), another antifa-allied gun group, to inquire about bump stocks. A bump stock is an attachment for semiautomatic rifles that allows them to fire faster.

Betts expressed a longing for climactic confrontation. In response to an essay by left-wing *Intercept* writer Mehdi Hassan titled "Yes, Let's Defeat or Impeach Trump—but What If He Doesn't Leave the White House?" Betts wrote, "Arm, train, prepare." In June 2019, Betts tweeted: "I want socialism, and I'll not wait for the idiots to finally come round understanding."

On the day of Willem van Spronsen's terrorist attack, Betts called him a "martyr." In line with antifa views, Betts had a cosmic hatred for border security and ICE. "Cut the fences down. Slice ICE tires. Throw bolt cutters over the fences," he wrote in a tweet. In the week leading up to his shooting, he retweeted posts that referred to U.S. migrant detention centers as "concentration camps"—again repeating what Congresswoman Ocasio-Cortez and van Spronsen had said. Other posts he shared eulogized van Spronsen as an "elder comrade."

And also illuminating is who Betts was repeating and interacting with on Twitter. He frequently shared posts from freelance writer Kim Kelly. The frequent *Teen Vogue* contributor has written an essay on the far left embracing guns. She's also authored a glowing profile of anarchists and argued many times on abolishing prisons. She referred to van Spronsen as a "comrade."[338] And in a now-deleted tweet, she defended him and called for others to take inspiration from his attack.

"As Van Spronsen and the many other heroic comrades before him have made clear, there are many ways to fight back against a violent fascist regime. Perhaps it's time for more of us to put our thinking caps on," Kelly wrote.[339] Another far-left writer Betts interacted with was Emily Gorcenski, a writer formerly known as Edward Gorcenski. Gorcenski gained notoriety among antifa and left-wing circles for identifying and releasing the personal details of people she says are alt-right. She has also expressed support for extremism on social media.[340] She calls for the far left to embrace weapons. This is an antifa doctrine that appealed to Betts. One of the tweets he shared from Gorcenski read, "What I'm saying is armed community self-defense is not only good, it's necessary."[341] He retweeted another post by an anonymous antifa account that read, "antifascist action is self defense. It is good, it is righteous, and it is necessary."

In the final weeks of Betts's life, he promoted posts that demonized Texas Senator Ted Cruz and Lousiana Senator Bill Cassidy's resolution against antifa extremism. He shared numerous posts in support of antifa, including one that had a photograph of the antifa Iron Front symbol. He also retweeted content from antifa accounts themselves, like Antifa International.

Those who dismiss the mountain of evidence of Betts's antifa views will say it existed only online. That is wrong. Betts put his militant antifa beliefs into practice by volunteering as armed black bloc security. In May 2019, he was one of around five hundred people who came to counter a tiny Ku Klux Klan rally in Courthouse Square in Dayton. He came masked and carried a modified pistol that is likely the same one he later used to kill in August. Hasan Karin, a person who personally knew Betts, told local media he bumped into Betts briefly and they talked.[342] This revelation was not widely reported. Instead, the mainstream media focused on what high school peers remembered of Betts's alleged misogyny seven years prior. The goal was to shift attention away from antifa and onto other theories for the shooting.

The FBI has still not revealed the findings of their investigation into Betts's shooting, but they did disclose that it was clear he had been exploring "violent ideologies."[343] The last tweets Betts liked on Twitter were responses to the El Paso shooting, which had just occurred hours before. The posts he liked called the attack "domestic Nazi terrorism" and linked the shooting to President Trump.

A year after the El Paso mass shooting, the hashtag #ElPasoStrong trended on social media. It was created to remember and honor the victims of the far-right shooting. Many media outlets published stories of how Latinos were affected. However, a day later, no #DaytonStrong campaign materialized. This wasn't any surprise to me. Some victims are valued more in the eyes of the American media than others.

Michael Reinoehl

In 2020, Portland, my hometown, was in the national and international news for all the wrong reasons again. Dozens of cities had Black Lives Matter–inspired protests or riots break out in response to George Floyd's death, but Portland stood out above all in that the violence was maintained for months.

Spending time in CHAZ in Seattle, I had already seen up close what happens when city officials make law enforcement retreat from the public. Anarchists and other extremists move in and establish their own rules. And they aren't shy about using violence. In fact, they revel in it. As in CHAZ, those who fashion themselves "security" for racial justice are often the most violent, cruel, and brutal. On August 29, 2020, three months into the daily violent protests in Portland, a 48-year-old volunteer security person for BLM-antifa killed a Trump supporter in downtown.

Michael Forest Reinoehl shot Aaron "Jay" Danielson, 39, using a pistol at near-point-blank range after lying in wait for him around a street corner. The shooting was caught on camera from a distance by a livestreamer. A person believed to be Reinoehl shouted: "We've got a couple right here!" Two shots rang out, and Danielson fell face-first to the ground.

The shooting occurred in the context of left-wing versus

right-wing clashes in Portland. Earlier in the day, hundreds of vehicles gathered in Clackamas County, near Portland, for a grassroots-organized Trump 2020 Cruise Rally. It was a mass vehicle caravan rally celebrating all that antifa hate: President Trump, America, and law enforcement. The day was peaceful as drivers made their way out of a mall's parking lot and onto a route that took them in and around the Portland area. But trouble was waiting when they decided to drive into downtown Portland.

Drivers displaying the U.S., Trump, and Gadsden flags were met by crowds of masked antifa rioters who came prepared with projectile weapons. Similarly, the drivers and their passengers were ready for confrontation with their own tools and weapons. Antifa rioters hurled eggs and rocks at the caravan participants. They also sprayed cars and passengers with urine from water guns. Some of them tried to stop the vehicles by standing in the road and pushing against the cars. In response, the caravan participants used pepper spray and shot people with paintballs. No one sustained real injuries, and it was another spectacle into the political clashes that have come to define Portland since 2016.

By around 8:30 p.m., the caravan vehicles were gone. But some of its participants walked around. Aaron Danielson walked with his friend Chandler Pappas. Both had participated as passengers in the caravan earlier in the day and are affiliated with Patriot Prayer, the Portland-area conservative group.

According to the criminal complainted, against Reinoehl, at approximately 8:44 p.m., he was walking ahead of Danielson and Pappas. He looked back at them and reached toward his waistband. Portland Police detective Rico Beniga wrote in the affidavit:

REINOEHL turns into the garage entry and reaches toward his left front waist area. REINOEHL conceals himself, waits, and watches as Danielson and Pappas continue walking by. Danielson and Pappas do not appear to interact or communicate with anyone and continue southbound on SW 3rd Avenue....

After Danielson and Pappas walk by, REINOEHL begins to emerge from garage while still reaching toward the pocket or pouch on his waistband. Subject #2 looks back toward REINOEHL. Danielson and Pappas cross westbound across SW 3rd Avenue and REINOEHL and Subjects #2 follows them. The shooting occurs shortly thereafter and is not captured on the surveillance video.[344]

When news spread on social media that someone had been shot, antifa accounts and antifa-sympathetic journalists erroneously spread the claim that a black comrade had been killed by a Trump supporter.

"The far-right have been building up to this for the last three weeks. The [Portland Police Bureau] encouraged this escalation," tweeted Rose City Antifa.[345] PopMob tweeted: "As we process our trauma over this tragic turn of events, let's remember the importance of standing together as a community in opposition to fascist violence."

Within a few hours, it was revealed that the homicide victim was a conservative who vocally supported law enforcement and the president. Photos of Danielson's body on the ground showed he had a "thin blue line" patch on his clothing, a symbol of support for police, and a hat bearing the insignia of the Patriot Prayer group. As soon as that news spread among antifa, the somber mood in the crowd, which by now gathered outside the Justice Center, became celebratory.

"I just got word the person who died was a Patriot Prayer person—he was a fucking Nazi!" shouted a woman on a bullhorn outside the federal courthouse. People shouted, "Yeah!" in response. She continued: "Our community held its own, and took out the trash. I am not going to shed any tears over a Nazi." Even though none of the antifa knew the identity of the deceased at that time, it didn't matter. They only needed to know that he was a Trump supporter. They celebrated his death through dancing, song, and the burning of American flags.[346]

In the immediate hours after Danielson's murder, internet sleuths went to work analyzing the blurry stills showing Reinoehl, who was unknown at the time, running from the scene in the livestream video. Based on his distinctive clothing, they found other clips from earlier in the evening showing him walking around downtown, at times pumping his fist in support of BLM, and frequently having his hand ready on a concealed gun.

What positively identified him to internet sleuths as well as law enforcement was a large tattoo of a black power fist on his neck. From there, people discovered a July 27, 2020, Bloomberg News video interview featuring Reinoehl.[347] His face and tattoo are seen clearly. Crowdsourcing the investigation moved much quicker than what police were saying, who at that point had not even named Danielson as the victim yet. Meanwhile, the shooter was now on the run.

Once I confirmed Reinoehl's name, I immediately searched online for his social media accounts. Though most antifa are quick to conceal and hide their online presence, Reinoehl still had an active Instagram account where he had posted throughout the summer riots. Within seconds of skimming his posts, it confirmed what I suspected all along. Not only was he obsessively in support of BLM, he identified himself as "100 percent antifa" and wrote long posts about the need for violent revolution. On June 16, 2020, Reinoehl wrote:

> Every revolution needs people that are willing and ready to fight. There are many of us protesters that are just protesting without a clue of where that will lead. That's just the beginning that's where the fight starts. If that's as far and you can take it thank you for your participation but please stand aside and support the ones that are willing to fight. I am 100% ANTIFA all the way! I am willing to fight for my brothers and sisters! Even if some of them are too ignorant to realize what antifa truly stands for....
>
> We truly have an opportunity right now to fix everything. But it will be a fight like no other! It will be a war and like all wars there will be casualties. I was in the army and I hated it. I did not feel like fighting for them would ever be a good cause. Today's protesters and antifa are my brothers in arms.[348]

For the record, Reinoehl did not serve in the U.S. Army.[349]

His other posts on Instagram reflect the same themes of viewing the current riots as part of an armed struggle for revolution. Though he was never known to dress up in black bloc, what is more important is that he espoused antifa's ideology. While calling for the abolishment of police, Reinoehl was auditioning for a role in what BLM-antifa would replace police with: armed community "self-defense." Not only has this resulted in deadly consequences in Seattle's CHAZ, others were nearly killed in Portland.

On August 16, 2020, an associate of Reinoehl, Marquise "Keese" Love, was part of a BLM "security" detail in downtown Portland that patrolled the area around the Justice Center, as they had done for many weeks. The day had been marked by extremist speeches featuring local activists like Letha Winston, the mother of Patrick Kimmons. Kimmons, a 27-year-old gang-affiliated black Portlander, was shot and killed by Portland Police in 2018 after shooting two people in downtown and aiming his handgun at responding cops.[350]

Since then, numerous BLM- and antifa-organized violent protests have been held in the city to "demand justice" for Kimmons, even though a Multnomah County grand jury determined the shooting was justified. Still, on August 16, Kimmons's mother incited the crowd by telling them that "this is a war, guys…We're getting ready to get armored up around here."[351] She later added in her speech: "I know you [cops] got a gun, but so do I."[352]

That night, Marquise Love and a marauding security team that included other agitators chased a videographer from the Justice Center to the nearby 7-Eleven. There, they beat up a transgender woman.[353] Two of the people who attempted to help her were Adam Haner and his girlfriend, Tammie Martin. Both ended up getting beaten by the mob. Haner was chased down in his car, causing it to crash in the middle of downtown. The security team then ran up to him and called him a racist and "white supremacist" while beating him.[354] Marquise Love, wearing his vest with the word

"SECURITY" on it, was recorded on video doing a roundhouse kick to Haner's head that knocked him unconscious. Independent videographer Drew Hernandez recorded these beatings discreetly and at great risk to himself. His video showed Haner laying unresponsive in a pool of his own blood.[355] Haner was taken to hospital and survived. Love is so far the only one convicted for that assault.

Reinoehl was part of this volunteer security crew with Love, though he did not appear to be present on the night Haner was beaten. However, they have attacked others throughout July.

Reinoehl's Bloomberg News interview that helped the public and investigators identity him provided an account of how he got shot in the arm. On July 26, 2020, two men who wanted to observe the protests began recording on their phones in Lownsdale Square, a public park that became the operations zone of BLM-antifa. One of the men, Aaron Scott Collins, was suddenly accused of being a Nazi, and the mob called for others to steal his phone.[356] Collins was hit with a skateboard and knocked down. While he was on the ground, the security team tried to steal his handgun, which was legally owned. Reinoehl was one of the people who tried to grab the pistol. Love was there as well.

The gun discharged during the struggle, and Reinhoehl was grazed in the arm by the bullet. The security team continued to beat the two men and eventually stole Collins's gun. Collins was taken to hospital by ambulance, where he received treatment for a head and bleeding mouth injury. No one was ever arrested over the assault and robbery. In the Bloomberg video, Reinoehl even admitted to not knowing what started the altercation when he decided to participate in the attack.[357]

The last few months of Reinoehl's life before his deadly shooting show he was a violent man with no regard for the well-being of others. Over and over, authorities failed to prosecute or jail him, even when they had several opportunities to. This is the travesty in the killing of Danielson. It could have been prevented.

Nearly two months before the killing of Danielson, Portland

Police actually had Reinoehl in custody—but he was let go. On July 5, 2020, during the start of violent riots outside the Mark O. Hatfield Federal Courthouse, Reinoehl was detained and cited for possessing an illegal and loaded gun in a public place, resisting arrest, and interfering with police. He was photographed fighting cops while they subdued him to the ground. In the photo released by Portland Police, his pistol is seen on the ground next to him. A source tells me that police released Reinoehl because he claimed to be injured. The Multnomah County District Attorney's Office then dropped all of his charges for unknown reasons.

But that wasn't the only missed opportunity to stop Reinoehl. On June 8, 2020, he and his teenage son were racing in separate vehicles in eastern Oregon. Reinoehl was stopped by a state trooper, who saw his 11-year-old daughter as the passenger.[358] According to state police, they found prescription drugs, marijuana, and an illegally possessed loaded Glock pistol. Reinoehl had a warrant for that arrest due to his failure to appear in court. But he was never apprehended.

Authorities in Oregon missed three opportunities to arrest and prosecute Reinoehl before he went on to kill. Just the day prior to the August 29 murder, he even attended the BLM-antifa riot outside Mayor Ted Wheeler's home. He was photographed with his young child, who was brandishing a baseball bat.[359]

Immediately after the killing, Reinoehl went on the run. He fled out of state to Lacey, Washington, about two hours north by car. Five days later, he emerged in a VICE News interview with sympathetic left-wing journalist Donovan Farley. In the interview from an undisclosed location, Reinoehl admitted to the killing, saying: "I had no choice. I mean, I, I had a choice. I could have sat there and watched them kill a friend of mine of color. But I wasn't going to do that."[360] He said that Danielson threatened him with a knife even though no evidence supports the claim. In fact, the video surveillance seconds before the shooting showed him waiting for Danielson and following him.

Reinoehl also admitted to being a fugitive, saying he was not turning himself in because he thinks police are collaborating with right-wingers. As mentioned earlier in this book, the rejection of police is a central tenant of antifa ideology. They do not allow comrades to cooperate with law enforcement.

The night that the rest of Reinoehl's interview was set to air, I received word from law enforcement sources that U.S. Marshals had killed him in Washington state. A federal task force made up of local officers located Reinoehl in an apartment. He was wanted for the second-degree murder of Danielson. The U.S. Marshals Service said Reinoehl was killed after leaving the apartment armed with a handgun.[361] As of this writing, it is unknown if he fired any shots. However, a .38-caliber pistol was confirmed found on his body.[362]

Like the antifa killers who came before him, Reinoehl was instantly made into a martyr by antifa in Portland. The night he was killed, BLM-antifa rioters attacked a police building in southeast Portland. On the ground outside the police building, they graffitied over and over: "You murdered Michael Reinoehl."[363] On Twitter, the account belonging to NYC Antifa responded to his death by writing angrily, "What the actual fuck."[364] Antifa doxing activist Emily Gorcenski simply tweeted, "Fuck Nazis," echoing Reinoehl's beliefs that motivated him to kill.[365] The morning after, while driving around Portland, I saw a large graffiti message on the side of a police building that read, "Long live Mike."

Graffiti in downtown Portland near the Justice Center.
Photo: Andy Ngo

Pool noodles were filled with nails to pop police vehicle tires. Photo: Portland Police Bureau

An antifa militant stalks the author's family home.
Photo: Andy Ngo

Confiscated weapons and tools from a rioter in July show fireworks, slingshots, a crowbar and a knife. Photo: Portland Police Bureau

CHAPTER 10

Doxing

H ALLOWEEN NIGHT 2019 was something like out of a horror film. All the lights in my home were off. The doorbell rang while I was lying in bed. I ignored it, thinking it was an overzealous trick-or-treater. But the ringing continued. And then it turned to loud banging on the door. Something wasn't right. I reached for my phone to dial 911. My family's address and my personal number had been doxed by antifa accounts on Twitter months earlier.

Against my better judgment, I put down the phone. I didn't want to traumatize a doorbell-ringing child or family with an entourage of police. I walked toward the front door. By now the pounding moved on to the windows. It wasn't a trick-or-treater. Looking through the peephole in the dark, I saw a group of six people dressed in black bloc. They all wore the same paper printout mask of my face. I recoiled and called the police, but by the time they arrived, the antifa visitors were gone. A police report was taken but as usual for Portland Police; nothing ever came of it. I don't know what their goal was that night. Was it to try to break inside? Or was it only to make me feel unsafe at my family's home?

I suspect the latter given what the security footage showed: the masked group gathered around and stared down the camera. The message was simple: we're watching you.

WITH THE EXCEPTION OF A few senators and congressmen, Republicans didn't really start caring about antifa until the riots in 2020. Democrats and the mainstream media, on the other hand, have done everything to obfuscate or deny antifa's existence. The paradox this sets for the public is that antifa are simultaneously over- *and* underestimated. That is, the threat of antifa violence is often exaggerated and has led to small panics, such as when armed citizens in Montana and Idaho in June 2020 held rallies to keep antifa out over unsubstantiated online rumors.[366] Then in September 2020, antifa were blamed in viral online rumors for starting devastating wildfires in Oregon. (There were several people arrested for arson, but political motives were not been established.[367]) There is a risk of the American right turning antifa into a boogeyman that is then blamed for everything. That is a mirror reaction to antifa blaming all ills on nonexistent fascists.

Obviously, I am not an apologist for antifa. I've been warning for years that they're a violent extremist movement that believes in using terrorist attacks to further their political agenda. I've suffered for being outspoken on this. But I'm also careful to not attribute fault to them when there is no evidence.

More importantly, I don't believe the violence is all we should be worrying about. In fact, the overfocus on violence, which ebbs and flows, causes us to neglect the other half of the picture: the threat they pose to the public and the republic through entirely nonviolent means. In fact, this is the domain where they are most able to advance their goals.

It's clear when antifa assault others with weapons. But few notice when they slowly brainwash communities through propaganda.

When antifa showed up to my family's home on Halloween

night wearing printout masks of my face, it was one of the most terrifying experiences of my life. And yet they were nonviolent and likely didn't even break any law. This is what I'm trying to communicate to readers: antifa deploy diverse tactics to achieve their agenda. With and without violence, they are able to terrorize victims and even force the hand of the state.

"DOXING" AS A SLANG TERM has only recently entered popular usage. Though there is nothing new about online harassment, the ability for social media posts containing private information to go viral makes doxing a new phenomenon. Twitter in particular easily allows posts to be widely shared through networks of anonymous accounts, something not as easily achievable on Facebook. Most high-profile accounts can evade terms of service violations (e.g., the posting of personal information) by retweeting, or sharing, a post made by someone else. The throwaway account that releases someone's address and phone number or a venue's contact information for an event might get banned, but the individuals massively amplifying the information for purposes of harassment are not.

From my initial exposure to antifa in late 2016, I was stunned at how fast and effective they are at identifying their enemies and releasing all the "research" in the form of doxes. In fact, one way antifa gain street cred is through their ability to gather counterintelligence. Stanislav Vysotsky, an associate professor of sociology and criminology at the University of Wisconsin who wrote one of the few scholarly books on American antifa, found that "these types of information and intelligence gathering practices are the core of antifascist activism."[368]

Indeed, on Twitter, groups like Rose City Antifa release long threads identifying attendees of right-wing public rallies, where they work, to whom they're married, with whom they're friends, what kind of car they drive, and so on. From there, the threads are shared hundreds or thousands of times where they're able to crowdsource additional personal information.

Through going to dozens of antifa protests and riots, I learned that they expend significant resources on reconnaissance. Most of the time, it is subtle. Unmasked, casually dressed antifa "spies" use cameras with zoom lens to photograph the faces of people they suspect are "fascists." These images are later poured through and scrutinized for details and cross-referenced with events going back months or years. Even in my early days as a student journalist, I remember seeing these antifa photographers trying to discreetly photograph me to determine at a later point whether I was an "ally or foe."

As a photojournalist, it's important for me to state firmly that there is nothing illegal or unethical about photographing people at public protests. That's what I do as well. But antifa use their images explicitly to harm targets. The point is not to document reality but to gather intel to get someone assaulted, fired, or stalked. For this reason, they do not photograph their comrades, who are often engaging in criminal activities. When they are accidently filmed, any distinguishing features or clothing are pixelated.

While the information antifa groups release on social media is usually obtained through public and open sources, they share it with a community of extremist vigilantes. The information often makes it way to the public in the form of homemade wanted posters that are plastered around town. The goal is to encourage mob violence against individuals spuriously accused of being Nazis.

In spring 2019, antifa and their allies sparked a hate crime panic in Portland by amplifying unverified rumors that LGBT people were being beaten, kidnapped, and killed on the streets. It began with an anonymous claim by a transsexual woman who said she was beaten on the head by transphobic men with a bat. The shocking allegations were accompanied by a GoFundMe fundraiser, which raised thousands of dollars. Through my reporting, I discovered the claim was made by a far-left trans activist.[369] The police report did not match her sensational fundraising claims. The responding police officer noted that she was intoxicated and had no memory of what happened. Her injuries were consistent with someone who passed out drunk and fell down.

However, within days, another shocking allegation emerged online. A self-described fat queer activist said her partner was beaten by "two young white men" driving a maroon SUV during the day in a busy southeast Portland intersection. She claimed to have reported the assault to police, but I checked and there is no record of that. In fact, she refused to cooperate with law enforcement, who had reached out to her after seeing the viral allegations online. Following these two outrageous stories, more than a dozen other sensational, vague claims of hate crimes in Portland were circulated on social media. They prompted a response from Mayor Ted Wheeler, LGBT groups, and also the Democratic Socialists of America.

In addition to amplifying baseless rumors, antifa actively stoked the flames by blaming random individuals pulled from their dossiers. Through digital and real-life flyers, they printed names and photographs of white men they had doxed from right-wing rallies.

"These are the faces of the attackers that have been terrorizing the queer/trans community lately. If you see any of these faces in public, hit them with a brick, because the police don't do anything to stop it," read one widely shared post on Instagram. One of the men falsely accused was 35-year-old Robert Zerfing, of Battle Ground, Washington. Antifa accused him because he was photographed in the past driving a maroon SUV to a conservative rally. It was a vague vehicle match based on an activist's Twitter accusation. Zerfing showed me evidence his SUV had been repossessed months prior to her allegation. His personal information was released publicly by antifa, and he received countless calls and threatening text messages. They also had his address.

Most of antifa's doxing and intimidation tactics skirt the line on criminality. Soon after the Halloween visit, I received a voicemail from an unknown number while I was at a conference in Florida.

"Is this the bootlicker that lives at..." said the man. He stated my address and proceeded to curse me out. I called Miami Police and was informed there is "nothing illegal" about saying an address. She wouldn't dispatch an officer to take a report.

In Portland, all the reports I've made to police of similar threats are never followed up. Even threats of death or bodily harm are dismissed as "freedom of speech" if they lack specificity. The lack of accountability for antifa's doxing and harassment campaigns has emboldened them to publicly incite violence against their enemies. Throughout 2020, "Murder Andy Ngo" and "Kill Andy Ngo" have been routinely written on buildings in downtown Portland. Police take reports as a matter of policy but do nothing.

ONE OF THE DOXING-ADJACENT strategies of antifa is to issue community "alerts" on Twitter and chat rooms on the real-time physical whereabouts of a particular person or group. This tactic is known as "cyberswarming." The target can be any person they accuse of being a cop or fascist. The tweets usually use a hashtag that begins with "Defend" and then the city name. For example, #DefendPDX is used for Portland targets. The intent of antifa is clear: they want comrades to immediately mobilize to confront, follow, or assault the target. The goal, as they say, is to make "fascists" afraid of being in public. But all too often their Don Quixote–like hunts for fascists lead them to harass people carrying out their regular activities that have nothing to do with politics. For example, during the summer 2018 antifa siege of the Portland Immigration and Customs Enforcement facility, one ICE officer was identified, followed, and harassed in a parking lot when he picked up his daughter from camp.[370]

I've also been a victim of antifa's cyberswarming. Antifa accounts on Twitter amplify tweets from Portlanders who claim to see me at particular locations around town. Often they are wrong and put innocent people at risk. For example, at an antifa protest in July 2020, black bloc militants accosted a random Asian male they mistook for me.[371]

"Do you think that I'm Andy Ngo? Is that what you're thinking, you racist c***s?" the man said in a video capturing the incident in north Portland. "This is the second time that's happened to me, third time that's happened to me at protests."

But sometimes they do find me and call attention to my whereabouts. In May 2019, I was physically attacked and robbed while at a Portland gym. On my way down the stairs to leave, I was suddenly drenched with a liquid that came from above. I ran upstairs and saw the assailant, who still had a bottle in hand. That man was John Hacker, a far-left activist who attends antifa and BLM rallies in Portland.

He cursed me out and accused me of putting protesters at risk with my reporting. I readied my camera to document the confrontation. The gym's management stepped in front of Hacker, at which point he moved in to hit me, knocking my phone to the ground. Next, he grabbed the device and tried to leave but was stopped by a gym staff member. I called the police over the incident, and an officer took a report, but nothing was ever done despite Hacker's identity being known and the assault and robbery being witnessed by others.

The insidious nature of much of antifa doxing and doxing-adjacent tactics is that they often don't violate criminal statutes or social media policies. You cannot get banned from Twitter for disclosing where you see someone. Likewise, it is not a violation to retweet a post from someone else who publishes actual private information. Driven by intense hatred, antifa want their targets to fear living a normal life. This is their terrorism without violence.

Former Portland Police Assistant Chief of the Investigations Branch Jami Resch, former Chief Danielle Outlaw and Mayor Ted Wheeler in 2019. Photo: Andy Ngo

The heavy-duty steel fence was torn apart on July 26, 2020, by hundreds of rioters using rope. Photo: Andy Ngo

CHAPTER 11

The "Democratic" Route

THIS IS WHAT NEW YORK DEMOCRATIC representative Alexandria Ocasio-Cortez said in an Instagram video after the Democratic National Convention in August 2020:

> I think it's important for us to talk about the deeper issues of this election, because let's keep it real: We need to win in November. November is about, in my opinion, stopping fascism in the United States. That is what Donald Trump represents.[372]

Ocasio-Cortez was not being facetious. Her comments elsewhere since she entered and rose to national prominence in 2018 repeat a theme: the Trump administration is fascist and must be defeated by any means necessary. She routinely calls for the abolishment of Immigrations and Customs Enforcement (ICE), defunding police, and ending capitalism.[373] In fact, no other politician as high profile as she has managed to mainstream the antifa agenda, making it politically palatable and even advantageous to espouse radical, extremist views.

Ocasio-Cortez is a member of the Democratic Socialists of America, the political party that openly participates in events with antifa and sets up booths in illegal autonomous zones. In August 2019, Ocasio-Cortez and Massachusetts congresswoman Ayanna Pressley promoted a fringe bail fund for antifa and other violent suspects arrested at a riot in Boston on their Twitter accounts. For Ocasio-Cortez, it's not just about radical rhetoric; she believes in action through mutual aid. Those she helped fundraise money for included antifa black bloc militants who attacked participants and police at a tongue-in-cheek Boston Straight Pride Parade.

"One way to support the local LGBTQ community impacted by Boston's white supremacist parade? Contribute to the Bail Fund for the activists who put themselves on the line protecting the Boston community," she tweeted.[374] This wasn't just a one-off. In June 2020, she encouraged her 6.5 million followers on Instagram to donate to groups like Unicorn Riot, an antifa media collective that mixes propaganda and news content.[375]

It should be no surprise that her militant opposition to U.S. border enforcement, like calling migrant detention centers "concentration camps," was echoed by antifa terrorists Willem van Spronsen and Michael Reinoehl. But with the protection of the media, she has never had to answer for her incitement against government agencies.

Immediately after the death of Justice Ruth Bader Ginsburg in September 2020, she stated in an Instagram live video: "Let this moment radicalize you." However, it's not only Ocasio-Cortez who has successfully injected antifa-style politics into the mainstream. What we are witnessing are antifa ideologues, supporters, and sympathizers realizing the efficacy of state and social subversion through the legal democratic process.

Most hard-core antifa do not accept working within the legal framework—for example, elections—but they increasingly recognize that this route should be tolerated for success. Violence and riots may achieve certain goals in the short term, such as terrorizing the opposition into silence, but it is the nonviolent democratic route that provides mainstream legitimacy. In that regard, antifa's biggest victories have not been their successes in shutting down events or brawling with "fascists," but rather the acceptance and tolerance they've gained in the mainstream left. Indeed, if the riots of 2020 prove anything, it's that a sizable portion of Democratic politicians, intellectuals, academics, and journalists find riots and looting justifiable if committed in the name of "racial justice."

BEFORE OCASIO-CORTEZ'S congressional election win in June 2018, there was already a high-profile politician working to mainstream antifa: Keith Ellison. From 2007 to 2019, Ellison served as U.S. representative for Minnesota's 5th Congressional District. He also served as the deputy chairman of the Democratic National Committee, second in command to Tom Perez. As a black convert to Islam, Ellison has long enjoyed the media spotlight for being an American Muslim in Congress. And this has helped overshadow his history of radical views.

When Ellison was a student at the University of Minnesota Law School, he wrote extreme essays under a pseudonym in which he defended anti-Semitic Nation of Islam leader Louis Farrakhan and made arguments for a creation of a black ethno-state carved out of the American South.[376] Ellison toned down his rhetoric as he developed a mainstream professional career, but occasionally his mask slipped. In January 2018, the then congressman tweeted out a photo of his endorsement of Mark Bray's *Antifa: The Anti-Fascist Handbook*. In the post, he is seen smiling along with the text: "At [Moon Palace Books] and I just found the book that strike [*sic*] fear in the heart of @realDonaldTrump."[377] His message wasn't just chilling for an endorsement of a book that donates proceeds to an international antifa fund; his words echo Quran 8:12, a verse often quoted by Islamic State and other jihadist groups to justify terrorism ("I will strike fear into the hearts of disbelievers"). Ellison proudly kept the tweet up for more than a year and a half. He deleted it after news broke of my beating in June 2019 for unknown reasons.

In January 2019, Keith Ellison took office as the attorney general for the state of Minnesota. He was in office throughout the devastating George Floyd riots in his state and even fueled a conspiracy theory that a cop dressed as antifa to incite riots. In late May 2020, one of the conspiracy theories spread online was that a black bloc rioter filmed in Minneapolis was actually an undercover St. Paul cop. It was false.

"This man doesn't look like any civil rights protestor [sic] I have ever seen. Looks like a provocateur. Can anyone ID him?" Ellison tweeted with a link to the video showing the masked man holding an umbrella and breaking windows.[378] In late July 2020, the Minneapolis Police Department said they possibly identified the rioter as someone with "white supremacist" ties, though curiously he has never been named, arrested, or charged.

Since becoming the chief prosecutor in Minnesota, Ellison has been careful in hiding his radicalism. But the outspoken extremism of his son, Jeremiah Ellison, who serves as a member of the Minneapolis City Council, is emblematic of where antifa see themselves making the most gains: local governments.

"I hereby declare, officially, my support for ANTIFA," tweeted Jeremiah on May 31, 2020, in response to Trump announcing his intent to "designate" antifa a terrorist organization.[379] The Minneapolis City Council, all occupied by left-wingers, later advanced antifa's political agenda by voting to "dismantle" the Minneapolis Police Department. Repeating the talking points of BLM-antifa, City Council president Lisa Bender said, "We are here because here in Minneapolis and in cities across the United States it is clear that our existing system of policing and public safety is not keeping our communities safe."[380] A veto-proof majority of the council voted in support of the proposal. In the months since, violent crimes have spiked in the city.[381]

Jeremiah Ellison isn't the only family member of a high-level

Democratic politician to have ties to antifa. The son of Virginia senator and former vice presidential candidate Tim Kaine was arrested at an antifa riot at the Minnesota State Capitol in March 2017. Linwood Michael Kaine was part of the black bloc who set off fireworks and smoke bombs in the capitol building to shut down a rally in support of Trump. He eventually pleaded guilty to obstructing the legal process. His charges of concealing identity and fleeing were dismissed. Kaine was only sentenced to a year of probation.[382]

ONE OF THE IMMEDIATE political consequences of George Floyd's death was the rush by left-wing city councils to defund police departments. It didn't just happen in Minneapolis. Seattle's City Council also voted to defund its police department. In August 2020, they voted seven to one to slash millions from the Seattle Police Department budget. This is after the city lived through the deadly no-police experiment of the Capitol Hill Autonomous Zone (CHAZ). The only council member who voted against the cuts was Kshama Sawant, the highest-profile member on the council. The 46-year-old Indian immigrant and member of the Socialist Alternative party didn't oppose defunding police, however. She believed the cuts didn't go far enough.

Sawant regularly condemns capitalism and makes excuses for antifa rioters in her city who destroy businesses, assault cops, and loot.[383] She's not alone in doing so. Fellow council member Tammy Morales told her colleagues in a public meeting in reaction to the outbreak of riots: "[What] I don't want to hear is for our constituents to be told to be civil, not to be reactionary, to be told looting doesn't solve anything."[384]

Statements like these give fuel, momentum, and legitimacy to antifa's violence. After CHAZ was dissolved, BLM-antifa rioters continued to organize weekly riots targeting businesses, police stations, the police union hall, and even the home of the union's president, Mike Solan. The militants have also tried to barricade officers inside the East Precinct using quick-drying cement while simultaneously setting fire to the building.[385] Those on city council did not and do not condemn the violence against police.[386]

IN PORTLAND, a similar political story is playing out. The city's establishment Democratic mayor, Ted Wheeler, came into office in early 2017. Though his history as a politician showed him to be a run-of-the-mill liberal from a wealthy family background, he's moved left since coming into office to try to appease the loud, insatiable far left in Portland. He has adopted their rhetoric, speaking frequently about white supremacy, white privilege, white racism, and fascism.

Under his leadership as the police commissioner (a dual role for the mayor in Portland), police have been made feckless. Morale is out the window. Police operate under a directive that they should avoid active policing of demonstrations if their presence is perceived as an "agitation."[387]

"If we identify that we might be the problem, that we might be the agitation there, we will remove ourselves physically from [the protest] to try to de-escalate, " Captain Craig Dobson said at a press conference in August 2019. News flash: antifa and their sympathizers view all law enforcement as an agitation. By pulling back on policing violent protests, antifa are given the permission to riot every day. And that's exactly what they did through most of 2020.

But it's not only Mayor Wheeler who has empowered antifa. To his political left is council member Jo Ann Hardesty. As the first black woman elected to Portland City Council, Hardesty has used her race as a bludgeon against the mayor and the city's majority white population. She's been championed by antifa ideologues in Portland, who view her as an ally in city government given their shared hatred of police.

Hardesty routinely criticizes law enforcement and makes excuses for antifa violence. When BLM-inspired rioting and looting first broke out in late May, Hardesty organized a press conference in place of the mayor, who was out of town, where she announced a conspiracy theory that white supremacists were behind the city's violence.

"When we allow white nationalists and white supremacists to infiltrate our peaceful protest…and then create the kind of chaos and damage in our community, we must make that stop," Hardesty said. This was completely baseless as evident by those who have been identified in the arrest records. Then in July, Hardesty took her conspiracies further. After weeks of daily riots and violent protests, she was quoted in *Marie Claire* saying that Portland Police officers were the ones starting fires to blame peaceful antifa protesters. "I believe Portland Police is lying about the damage— or starting the fires themselves—so that they have justification for attacking community members," she said in the interview.[388] Chuck Lovell, the police chief, publicly asked her for evidence of the shocking claim. She later admitted she had none.

Rhetoric like this from elected officials provides morale and legitimacy to antifa. But sometimes politicians even actively take steps to aid them directly. In response to the city's riots, Mayor Wheeler banned Portland Police from cooperating with federal law enforcement during the height of the riots in downtown in July 2020.[389] In September 2020, he issued another directive banning Portland Police from using tear gas for crowd control. When the police chief attempted to push back, Wheeler publicly admonished him. In a statement from his office, he said: "The Portland Police Bureau's decision to put out a press release questioning my direction was a serious breach of protocol and an inappropriate use of City communications resources. I made it clear, in no uncertain terms, to the Chief that this cannot happen again."[390]

BEFORE PORTLAND ANTIFA EMBOLDENED themselves to influence local government, they did a test run at the neighborhood level. In 2017, a group planned and successfully took over a northeast Portland neighborhood association that has a direct line to city council. Jonathan Ogden, one of the board members at the time, spearheaded this effort. In a leaked document authored by Ogden, he wrote about how to silently take over neighborhood associations with the goal of creating "autonomy" areas.

"Using the legal framework already in place in Portland, the Neighborhood Action Councils would take up the task of select members coordinating and sustaining a majority within each Neighborhood Association, as well as create proposals to have brought to the council that will further goals in line with the overall vision of popular self-determination," Ogden wrote in the March 2017 document.

In order to carry out the plan, he wrote that they would need to organize for elections, field candidates, crowdfund money, and "coordinate a response network able to swarm votes." The document included a proposed yearlong project timeline that concluded with a "revolution summer." The plan was ambitious, and in many ways it was modeled on how the antifa paramilitary controlled certain neighborhoods in the interwar years of Germany. Simply put, the goal was to create lite versions of anarchist-communist communes within the city.

Ogden's plan was a success. In October 2017, Ogden and a group of allied candidates from his antifa network won elections in the Montavilla Neighborhood Association. Together, they now formed a bloc and political majority on the association. Political moderates in the community and those aligned with the "old guard" tell me it was indeed a "takeover." They're afraid to speak on record but say there were irregularities in the voting process, suspecting that dozens and dozens of voters who didn't actually live in the neighborhood were brought in. Those elected or reelected to the board included Micah Fletcher and Johnnie Shaver, respectively. Fletcher is a Portland activist who fought a mentally unstable man named Jeremy Christian on a moving train in 2017 because he believed he was a white supremacist. The incident resulted in the deaths of two other men when Christian began stabbing the people around him in a fit of rage. Fletcher was seriously injured and survived. Christian was convicted of the killings and sentenced to life in prison without the possibility of release or parole.[391]

Johnnie Shaver, the other activist reelected to the Montavilla Neighborhood Association, wrote prolifically on Twitter using a pseudonym. She posted explicit support for antifa causes and against the right.[392]

To celebrate their neighborhood electoral success, the antifa network held a celebration in a local bar. One of the attendees of that gathering was antifa street brawler Sean "Armeanio" Kealiher.[393] Kealiher gained infamy in the Portland area for being one of the Rose City Antifa members who regularly brawled on the streets during riots. He also released writings online using a moniker in which he urged for terrorist attacks against cops and bombings on schools.[394] He was killed in mysterious circumstances outside the Cider Riot antifa pub in October 2019. Witnesses to the hit-and-run incident refuse to cooperate with law enforcement per antifa rules. Online, antifa accounts urged comrades to delete any communications they had with Kealiher.[395] To date, the homicide remains unsolved.

The Mark O. Hatfield U.S. Courthouse is entirely vandalized by rioters. Photo: Andy Ngo

A protestor threw a drink at Andy Ngo's face at an antifa protest in June 2019. Photo: Chelly Bouferrache

CHAPTER 12

Information Warfare and Propaganda

MUCH OF ANTIFA'S PROPAGANDA is explicit and in-your-face. The chants, the graffiti, and the symbols. They can show up anywhere: on buildings and clothing and even at sports games. One of the strategies antifa used to mainstream their symbols and messaging has been through infiltrating the official fan clubs of American soccer teams. Modeled after the European-style politicization of soccer fan organizations, antifa ideologues have taken over the Emerald City Supporters and the Timbers Army. Both are official fan clubs for Major League Soccer (MLS) teams, the Seattle Sounders and the Portland Timbers, respectively.

The soccer fan clubs have reserved seating, where members coordinate cheers, chants, and flag waving together.[396] It is normal to see dozens of people displaying the antifa two flags logo and the Iron Front symbol at games. They also drape the symbols over huge banners in the lower sections, displaying the propaganda for television cameras.

In August 2019, MLS banned political symbols but reversed course after just a month following boycotts, massive pushback, and negative press coverage.[397] The media coverage of the issue was favorable to antifa and the fan clubs, who called the logos symbols of "anti-racism" and "anti-fascism."

If antifa's operationalized tactics can be described as a multiprong machine working through violent and nonviolent means, the lubricant keeping it all going is information warfare. A military concept, information warfare refers to the use, denial, exploitation, or manipulation of information against an opponent.[398] That includes hiding information as well as spreading disinformation and propaganda to wage war. And no one does propaganda for antifa than sympathetic journalists and useful idiots. In my first year covering the antifa beat, one of the things that shocked me as much as street violence was the alternate reality local and national press presented on antifa.

Why do citizens of cities like Portland or Seattle have tolerance for a transparently violent, extremist movement? For the majority of residents living in areas affected by antifa's violence, they actually don't see the real antifa. The fighting and rioting are isolated to small areas and for limited hours of a day. It actually is possible to live a normal life without ever realizing there are riots happening in another part of the city. Even with an extraordinary example like Seattle's CHAZ, if one did not travel through Capitol Hill, there would be no reason to believe it was besieged by extremists.

Video recordings and livestreams by independent media journalists have been exceptionally informative. Those videos provide the up-close, raw, and uncensored look into antifa's extremism. Antifa know this and have made it a priority to keep out journalists like myself, even releasing manuals on how to obstruct the work of unapproved press.[399] But more importantly, they've made key allies in the media to counter negative coverage, amplify their propaganda messaging, and discredit their shared opponents.

The American public has been inundated with nonstop propaganda that obfuscates and lies about antifa, simultaneously presenting them as anti-fascists fighting racism and a figment of the right's imagination. How many people who have heard of antifa actually know the movement is made up of organized networks of anarchist-communists who have the goal, training, and determination to overthrow the U.S. government?

Fake News

If you're an average apolitical American, these and similar headlines are probably what you've skimmed about antifa at some point since 2017: "Anti-fascists will fight Trump's fascism in the streets"; "Hurricane Harvey: antifa are on the ground in Texas helping flooding relief efforts"; "Reminder: If you're not antifa, you're pro-fa"; "Anti-fascists linked to zero murders in the U.S. in 25 years"; "Who caused the violence at protests? It wasn't antifa."

This is just a small sample of headlines from antifa-related stories that ran in the media from the *Guardian* to the *Washington Post* since 2016. If one isn't tuned to the nuances of the American political and culture war, for example, people like my own parents, the default position is to view antifa as the "good guys." With the obligations of family life and work, few have time to actually investigate beyond the headlines and leading paragraphs.

The role of the media is to inform the public. But too often when it comes to antifa, we are fed incorrect information. I don't believe most liberal journalists set out to intentionally mislead their audiences and readers about antifa. I think it is pure ignorance that leads news personalities like MSNBC's Joy Reid or CNN's Chris Cuomo to repeat some variation that "antifa" is "just short for 'anti-fascist.' "[400]

But something different that I observed in my years of reporting on antifa is the existence of whole networks of writers and so-called journalists who intentionally spread pro-antifa messaging. Their stories go beyond mere bias and into the realm of propaganda. Most do it as ideological fellow travelers on the far left, but some I've learned are actually members of the militant antifa movement.

In an earlier chapter, I referenced former National Public Radio contributor and current *Teen Vogue* writer Kim Kelly as an example of a journalist whose writing is sympathetic to the radical left.

"One of my greatest hopes is that the work I'm doing at @TeenVogue and elsewhere provides that spark for someone else someday," she tweeted in November 2019.[401] The example of Kelly is egregious, but she isn't an outlier.

Unpersoning

One of the eye-opening experiences after my beating by antifa thugs in 2019 was the number of journalists who began targeting me with such animosity and viciousness that they were indistinguishable from antifa accounts. Journalists I never interacted with pursued me with an obsessiveness I can only describe as a personal vendetta. Their goal has been not only to delegitimize me as a journalist but to make me a toxic figure that others would be afraid of associating with. They pursued that goal through writing lies and half-truths and even inciting violence.

Two months after my June 2019 attack, a damning story seeking to "expose me" was published on the blog site of Portland Mercury, a local left-wing alternative paper. "Ben," an antifa activist using a pseudonym, told the story's author Alex Zielinski that for nearly two years he had been a "spy" in Patriot Prayer, the right-wing Portland-area group. He made the shocking allegation that I made a pact with Patriot Prayer's leader Joey Gibson for mutual protection.

"There's an understanding that Patriot Prayer protects him [Ngo] and he protects them," alleged Ben in the story. To provide evidence for his claim, the paper was supplied with an "undercover" video he filmed. Recorded on May 1, 2019, it showed a group of Patriot Prayer associates milling around a Portland street and discussing where to go. For some brief moments, I can be seen walking by in the background.

Here's what really happened. On that day, antifa and other far-left groups organized May Day–related protests throughout Portland. A group of right-wingers organized their own separate flag-waving rally. I covered both sides, who were in different parts of the city. Toward the end of the day, I was informed in a private message by an independent left-wing journalist that the group of right-wingers might go to Cider Riot, a pub where Rose City Antifa had organized an after party. I followed the right-wing group, who walked around aimlessly for an hour in northeast Portland. I did not hear what they were saying. I was on my phone reviewing the footage and photographs I recorded earlier in the day.

Eventually, they walked to Cider Riot, where around fifty antifa immediately masked up. Soon after, a mutual street brawl broke out between the factions. I filmed the fight but was stopped after a masked antifa woman from the pub blinded me directly with bear mace. Another journalist, Oregon State student Noah Bucchi, had his camera smashed with a weapon by a person in black bloc. He was then assaulted by several antifa when he tried to follow and identify his assailant.

I was a victim of antifa's violence that day. But the *Portland Mercury* made me out to be a sinister coconspirator of a violent attack on the pub. It was a bogus claim. I was never reached for comment, and without knowing who "Ben" was, I couldn't even address my accuser.

The network of antifa-supporting journalists is powerful not only because they work with media sites or papers but also because their smears are laundered between one another and amplified far beyond the original publication. The smears eventually become citations in a Wikipedia entry or the first results in a Google search.

Anytime someone looks me up online, they will see the false smears first. "Super awkward for right-wing blogger Andy Ngo to make a cameo in video of plot against antifa," read a headline by Tess Owen in VICE News. Courtney Hagle of Media Matters for America wrote, "Media presented far-right grifter Andy Ngo as a credible journalist. He was just caught covering for far-right extremists as they plan violent attacks."

I doubt these writers actually watched the full eighteen-minute video that was selectively released by "Ben." Fortunately, at least one journalist did. *Reason* magazine's Robby Soave watched the video and analyzed its content in a report in September 2019:

> [T]he message coming from left-of-center media was clear: Patriot Prayer planned the Cider Riot attack, Ngo was tacitly involved, and Ben's video proves it.
>
> The problem, of course, is that the video—which mostly depicts a small group of people standing around, discussing which side of the street they should walk on when and if they approach antifa, and conversing with the undercover Ben—proves no such thing. I have watched it from start to finish at least five times, and it does not even establish that the group of right-wing agitators planned an attack—let alone that Ngo was aware of such a plot. Indeed, the Portland Mercury article that received such rave reviews from The Daily Beast, Vice, Media Matters, and others makes little effort to explain what was so damning about the video, and Zielinski spends much of her article lionizing Ben's actions without offering any independent scrutiny of his claims.[402]

Alex Zielinski, a former reporter for the defunct hard-left ThinkProgress news site and author of the *Portland Mercury* hit piece, has played an important role in normalizing antifa in Portland. I believe that her coverage since she became the paper's news editor protects antifa, amplifies their talking points about "fascists" in Portland, and joins in demonizing antifa's opponents. Sometimes this manifests in shockingly cruel ways.

Soon after Aaron "Jay" Danielson was shot and killed by antifa shooter Michael Reinoehl, she misidentified him as a different man who she says supported terrorism.

"Bishop, whose legal name is Aaron Danielson, made headlines in 2017 when he brought a rifle to a Patriot Prayer rally in downtown Portland. Bishop was also a strong support of Jeremey [*sic*] Christian, the white supremacist who killed two men and critically injured another on a MAX train in 2017," Zielinski reported.[403] She later had to issue a correction, which happens to all journalists, but her mistake is emblematic of a pattern.

Beyond writing hit pieces and insults on social media, Zielinski's tweets may have actually put me in physical danger.[404]

Since antifa beat me in 2019, I've had to develop discreet ways to cover their demonstrations and riots. This can involve dressing like them, but doing so is extremely risky. Antifa have informed their members and supporters to look for people who match my body shape and height. They've accosted the wrong people on several occasions, but they've also been right.

At a violent downtown protest in June 2020, antifa knew I was there and passed this information either directly or indirectly to Zielinski. While I was undercover and on the ground, she tweeted to tens of thousands of people: "Heads up all, it looks like Andy Ngo is here, wandering around with [KOIN News] reporters. I don't think they're aware."[405] The second part of Zielinski's tweet informed everyone exactly where I could be found at that moment. The KOIN News crew stood about a block away from the demonstration and wore markings that identified them as part of the news station.

After Zielinski sent her tweet, whether or not it was her intention, several people began to repeatedly shine a powerful green laser capable of permanent vision damage at my eyes. The mob began to gather across the street to confront me. I barely got out safely by pleading with a local reporter I just met to leave with her in her car.

I WISH I COULD SAY THAT Kim Kelly and Alex Zielinski are the radical exceptions in journalism. But they're just two examples among a cabal of messengers who work in media and have the ability to launder their narratives far and wide. The damage they've done in making the public ignorant and misinformed on antifa has been immense. But as left-wing writers in an industry run mostly by people on the left, their bias does not count against them.

Take, for example, Harvard-educated Talia Lavin, a former fact-checker for *The New Yorker* magazine and an open antifa activist.[406] In 2018 she falsely accused Justin Gaertner, a combat-wounded U.S. Marine veteran and Immigration and Customs Enforcement (ICE) forensics analyst, of having a neo-Nazi tattoo. She was absolutely wrong. The cross tattoo Gaertner has on his elbow is a symbol for his platoon. He was severely injured by IEDs in Afghanistan, resulting in him losing both his legs. Lavin's mistake earned a rare and well-deserved public rebuke from ICE.[407] She resigned in disgrace from the *New Yorker* and, in a series of tweets, made herself out to be the victim where she asked for donations.[408]

A mistake of that magnitude would be a career ender for any journalist perceived to be on the center or right. But Lavin enjoys the leftist privilege of failing upward. After resigning from the *New Yorker*, she was given the opportunity to write freelance for a number of large publications. Her area of writing and research? "Far-right extremism." In March 2019, Lavin was hired as an adjunct journalism instructor at New York University to teach an upcoming course on "Reporting on the Far Right."[409] Her course was later canceled because only two students had signed up.[410]

On multiple occasions throughout 2019 and 2020, Lavin's

reporting that I collaborated with a terrorist group was false and contributed to the danger I faced.

"Andy Ngo is best known for providing kill lists to Atomwaffen and being a threat to our communities," she wrote in June 2020 on Twitter.[411] The lie was retweeted more than a thousand times. Atomwaffen is an American neo-Nazi terrorist organization. I have never had contact with that group or any terrorist organization. The lie was first started by antifa accounts after my beating in an attempt to convince their followers that I deserved the assault. Antifa militants have projected the message on public buildings in Portland and distributed flyers with the lie.[412] It has inspired others to call for me to be killed.

Identifying Antifa Press

Without being familiar with the history of particular journalists, a good indication of their support for militant antifa can be seen through observing how they're treated at BLM-antifa protests and riots. If they are allowed to freely interview, record, or photograph, that is a good sign the journalist produces antifa-approved content.

Antifa are instructed to be untrusting of journalists, even liberal ones who are sympathetic to them. They fear being identified by law enforcement through the journalists' published work. This became such a perceived issue by antifa during the 2020 riots that the Freelance Journalists Union of the Industrial Workers of the World (IWW) issued a list of directives to "journalists covering the ongoing uprisings."[413]

"If a comrade asks you to stop filming them, stop filming them. Generally speaking, our cameras should be trained on law enforcement and reactions, not to unintentionally incriminate comrades," read the announcement. "If you accidently capture comrades on film, obscure their faces, tattoos, and all other identifying characteristics before publishing."

These rules fly in the face of journalistic ethics in that they put reporters into an explicit advocacy role where their mission is to protect one particular side, literally. This is not reporting, it is propaganda.

One journalist I've observed following these directives is Robert Evans, a Portland-based staff writer with the left-wing investigative online outlet Bellingcat. He is a former editor at humor site Cracked and currently hosts several podcasts. Evans is popular with the far left and antifa on social media, who regularly boost his content.

On July 19, 2020, Evans disputed someone's characterization of the arson attack on the Portland Police Association (PPA) during a night of rioting by antifa. User "@JRehling" tweeted: "Tonight, there was a fire at the Portland Police Association building while police clashed with protesters. The Reichstag Fire in Berlin in 1933 was used as a pretext for mass arrests of Nazi Party opponents." In response, Evans wrote: "This is bullshit. I was there. The burning of the PPA was an intelligent, deliberate and successful action by well organized activists. Do not take this away from them. The PPA was a well chosen target and burning was a justified act of protest against a valid target."[414] Evans later deleted the tweets.

Despite his open support for violent extremism, Evans was profiled by the *New York Times* due to his coverage of the Portland riots.[415] The biased narratives and even falsehoods propagated by local journalists don't stay local—they are amplified by legacy media on the East Coast, which then pass that narrative onto the international press. Despite Evans's extremism, he's been awarded mainstream legitimacy.

I did not like Trump's 2019 comment describing the mainstream media as "truly the enemy of the people," but one can see the basis for that sentiment when looking at how transparently extreme ideologues are presented as the arbiters of truth. Evans isn't the only far-left writer to get this treatment.

While it's bad enough that there are journalists who express support for violent antifa, there are some journalists who are actually more than just supporters. One such person is Portland-based writer Shane Burley. He's the author of *Fascism Today: What It Is and How to End It* and has written essays for NBC News, *Jacobin*, Al Jazeera, Daily Beast, and other mainstream outlets. He's also a member of the IWW Freelance Journalists Union.[416]

In an August 2019 op-ed on the UK *Independent* news site titled "I Was the Target of Alt-Right Death Threats across the Internet—Here's What Happened Next," cowritten with Portland State academic Alexander Reid Ross, they wrote:

> In a tweet, *Quillette* contributor Andy Ngo attempted to identify us, and others, as covert "antifa ideologues" posing as experts for willing journalists, all of whom, apparently, have joined together in a plot to create some kind of media-antifa industrial complex. Ngo is known for saying that antifascist activists are a violent menace who are being aided by the right, and a look at his podcast and social accounts gives us the impression of a man set on discovering antifa-bias in the media.[417]

The essay goes on to say how the writers have allegedly been threatened because of my accusation. I denounce all criminal harassment and threats against anyone. And I stand by my statement. I did accuse Burley and Ross of being "antifa ideologues." But that's actually an understatement. As documented in the "Rose City Antifa" chapter of this book, both men were instructors at Rose City Antifa recruits.

In June 2020, NBC News published an opinion essay by Burley arguing against President Trump's decision to designate antifa a domestic terrorist organization.[418] Burley's essay was perfectly fine as an opinion piece, but nowhere is it disclosed that he has direct ties to an actual formalized antifa organization. I emailed the opinion editors at NBC to inquire if they were aware of this. I included evidence in the email. They did not respond.[419] Burley was reached for comment as well, but he did not respond to me.

MY EXPERIENCES WITH JOURNALISM and so-called journalists since the June 2019 beating have been sobering and eye-
opening. I'm not only attacked for my criticism of antifa, I am targeted
for doing what those reporters should be doing: reporting the truth.

In September 2020, I was the subject of yet another hit piece
in the local press. Portland paper *Willamette Week* published a
report by Sophie Peel titled "Portland Protesters Say Their Lives Were
Upended by the Posting of Their Mug Shots on a Conservative Twitter Account."[420] One of my side projects is to chronicle the names,
charges, and booking photos of those arrested at riots. Portland's
paper of record, the *Oregonian*, announced in summer 2020 that it
would no longer publish mugshots, following the trend of protecting the identities of antifa and accused rioters. But the public has a
right to know.[421]

The arrests are important not only because the public should
know who meets the standard for arrests but also because they're
often the only way antifa are ever unmasked, literally. The *Willamette Week* story interviewed several people arrested at riots
who blamed me for the backlash or repercussions against them.
One woman made the shocking allegation a man carrying a gun
showed up to her family's home after I publicized her arrest. The
story said her mother called police. But I checked with Portland
Police and the Portland Bureau of Emergency Communications.
They informed me there was no record of a phone call from the
woman's home or any associated phone numbers. *Willamette
Week* was forced to issue a correction to acknowledge this after I
repeatedly contacted the news editor.

As *Unmasked* demonstrates, antifa can terrify, dox, harass,
and intimidate without any use of force. They've been particularly
effective because they have infected one of the most important
institutions of a free society: the press. Ironically, media is now
often used to undermine public support for free speech and the
nation's norms, culture, and history.

Binh Ngo circa late 1950s.
Photo: Andy Ngo

Mai and Binh Ngo on
their wedding day in 1980
Photo: Andy Ngo

Mai Ngo circa 1974.
Photo: Andy Ngo

Afterword

I N 1979, a young Vietnamese couple arrived in the United States as asylum seekers. Though both originated from the same province in southeastern Vietnam, they actually met each other during their six-month stay at a camp run by the United Nations High Commissioner for Refugees (UNHCR) near Tanjung Pinang, Indonesia.

A few years prior, their union would have been unusual and seen as a mini-scandal. Mai, the woman, came from a middle-class, nouveau-riche family who owned a jewelry business in Vung Tau, a beach town popular with tourists from Saigon. Binh, on the other hand, was born into a poor family in Long Dien, a small town near Vung Tau. His father, a Hakka immigrant from southern China, died when he was a child.

Before the fall of Saigon in 1975, the two would likely not have met. Their origins and upbringing placed them at different social strata. As a girl, Mai excelled academically. She loved history, literature, and music. She was trained to play the mandolin. She learned English. Her older brother was one of the few Vietnamese students granted the opportunity to study at university in France. Mai herself was preparing to be part of the early generation of Vietnamese young women to go to university. In contrast, Binh was educated to only around 15 years old. He needed to enter the workforce as a teen to help support his single mother, nieces, and nephews.

While their origins and upbringing placed them at opposite ends of South Vietnamese society, Mai and Binh would soon know destitution together. By the early 1970s, the United States reduced the number of American troops in Vietnam, leading to a withdrawal by 1973 under President Richard Nixon. Though not suffering large defeats, morale was devastatingly low among the Americans as the war dragged on and on. At that time, it was America's longest war. Nearly fifty thousand American troops were killed in action, and countless others were suffering from debilitating injuries, PTSD, and drug addiction. Ongoing anti–Vietnam War protests and negative press coverage at home coupled with the Nixon administration's scandals shifted U.S. priorities elsewhere.

Without continued massive American military support, the South Vietnamese army was unable to hold off the assault by the People's Army of Vietnam, along with their guerilla communist forces in the South. On April 29, 1975, the communists rolled into Saigon, the South's capital, with tanks. They captured key locations with ease.

In those final hours, only the most well-connected and fortunate elites had the means to evacuate on the few remaining helicopters. Everyone else could only watch or listen by radio.

The uncertainty and chaos ended quickly. By the following day, the Presidential Palace, South Vietnam's equivalent to the White House, was captured. The three-striped yellow-and-red flag of South Vietnam was taken down, never to be flown again in the country. After nearly twenty years, the war was over. It was a humiliating defeat for the Republic of Vietnam (South Vietnam) and the Americans. The world's strongest military could not overpower the forces of a developing Asian country aided by the vastly inferior militaries of China and the Soviet Union.

The few Vietnamese who fled or emigrated before April 1975 were lucky. What began next was the process of reunification under communist rule. And the victors had plans for the counterrevolutionaries.

Prison Camps

In the months after the fall of Saigon in 1975, hundreds of thousands of South Vietnamese were ordered to register for mandatory "reeducation," euphemistically named by the new government. Those targeted were led to believe the classes would last mere days. The detainees were actually sent to prison camps in remote regions of the country as punishment for "counterrevolutionary" behavior and "collaborating" with the enemy (the United States). Detention periods lasted months at their shortest and up to seventeen years for some. The communist government targeted those who were accused of having any affiliation with the former South Vietnamese regime. This included government employees and all military people but also expanded to include religious leaders and the middle class.

Binh, then 21, was swept up in the dragnet. Though he only served as a rookie police officer assigned to desk duties in Ba Ria, the Vietnamese government targeted law enforcement linked to the former regime. Binh spent the next year laboring in the jungle fields of Bau Lam, a rural commune in the southeast of the country. They were forced to farm crops they never got to eat.

Prisoners were underfed or starved and housed in conditions that exposed them to weather, disease, and pests. Binh recalls how he and the other prisoners had their skin ravaged from chronic exposure to fleas and mosquitos. There was no medical aid, turning small cuts and bites into vectors for infection.

In 1982, human rights activists Ginetta Sagan and Stephen Denney from the Indochina Center of the University of California, Berkeley attempted to shed light on the plight of Vietnamese political prisoners, which was largely unknown in the West.

"Re-education as it has been implemented in Vietnam is both a means of revenge and a sophisticated technique of repression and indoctrination which developed for several years in the North and was extended to the South following the 1975 Communist takeover," they wrote.[422] Indeed, forced suffering and misery were the function of the camps. Prisoners were dehumanized as punishment for being so-called counterrevolutionaries. Those caught attempting to escape were shot and killed. The few who successfully escaped the borders of the camp found themselves lost in the middle of a jungle, forcing them to return to the prison they'd fled.

Another subcategory of prisoners was the middle and upper classes who owned commercial enterprises. Their businesses, which often doubled as their homes, were confiscated without compensation. Mai, her parents, and all the siblings, ranging from young adults to young children, were sent to prison camp for this reason. The family owned a jewelry business—a product of hard work within a generation rather than through inheritance or nobility. But it was of no difference to the government. It was argued that the family's wealth was acquired through the exploitation of workers. The family's savings, possessions, and home were seized in a raid. Mai's eldest brother, San, was sent to a prison camp in North Vietnam for his work with the South Vietnamese intelligence services. No one knew where he was exactly or whether he was even alive. The rest of the siblings, including Mai, were sent to a converted prison camp near their former home.

Age provided no mercy. Young children were punished along with their parents. Mai was 16 at the time and still vividly remembers the rats running on the ground where they slept. Worst yet, the camp was infested with fire ants. On one occasion, Mai woke up with a burning sensation within her head. Fire ants had crawled into her ear canal. She cried from the pain. Mai's mother was help-less. A fellow prisoner suggested pouring water in Mai's ear to see if the ants could be agitated out.

Dean, the youngest sibling in the family at 10 years old, suffered from infected skin rashes on his groin. There was nothing to clean or treat the wounds, which had developed into open pustules. On another occasion, Mai woke up with a sharp piercing pain on her toe. It was bleeding.

"That's a rat bite," one of her brothers said. The bite became infected and her foot swelled up, making each step painful. She was still required to perform the daily task of transporting water from the well using buckets.

The family languished in the camp for the next fourteen months. Relatives were too afraid to visit, fearing they would also be impris-oned. Only poor family friends with nothing to lose braved the journey. One time they brought sugar byproducts as a treat for the children. The camp served the prisoners salted gruel made from boiling spoiled rice grains.

In addition to the hard labor, there were interrogations, with particular attention focused on the young.

"Tell us where your parents hid the jewelry and we'll let you leave," camp officials told Mai and her siblings. They believed the family hid jewels and gold beyond what had been confiscated.

In addition to forced labor in the camps, prisoners were subject to intense indoctrination. Day in and day out, they had to read and repeat communist texts. They were required to confess their alleged "sins" against the Vietnamese people. The more depraved one could portray oneself, regardless of truth, the better the con-fession would be received by camp leaders. The goal of the indoc-trination classes was to break the will, spirit, and individuality of prisoners so that they could be reformed into "proper" socialist citizens.

Boat People

From the late 1970s all the way through the 1980s, hundreds of thousands of Vietnamese fled the Socialist Republic on cramped, unseaworthy boats to nearby countries that didn't want them. Untold numbers of people perished at sea. The UNHCR estimated that up to four hundred thousand died fleeing Indochina on boats.[423] But death wasn't necessarily the worst fate, according to some survivors. The Gulf of Thailand was infested with pirates who specifically targeted refugee boats. In addition to being robbed, the females were gang-raped and survivors would sometimes be abducted if they weren't killed. The dangers were no secret to families who contemplated leaving. But to them, the risk was worth taking.

Even after destitute prisoners were released from camps, they faced continual state-sanctioned persecution through extended probation periods where they were surveilled, could not leave the country, and could not send their children to school. The mismanaged socialist economy also brought about food shortages throughout the country, something South Vietnamese had not previously experienced. Those on probation were not allowed to receive government food rations. If one expressed dissident views during the probation period, they could be sent back to prison camp. Faced with such oppressive conditions, hundreds of thousands chose to risk death by fleeing on derelict boats. These refugees became known as "boat people."

By 1979, conditions became dire enough that Binh, Mai, and their families made arrangements to abandon everything for a last escape. Mai had already attempted—and failed—to leave on three previous occasions. Bad weather or broken equipment forced the boats to return to shore.

"I told my sister that if this time were to fail again, I'd give up," she says. Binh's family borrowed money from extended relatives to finance his trip. It cost an average of $3,000 U.S. dollars, paid in 24-karat gold bars at the time, for the exit papers and travel cost. Adjusted to 2020, that is more than $11,000—an astronomical amount for those in a developing country at the time.

Mai and Binh, who did not know each other, were cramped with dozens of others in a small boat that departed from the southern coast of the country. The boat headed toward Malaysia, a five-day trip at sea. Belongings of value were confiscated or stolen at refugee camps, leading refugees to creatively sew thin jewelry bracelets in the seams of their clothing. Mai's family chose to hide what few diamonds they had left in the cruelest—and most desperate—of ways. Her parents had a dentist extract teeth from both her and her younger brother to hide diamonds. Each sacrificed tooth housed one tiny diamond. With the uncertainty of where the children would ultimately settle, Mai's parents were desperate to ensure that they had something of value to pawn off.

After days at sea in cramped conditions where seasick passengers vomited on each other, they arrived in Malaysia. But the Indochinese refugee crisis had stretched neighboring countries and their camps to a breaking point. After several weeks of moving the new arrivals from camp to camp, the Malaysian authorities forced them back out to sea, this time on boats that were damaged and flooding. The intention was to make it a one-way trip. They shot at the boats when they attempted to turn back toward Malaysia. The only choice was to continue onward to neighboring Indonesia.

After a day and a half, they finally arrived at the Riau Islands, where there was an established UNHCR camp. It was here that Binh and Mai met and began a relationship that turned into romance. Mai, now a 19-year-old woman, was attracted to Binh's kindness.

Every morning, those running the camp dumped a large batch of freshly caught fish on the ground for a first-come-first-serve scramble among the refugees. Aggressive men usually made off with the best fish, leaving the undesired sardines and bait as left-overs for the rest. Binh sought to impress Mai by jousting with the other men for the best fish to give to her. He also helped her fetch water from the well, a laborious task involving travel using buckets attached to a carrying pole. In turn, she would lend him her oil stove and cooking pot, items she purchased by pawning off her small bits of jewelry. Over the next half year, they continued to bond on the island. When it was determined that both would be settled in the United States, where they had distant relatives, they made tentative plans to continue their relationship in their future home.

Land of the Free

From 1975 to 1997, the UNHCR estimates that more than eight hundred thousand Vietnamese refugees were housed in camps throughout Southeast Asia and Hong Kong. The majority were boat people. The United States, Australia, and Canada welcomed the majority of them, with a smaller number settling in Western Europe. Before the 1970s, there was no history of Vietnamese migration to the West. Today, they form the fourth largest Asian American ethnic group in the United States.

By the end of 1979, Mai and Binh were on flights toward the West Coast of the United States, with layovers in Hong Kong, Taiwan, and South Korea. Binh was settled in Portland, Oregon, while Mai was sent to San Francisco. The following year, they wed in San Francisco's Chinatown district. Shortly after, Mai moved up to Portland to live with her husband.

Life in a new country with an unfamiliar culture and language was difficult, but they cherished the new freedoms they had: free-dom of speech and freedom of expression. "America is number one," Mai would always say. Binh worked at an assembly line in a factory where he befriended other Asian immigrants. The work was hard manual labor, and English was not a required skill. Mai took a position as a vegetable washer in the kitchen of a downtown hotel. At night, they took English classes. Together, they earned a meager income. It was enough to rent a small apartment that was shared with another Vietnamese family. They were homesick for their family and friends, whom they had no way of contacting. And they missed the food. There weren't any Vietnamese or Asian supermarkets in Portland in the early 1980s. Initially, it was particularly difficult for Mai to adapt to the tastes of American cuisine, though over time she acquired a liking of spaghetti with Bolognese sauce.

The United States continued to resettle tens of thousands of Vietnamese refugees all the way into the early 1990s. The diaspora communities established "Little Saigon" areas across the United States like in San Jose and Orange County, California.

My Story

By now, readers can surmise that Mai and Binh are my parents. Their story, and the story of the Vietnamese diaspora to the West, forms part of my story. Growing up, I heard vignettes from my mother's and father's prior lives, but I had no context to comprehend them. Occasionally, my mother talked about the horrors of being stuck in a boat for five days and nights at sea, unsure of when or how they would survive. She talked about the resentment she had against the Vietnamese communist regime. I didn't understand any of it.

Like many second-generation Vietnamese immigrants to the West, I coasted through life with little understanding of how my parents ended up here and the sacrifices they made. I was concerned with the material distractions of most youth, unaware of the culture, freedoms, and liberties that made society around me prosperous.

It wasn't until I was well into adulthood that I seriously

contemplated what it meant to be an American citizen. Is it merely an arbitrary legal label, as some people on the left claim? No. By sheer luck I was born into the small percentage of humanity to live in a society where liberty and equality are not just enshrined into the legal code but part of the culture and dominant norms. Here, conflicts are supposed to be solved through dialogue and mediation, not tribal warfare and vigilantism. My millennial peers are often ignorant to the fact that in much of the developing world, conflicts still end in tit-for-tat clan violence because citizens cannot depend on the state for justice. And more than a third of humanity lives in authoritarian states that are "not free," that is, their citizens are denied basic civil and political rights.[424]

The prosperity witnessed in the United States is not by accident. It is the result of the evolution of hundreds of years of enlightenment philosophy and deep political thought from founding fathers who crafted the Constitution and framework that uphold our rights. And even though my parents never achieved the wealth status associated with the American dream, they achieved the greatest dream they could hope for: freedom.

Communism, like fascism, is anathema to liberalism. By liberalism, I am not referring to leftism or the political ideology of contemporary American Democrats. I am talking about the political and moral philosophy of thinkers like John Milton, John Locke, and James Madison. Liberalism is the framework that allows for the protection of liberties, equality, property, free speech, and freedom of expression. How ironic that decades after Mai and Binh fled revolutionary communism, their son would encounter a virulent strain of the ideology in their adopted home in the United States.

June 29, 2019, was supposed to be just another left-wing protest in Portland, but that day I ended up hospitalized with a brain bleed because of violent masked revolutionaries who viewed me as a "reactionary." Antifa's choice of language in describing me that way echoed how my parents were labeled "counterrevolutionary" by the Vietnamese regime and punished accordingly.

The beating that day cemented my resolve in investigating the origins, ideology, and organization of antifa. I thought I already knew a lot after covering the movement on and off for two years, but through the course of research and writing this book, I realized that even I underestimated the danger of this movement.

A Message to Antifa

In January 2018, my father suffered a serious stroke. I was with him when it happened. I caught him before he fell down the steps of the front door. While waiting for the ambulance, I saw my father slipping away from me by the second. His speech slurred until I couldn't understand him anymore. His face contorted into an expression I barely recognized as my father.

My life was thrown upside down for the next year. I dropped out of my graduate studies program to care for him. The brain damage he suffered is extensive. He lost the ability to speak or move. His cognitive abilities are severely affected. My father, the man who sacrificed everything for my sister and me, survived the stroke. But we still lost him.

What I lament most is that he never saw his son succeed in life. He and my mother built a life for their future children from scratch as refugees in a foreign land. But for most of my adolescent and young adult life, I struggled with crippling chronic depression. He did not see me overcome that and grow to become a successful journalist who was invited to speak at Congress. The person I knew as my father is gone, but his American dream lives on in me. It gives me the resolve to overcome the assaults, intimidation, and death threats to continue my work.

In those dark times in the hospital in 2018, I watched my father and other patients in the Intensive Care Unit teeter on the edge of life and death. Some went over. It opened my eyes to the fragility of human life. Having never experienced the death of a loved one growing up and suffering from the hubris of youth, I was ignorant about mortality. In those nights in the hospital, however, what I saw was that every person, regardless of upbringing and politics, suffers pain, loss, and grief.

Antifa have sought to cast me not just as a fascist but also as heartless and cruel. The goal has been to damage my professional career and make me reviled wherever I go. I regret to say that the latter has worked. I've been shouted out of businesses and even assaulted at one. Antifa regularly stalk me and report on social media where I can be found. I'm angry at them, but I still see their humanity and don't wish them ill. I actually feel sympathy for those pulled and brainwashed into antifa's twisted ideology. They are often exploited and used by a movement that explicitly rejects the value of individuals in favor of the cause.

Antifa are often assumed to be upper-class spoiled brats by their detractors, but this isn't broadly true. I've looked through records and backgrounds of nearly a thousand people arrested at antifa riots to get a better sense of who they are. While some are indeed highly educated and in white-collar professions ranging from law to academia to health care, those who are involved in the street violence are disproportionately individuals dealing with housing insecurity, financial instability, and mental health issues like gender dysphoria.[425] Antifa could not give a damn if those people end up injured, imprisoned, or dead in the furtherance of their political agenda.

Since Donald Trump's 2016 election win, antifa's numbers have soared in the United States. This is reflected in not just the scale of their riots but also the frequency. Antifa is a household name in 2020 when they were virtually unheard of just five years prior. Fear and hatred drive left-wing people to antifa's extremist ideology—but there is more. They have grievances that need to be acknowledged. Some of it is indoctrinated through education and culture, but not everything can be blamed on that. Grievance ideologies resonate with millennials and Gen Z because of an economic reality they experience: crushing student debt, job insecurity, and the inability to ever afford a home.[426] I can understand why those who lose faith in the American idea—in liberal democracy—turn to extremist ideologies for solutions. The corruption in politicians and state institutions at times rattles my own confidence in the American rule of law and democracy.

For those who are vulnerable, antifa is more than appealing. It promises community, protection, and purpose.[427] It is organized like a zealous religious movement through the constant feeding of ideology and propaganda. They believe a communist-anarchist world utopia is possible. There would be no borders, police, prisons, racism, or fascism. All material needs would be met through community mutual aid, not through working in an exploitative capitalist system.

But the world antifa envisions is a literal "utopia." Translated from the original Greek, "utopia" means "no place." No society can function as antifa envisions. Their small-scale experiments at creating separatist anarcho-communist communes, have ended in disaster and death. Even when their anti-fascist ideology was instituted at the state level (e.g., in the former East Germany), the result was the creation of a sprawling spy apparatus that monitored the public and private thoughts of citizens for wrongthink.

Antifa will continue to grow after this book's publication. The groundwork has already been laid, and the ideology is mainstreamed and given legitimacy through Black Lives Matter and the Democratic Party. Still, I urge compassion for those who have been drawn into this violent extremist ideology. The hatred antifa feel toward their society, country, and fellow citizens comes from pain and resentment of their own lives.

One of the most disempowering mind viruses infecting America and the West at the benefit of antifa is grievance ideology. Through its control in every cultural and educational institution, it primes people to become perpetual victims. It makes them see grievance in every interaction. It turns pain and ignorance into hatred. It turns people into oppressors. Efforts by the Trump administration in September 2020 to address critical race theory via an executive order to ban federal contractors from teaching the poisonous ideology is a good first step.[428] But how do we address it in K–12 education? Higher education? The rest of society? What it will take is the bravery to say, "Enough!" Grievance ideology only has power insofar as it is seen as legitimate. It is not.

THE VICTORY OF REAL JUSTICE over antifa's version of "social justice" requires people to be held accountable for their crimes. The systematic demonizing and weakening of police departments and law enforcement across the United States have emboldened BLM-antifa to destroy and attack with near impunity. Law enforcement need to be given access to the training and tools for crowd control. Prosecutors must prosecute. Proclamations labeling antifa "domestic terrorists" provide red meat for a right-wing base but have little effect in legal practice.

Antifa's ideology, or any extremist belief system for that matter, cannot be banned per the First Amendment. Antifa have the constitutional right to espouse their hatred, as do racists and other bigots. I'm skeptical that additional legislation can be helpful when there are already laws that can be applied. The Racketeer Influenced and Corrupt Organizations (RICO) Act may be relevant; it was codified into American federal jurisprudence in the 1970s to prosecute the Mafia and others involved in organized crimes. Antifa, regardless of what they call themselves, are an organized criminal network of groups. It's not only the violent hooligans who should be prosecuted. Organizers exchange money and

resources with one another. They provide radicalization training and instructions on how to commit crimes. They cross state
lines.

The problems witnessed in Portland and other left-wing cities is
not the lack of laws but the lack of law enforcement. When the far
left say the American legal system is "broken," I actually agree with
them but for different reasons. Why are district attorneys, who are
elected politicians, determining who gets prosecuted? They have
every incentive to bow to the whims of the mob in order to stay in
office. There must be better independent oversight to hold rogue
prosecutors accountable.

The BLM-antifa narrative that police are murdering black and
brown people in epidemic proportions needs to be thoroughly
debunked. It is not supported by the evidence or data. This should
be the job of the media, but it has been they who fan the flames of
racial division through one-sided wall-to-wall coverage. The unend-
ing distraction from real issues that can otherwise be addressed
through evidence-based policy making has us chasing shadows.

ON NOVEMBER 14, 2020, thousands of people from across the
United States traveled to Washington, DC, for the "Million MAGA
March." The event was organized as a last-minute grassroots show
of support for President Trump, who was projected to lose the
2020 election to Joe Biden. Attendees wore patriotic gear, waved
Trump and American flags, and sang the national anthem. It was
peaceful and celebratory—until the sun began to set. As the participants dispersed and headed to their cars and hotels, they were
met by marauding gangs of Black Lives Matter and antifa black
bloc counter-protesters. Police had kept the two sides separated
during the day, but by now the militants were roaming the streets
for stragglers.

Over the course of several hours, individuals, families, and

groups of Trump supporters were singled out for harassment, robbery, and assault. The far-left agitators stole people's hats and flags
and set them on fire on the street. They pushed and punched people
to the ground. They hit them with sticks. Diners eating outside at
hotel restaurants had projectiles and mortar explosives thrown at
them. No one was spared. Those targeted included women, children, and the elderly.

The scenes of wanton violence against Trump supporters—
though shocking—were nothing new. During the 2016 presidential
campaign, people leaving Trump rallies in liberal cities, like San
Jose and Chicago, were stalked, robbed, and beaten. But the sym-
bolism of American citizens being assaulted with impunity for participating in the political process in the U.S. *capital* foreshadows
even darker times ahead for the nation.

For me, what I saw felt like a personal attack. I love America.
I am grateful for this country and its Constitution. Its people are
generous and welcoming. My family came from a society where
there is no tradition of freedom of speech or the rule of law.

America is worth preserving and protecting for future genera-
tions. Tragically, what I see is that it's becoming taboo to be patriotic or grateful to one's nation. Americans have been robbed and
assaulted in public for merely holding symbols of the United States.
As the George Floyd–inspired rioting broke out in Portland at the
end of May 2020, I saw a mob of so-called racial justice activists
beat a man peacefully carrying an American flag in downtown.[429]
They punched him in the face, knocked him to the ground, and
kicked him repeatedly on the head. He would not let go of that flag.

Antifa, its far-left allies, and useful idiots have convinced the
public that patriotism is synonymous with racism and fascism. I
reject that and call for all decent people to do the same. As much as
this book is about antifa, it's also a letter of gratitude to the nation
that welcomed my parents, penniless refugees from the Socialist
Republic of Vietnam, to become equal citizens.

Antifa seek to destroy the American philosophy and the literal state itself. They are finding some success. For those who are drawn to their siren calls of "anti-racism," "anti-fascism" and "equity," look to where their ideas have been put into practice. No one inherits a utopia or civilization. They inherit ash, blood, and feces-stained rubble.

1 "Rani Baker," who is verified on Twitter, was previously known as Ralph Stuart Baker III. She is originally from Texas and is extremely active in the Portland antifa scene. In 2014 she petitioned the courts to change her name to Agnesia Romilda-Lynn Baeddel. She has been seen attending protests with the Satanic Portland Antifascists group. Ruptly, "USA: Scuffles Erupt between Patriot Prayer and Antifa."

2 Antifa Sacramento, "Antifascist Prisoner Support."

3 Rose City Antifa, "Statement about June 29, 2019."

4 Victor Fiorillo, "D.C. 'Antifa Leader' Is Third Man Charged in Marine Attack in Philadelphia."

5 Fred Lucas, "Antifa Activist Facing Assault Charges Was Tied to Democratic Policymakers."

6 Donald J. Trump, "Major consideration is being given to...."

7 Katie Shepherd, "At IRE one of the tips from the 'Reporting on Hate' panel...."

8 Victor Garcia, "Ex-Antifa Member Slams Nadler for Calling Far-Left Group 'Imaginary': 'That's Just False.'"

9 Meg Kelly and Elyse Samuels, "Who caused the violence at protests? It wasn't antifa."

10 Lois Beckett, "Anti-Fascists Linked to Zero Murders in the US in 25 Years."

11 Marisa Schultz, "Dem Senator Walks Out of Ted Cruz's Antifa Hearing: 'I Don't Think You Listen.'"

12 Indianapolis Metropolitan Police Department, "IMPD Officer Involved Shooting."

13 Wayne Hubbard, "Justice for Sean Reed!"

14 David Hogg, "While white men stomp around with ar-15s in state capitals in front of police and face zero repercussions. Sean reed served his country only to die after being shot running away from the police. This is what a system looks like that protects and serves white supremacy."

15 Dreasjon Reed, "Just say the word I'm on they block like this."

16 Laura Rogers and Karen Moore, "Crowd Gathers in Indianapolis to Protest Death of Sean Reed in Police Shooting."

17 Jeremy Jones, "Gregory McMichael Murderer Ahmaud Arbery Seen at KKK Rally in 2016."

18 Diane Sandberg, "Family of George Floyd Seeks Independent Autopsy."

19 Andrew M. Baker, "Cardiopulmonary Arrest Complicating Law Enforcement Subdual, Restraint, and Neck Compression."

20 Neil MacFarquhar, "Minneapolis Police Link 'Umbrella Man' to White Supremacy Group."

21 Libor Jany, "Minneapolis police say 'Umbrella Man' was a white supremacist trying to incite George Floyd rioting." https://www.startribune.com/police-umbrella-man-was-a-white-supremacist-trying-to-incite-floyd-rioting/571932272/.

22 CrimethInc., "Why We Break Windows: The Effectiveness of Political Vandalism."

23 Jackie Salo, "New York Times Reporter Says Destroying Property Is 'Not Violence.'"

24 David Remnick, "An American Uprising."

25 CrimethInc., "Why We Break Windows: The Effectiveness of Political Vandalism."

26 Michael Biesecker and Michael Kunzelman, "As Trump Blames Antifa, Protest Records Show Scant Evidence."

27 Neil MacFarquhar, Alan Feuer, and Adam Goldman, "Federal Arrests Show No Sign That Antifa Plotted Protests."

28 Libby Torres, "Drake, Chrissy Teigen, and Steve Carell Are Just Some of the Stars Who've Donated to Bail-Relief Funds across the US."

29 Jonah Engel Bromwich, "The Minnesota Freedom Fund Has $30 Million and an Identity Crisis."

30 New York City Antifa, "Solidarity from NYC to . . . ."

31 Antifa Seven Hills, "HOW TO SUPPORT #Minneapolis DIRECTLY! . . . ."

32 Portland Youth Liberation Front, "From Portland to Minneapolis, for Youth Liberation! . . . ."

33 Pacific Northwest Youth Liberation Front, "BOOSTING Portland: Vigil for . . . ."

34 Ryan J. Foley, "Woman, 22, Killed at Protest as Civil Unrest Roils Davenport."

35 Jemima McEvoy, "14 Days of Protests, 19 Dead."

36 Revolutionary Abolitionist Movement NYC.

37 Larry Celona and Vincent Barone, "Black Lives Matter Protesters Riot in Manhattan, Cause $100,000 Damage: NYPD."

38 Anarchists Worldwide, "So-Called USA: Revolutionary Abolitionist Movement 10 POINTS of ACTION."

39 Associated Press, "Rayshard Brooks Struggled in System but Didn't Hide His Past."

40 Asia Simone Burns, "Police ID 8-Year-Old Shot, Killed; $10,000 Reward Offered in Case."

41 Gabrielle Fonrouge, "This Is Why Jacob Blake Had a Warrant Out for His Arrest."

42 Racine County Eye, "Police: K9 Dozer Helps Subdue Man Who Pulled Gun at Bar"; Shayndi Raice, "Jacob Blake Shooting: What Happened in Kenosha, Wisconsin?"

43 Jason Silverstein, "Kamala Harris Meets with Jacob Blake's Family in Wisconsin."

44 Lee Brown, "Armed Protesters Confront Armored SWAT Vehicle after Wisconsin Shooting."

45 Schaffer. Interview by Andy Ngo, October 2020.

46 Hernandez. Interview by Andy Ngo, October 2020.

47 Matthew Banta, "Hey you Patriot Fash...."

48 FOX 11 News, "Charges Filed against Man Accused of Defying Orders during Waupaca Protest."

49 Milwaukee Coalition Against Trump, "As protesters milled along the side of...."

50 Benita Mathew, "Neenah Man Charged with Bringing Smoke Grenades to Green Bay Rally, Accused of Pointing Rifle at Police in Waupaca."

51 David Aaro, "Kenosha Sees 175 Arrested during Civil Unrest so Far; 102 Had Addresses Listed Outside City, Police Say."

52 Louis Casiano, "Seattle-Based Activists Arrested in Kenosha after Filling up Gas Cans."

53 Guarente, "What It's Like to Eat Inside Seattle's Much-Discussed Protest Space."

54 Seattle Police Department, "East Precinct Protest Update."

55 Seattle Antifascists, "We need more people with guns...."

56 Project Veritas, "Militia Wing of ANTIFA Believes in Complete Abolition of the System Itself, Including Police."

57 Nicholas James Armstrong, "We can't wait till someone gets...."

58 "Andy Ngo, "Nicholas James Armstrong/Nikki Jameson was seen...."

59 Ngo, "Antifa Militant Seen with Illegal Gun in the 'CHAZ.'"

60 Jenny Durkan, "The Capitol Hill Autonomous Zone...."

61 Brandi Kruse, "CHOP: Seattle Mayor Walks Back 'Summer of Love' Comment."

62 Kelly Weill, "Local Businesses Love the 'Domestic Terror' Zone in Seattle, Actually."

63 Arrest Facts, "Solomon Samuel Simone."

64 Alex Kasprak, "Does This Video Show Raz Simone Handing Out Guns in Seattle's CHOP?"

65 Solomon Samuel Simone, "The president really put a hit on my head...."

66 Uhrs Gehriger, "America Under Siege: 'They Don't Want Law and Order. They Want Anarchy.'"

67 Shelby Talcott, "EXCLUSIVE: 'I've Been Scared Every Day': Seattle Resident Speaks Out about Life on the Border of CHAZ."

68 PubliCola, "FBI Says There Was Specific Threat against East Precinct; Durkan Letter Dodges Protesters' Three Demands."

69 Nellie Bowles, "Abolish the Police? Those Who Survived the Chaos in Seattle Aren't So Sure."

70 Jason Rantz, "Rantz: Alleged Seattle Arsonist near CHOP Arrested, AK-47 Found Nearby."

71 Joseph Schwartz and Jason Schulman, "Toward Freedom: Democratic Socialist Theory and Practice."

72 Sprout Distro, "Blockade, Occupy, Strike Back."

73 Portland Police Bureau, "To the group near N. Mississippi Avenue...."

74 Warzone Distro, "Against the Police and the Prison World They Maintain."

75 Sprout Distro, "Accomplices Not Allies: Abolishing the Ally Industrial Complex."

76 KOMO News Staff, "Best: SPD Response Times Have Tripled since Loss of East Precinct."

77 U.S. Department of Justice, "Man Charged with Arson for Setting Fire to Seattle's East Police Precinct during Capitol Hill Protest."

78 JoshWho News, "CHAZ Shooting Victim's Brother Claims Criminal Protesters 'Hid' His Brother from Him while He Was Dying."

79 Seattle Police Department, "Homicide Investigation Inside Protest Area."

80 Casiano, "Seattle Father Mourning Loss of Son Killed in 'CHOP' Zone Gets Calls of Support from Trump, Mayor Durkan."

81 Associated Press, "Seattle Mayor Proposes $20M in Cuts to Police to Help Budget."

82 David Gutman, "Durkan Proposes $20 Million in Cuts to Seattle Police as Part of Proposal to Balance Budget."

83 FreeCapitolHill, "The Demands of the Collective Black Voices at Free Capitol Hill to the Government of Seattle, Washington."

84 Ami Horowitz, "Inside CHAZ (the Capitol Hill Autonomous Zone)."

85 @MaliceBD, "2 guys in a stolen SUV shot up...."

86 @MaliceBD, "I know I shouldn't glorify...."

87 @JaredComrade, "Congratulations! I'm proud of you Anarchists…"

88 Angela King, Casey Martin, and Gil Aegerter, "1 Teen Dead, 1 Wounded in Shooting at Seattle's CHOP."

89 Seattle Police Department, "Group Causes Significant Property Damage and Commits Arson in Capitol Hill Neighborhood."

90 Solan, Mike. Interview by Andy Ngo, August 23, 2020.

91 Seattle Police Department, "Officer Involved Shootings (OIS) Dashboard."

92 Seattle Police Department, "Officer Injuries, Precinct Damage, Arrest Updates."

93 Seattle Police Department, "Updated: Officers Injured, 18 Arrested during Riot in SODO."

94 Rantz, "Rantz: Rioters Tried to Burn Seattle Police Alive."

95 Daniel T. Satterberg, "The State of Washington v. Jacob Bennet Greenburg, Danielle E. McMillan."

96 Yahoo Finance, "Seattle Police Chief Carmen Best Plans to Announce Her Resignation."

97 Portland Police Bureau, "Update: Information about Additional Arrests from May 30 Riot."

98 Ngo, "Masked militants ransacking the Justice Center…."

99 Ngo, "In downtown Portland, rioters…."

100 Brad Kalbaugh, "State of Oregon v. Amelia Joan Shamrowicz."

101 FOX 12 Staff, "New Data Shows Surge in Portland Shootings, with 488 So Far This Year."

102 Joel Finkelstein, Alex Goldenberg, Sean Stevens, et al., "Network-Enabled Anarchy: How Militant Anarcho-Socialist Networks Use Social Media to Instigate Widespread Violence against Political Opponents and Law Enforcement," 3.

103 Finkelstein, Goldenberg, Stevens, et al., "Network-Enabled Anarchy," 15.

104 Portland Police Bureau, "Destructive Crowd Topples Historic Statues in South Park Blocks, Breaks Windows, Arrests Made."

105 The Witches, profile.

106 Riot Ribs, profile.

107 Equitable Workers Offering Kommunity Support, profile.

108 OHSU4BLM, profile.

109 PDX Shieldsmiths, profile.

110 PDX Hydration Station & Umbrellacrosse Sticks, profile.

111 PDX Community Jail Support, profile.

112 Riot Ribs, "FOR IMMEDIATE RELEASE…."

113 Portland General Defense Committee, "PDX Protest Bail Fund."

114 Portland General Defense Committee, "GoFundMe Transparency."

115 Portland Police Bureau, "Update: During June 1st Demonstration 10 Adults Arrested and 6 Adults Cited."

116 Portland Police Bureau, "Justice Center—Police Raw Video."

117 Portland Police Bureau, "Several Weapons Seized Related to Down-town Demonstrations."

118 Teressa Raiford, "We Should Abolish Period."

119 Traci Yoder, "Legal Support for Anti-Fascist Action."

120 Influence Watch, "National Lawyers Guild."

121 Aimee Green, "21 Protest-Related Lawsuits Have Been Filed against Portland Police: Latest 3 Accuse Police of Harassing Critics."

122 Portland Police Association, "A letter to the editor....", https://www.facebook.com/PortlandPoliceAssociation/photos/a.386709091352814/2233132546710450/?type=3&theater.

123 Nick Budnick, "Portland Mayor Admonishes Police Chief after Public Clash over Tear Gas."

124 Portland Police Bureau and Portland Fire and Rescue, "Arson Fires 5/29/2020 to 6/8/2020."

125 Ted Wheeler, "We talked about agitation...."

126 Portland Police Bureau, "Update: Arrests Made for July 4th Demonstrations."

127 U.S. Department of Justice, "Seven Arrested, Facing Federal Charges After Weekend Riots at Hatfield Federal Courthouse."

128 Pacific Northwest Youth Liberation Front, "For real tho, the cops...."

129 Mia Cathell, "Journalist Attacked by 'Black Bloc' Militants at Antifa Riot in Portland."

130 Wheeler, "A number of people have asked if I...."

131 Ron Wyden, "The consequences of Donald Trump unilaterally...."

132 Kate Brown, "This is a democracy, not a dictatorship...."

133 Rebecca Ellis, "Portland Votes to Wall Off Local Police from Federal Law Enforcement."

134 Ngo, "For those who say I am lying about the 'mom'...."

135 Fosters Daily Democrat, "NH Man Gets 41 Months for Possessing Child Pornography in Maine."

136 Ngo, "Blake David Hampe, the accused #antifa stabber...."

137 Blake David Hampe, "I was marching very close...."

138 Multnomah County Sheriff's Office, "Blake David Hampe Booking."

139 U.S. Department of Justice, "Texas Man Charged with Assaulting Deputy U.S. Marshal with Hammer during Weekend Protests in Portland."

140 Ngo, "Trump-Loving Grandma Outs Portland 'Bomber' to Feds—and It's Her Own Grandson."

141 Portland Police Bureau, "Protest Blocks Streets, Officers Assaulted, Pelted with Rocks, Glass Bottles, Other Objects"; "Update: Multiple Suspects Charged with Assaulting Officers, Other Charges."

142 Sara Cline, "Portland Protests Set Up Clash between Journalists, Police."

143 C-SPAN, "Hearing on Protests across U.S."

144 Brown, "After My Discussions with VP Pence...."

145 Portland Police Bureau, "Arson Fire in Building, Riot Declared."

146 Portland Police Bureau, "24 Arrested, Officer Injured by Large Rock during Unlawful Assembly."

147 Portland Police Bureau, "Update: 12 Adults Arrested, 1 Juvenile Detained-New Criminal Tactic Used on Police Vehicles, Spike Devices Seized."

148 Tess Riski, "New Multnomah County District Attorney Mike Schmidt Must Decide Who Faces Criminal Charges amid Portland's Protests."

149 Multnomah County District Attorney, "District Attorney Mike Schmidt Announces Policy Regarding Protest-Related Cases."

150 Portland Police Bureau, "Protesters Break Windows, Burglarize Business, Start Fire in Apartment Building; Riot Declared."

151 Portland Police Bureau, "Ammunition and Destructive Devices Recovered at Lownsdale Square Park."

152 Portland Police Bureau, "59 Arrested during Riot."

153 Paul Best, "Staffer for Top Oregon State Lawmaker Arrested during Portland Riot."

154 Ngo and Mia Cathell, "Portland District Attorney Brings Charges Following Week of BLM-Antifa Arson Attacks."

155 Ellis, "Portland Mayor Ted Wheeler Bans Use of CS Tear Gas."

156 KATU Staff, "Protests Cost $23 Million in Damage, Lost Business, Portland Police Say."

157 Hannah Ray Lambert, "Policing Portland's protests: 1,000 arrests, handful of prosecutions." https://www.koin.com/news/protests/policing-portlands-protests-1000-arrests-handful-of-prosecutions/.

158 Multnomah County District Attorney, "Protest Cases."

159 Sarah Iannarone, "To those who say Antifa are...."

160 Laural Porter, "On Straight Talk, Portland mayoral candidate Sarah Iannarone declines to denounce violent protests, says protesters' outrage with police is valid."

161 Oregon Secretary of State, "General Election November 3, 2020." https://results.oregonvotes.gov/SearchResults.aspx?ID=610.

162 Portland City Council, "City Council 2017-03-22 PM."

163 @PDXDublin, "Heroe's American Café on...."

164 Multnomah County Sheriff's Office, "Unified Command press release on Nov. 4 unlawful assembly and riot."

165 Multnomah County Sheriff's Office, "Unified Command: Individuals target a City Commissioner's home, set fire at Portland City Hall."

166 Portland Police Bureau, "Mass Gathering Vandalizes Building in Laurelhurst Neighborhood." https://www.portlandoregon.gov/police/news/read.cfm?id=271330.

167 Rose City Antifa to "Lion"/Project Veritas, September 22, 2017.

168 Alexander Reid Ross, "Andy Ngo contacted me about a book talk...."
169 Caroline Victorin, "Johan's Green Card Fund."
170 Berger, Dan, "Outlaws of America: The Weather Underground and the Politics of Solidarity," google.com/books/edition/Outlaws_of_America/6KC36MHH3j8C?hl=en&gbpv=0, p. 117.
171 Torch Network, "About."
172 Torch Network, "Points of Unity."
173 Sprout Distro, "An Activist's Guide to Information Security."
174 Sprout Anarchist Collective, "What is security culture? A guide to staying safe..."
175 It's Going Down, "Time to Beef Up Defense against Far-Right Doxxing."
176 It's Going Down.
177 Don J. Hamerquist, Sakai, and Xtn., *Confronting Fascism: Discussion Documents for a Militant Movement.*
178 M. Treloar, "Portland History in Review: A Hundred Little Hitlers."
179 Rory McGowan, "Claim No Easy Victories: An Anarchist Analysis of ARA and Its Contributions to the Building of a Radical Anti-Racist Movement."
180 North Carolina Piece Corps, "The divorce of thought from deed: a compilation of writings on social conflict, white supremacy, and the mythology of free speech at UNC."
181 Al-Anani, *Inside the Muslim Brotherhood: Religion, Identity, and Politics.*
182 CRC Staff, "The Pro-Antifa Nonprofit Doxxing Conservatives."
183 The Third Position is a political philosophy developed after WWII that opposes both capitalism and communism. It emphasizes the need for mutually agreed-upon ethnic separatism and takes elements from the far right and far left.
184 Portland State University, "Portland State Ronald E. McNair Scholars Program."
185 Adam Rothstein, "Adam Rothstein's Info and CV."
186 Juan Conatz, "Between Infoshops and Insurrection: U.S. Anarchism, Movement Building, and the Racial Order."
187 Common Cause Ottawa, "With Allies Like These: Reflections on Privilege Reductionism."
188 The "Accomplices Not Allies" booklet was given out at CHAZ in Seattle. The cover stands out: it is a black-and-white drawing of a balaclava mask. The booklet lays out different types of problematic "allies" in radical-left movements. It argues that allyship should be done away with in favor of creating "accomplices" who are willing to be involved in direct action (i.e., criminal actions).
189 Incite!, "Why Misogynists Make Great Informants: How Gender Violence on the Left Enables State Violence in Radical Movements"
190 A questionnaire was provided only to male prospective members of Rose City Antifa to quiz them on their knowledge of intersectional oppression.

191 Chris Crass, "Against Patriarchy: Tools for Men to Further Feminist Revolution."

192 Planned Parenthood Advocates of Oregon, "Congratulations to Jacinda Padilla,...."

193 @LuminaryMilan, "Proof. Also like I literally went there...."

194 Sally Kohn, "My sense is that if Trump wins, Hillary supporters...."

195 CBS Austin, "DPS Identifies Six Arrested during Anti-Trump Protests at Capitol on Sunday."

196 Bert Hoppe, *In Stalins Gefolgschaft: Moskau und die KPD 1928–1933*.

197 Kevin McDermott and Jeremy Agnew, *The Comintern: A History of International Communism from Lenin to Stalin*; David Abraham, review of *Beating the Fascists*.

198 Hoppe, *In Stalins Gefolgschaft: Moskau und die KPD 1928–1933*; Günter Fippel, *Antifaschisten in "antifaschistischer" Gewalt: mittel- und ostdeutsche Schicksale in den Auseinandersetzungen zwischen Demokratie und Diktatur (1945 bis 1961)*.

199 Bray, *Antifa: The Anti-Fascist Handbook*, 24.

200 Patrick Moreau and Rita Schorpp-Grabiak, *Man muß so radikal sein wie die Wirklichkeit—Die PDS: eine Bilanz*. 166.

201 Jung Chang, *Wild Swans: Three Daughters of China*.

202 Alison Smale, "60 Years Later, Germany Recalls Its Anti-Soviet Revolt."

203 Richard Bernstein, "In Eastern Germany, 1953 Uprising Is Remembered."

204 Mary Fulbrook, "Stasi. The Untold Story of the East German Secret Police John O. Koehler," 9.

205 Jeremy Peter Varon, *Bringing the War Home*, 39.

206 Associated Press, "Germany: Left-wing violence and extremism on the rise."

207 Associated Press, "Germany: Left-wing violence and extremism on the rise."

208 Bundesamt für Verfassungsschutz, "Left-wing extremist following."

209 M. Mayer, "The Career of Urban Social Movements in West Germany."

210 BBC, "Berlin riot: 123 police injured in anti-gentrification protest."

211 Spiegel, "Polizei richtet Sonderkommission ein."

212 Nachrichten, "SEK-Chef über G20-Einsatz: 'Dann war Stille im Schanzenviertel.'"

213 Focus, "'Bin um mein Leben gerannt': Entsetzen nach linken Krawallen in Berlin."

214 Deutsche Welle, "Leipzig police probe 'attempted murder' of officer."

215 Berliner Morgenpost, "Verfassungschutz-Chef: 'Linksextreme würden notfalls töten.'"

216 Autonomism has its origins in postwar Italy. It is a split from communism, in which its adherents reject the traditional role of the state in implementing Marxism. After crossing into West Germany, it merged

with various antisocial and left-wing counterculture movements. Autonomism plays a significant role in antifa's contemporary ideology and organizational tactics, such as the black bloc.

217 Bray, *Antifa*, 47.

218 Steven, "1985–2001: A Short History of Anti-Fascist Action (AFA)."

219 Ewen A. Cameron, "David Powell, British Politics, 1910–35: The Crisis of the Party System," 181.

220 Nigel Jones, *Mosley*, 114.

221 Stanislav Vysotsky, *American Antifa: The Tactics, Culture, and Practice of Militant Antifascism*, 55.

222 Bray, *Antifa*, 66.

223 Bray, *Antifa*, 66.

224 Bray, *Antifa*, 66.

225 FBI, "Hate Crime in the U.S.: New Stats and a Continuing Mission."

226 Jack Levin and Jack McDevitt, "Hate Crimes."

227 Mike Carter, "Prosecutors Won't Retry Couple Accused in Shooting of Antifa Protester on UW Campus during Milo Yiannopoulos Event."

228 University of California, Berkeley, "Milo Yiannopoulos Event Canceled after Violence Erupts."

229 Karina Ioffee, "FBI Investigates Threat against Berkeley School after Teacher's Counterprotest at Neo-Nazi Rally."

230 Kris Turner, "Local terrorist activity suspected."

231 "UCB News: Campus Investigates Damage from Feb. 1 Violence."

232 Emilie Raguso, "UCPD Chief at Berkeley: 'Crowd Control Situations Are Different."

233 In 2017, Berkeley Unified School District middle school teacher Yvette Felarca became an unofficial spokesperson for antifa. She was already known as a leader in By Any Means Necessary, a Bay Area left-wing militant group, and she had garnered significant media attention for being caught engaging in political violence on camera. She was charged with felony assault and misdemeanor rioting relating to a brawl outside the California State Capitol in 2016. In February 2017, she went on *Tucker Carlson Tonight* to defend militant antifa tactics. In 2018, she was ordered by a court in Alameda County to pay former Berkeley College Republicans president Troy Worden over $11,000 in damages for filing a frivolous restraining order. In April 2020, Felarca participated in an online fundraiser for the Antifa International Defense Fund.

234 Berkeleyside staff, "Chaos Erupts, Protesters Shut Down Yiannopoulos Events, Banks in Downtown Vandalized."

235 George Kelly and Rick Hurd, "Bay Area College Professor Used U-Shaped Bike Lock in Beating, Police Say."

236 SHUTTERSHOT45, "Trump Supporter Smashed in the Head with U-Lock by Masked Antifa Thug in Berkeley."

237 Margaret Black, "Former College Professor Takes 3-Year Probation Plea Deal in Assault Case."

238 Southern Poverty Law Center, "Charles Murray."

239 Taylor Gee, "How the Middlebury Riot Really Went Down."

240 Gee, "How the Middlebury Riot Really Went Down."

241 Susan Svriuga, "Evergreen State College Reopens after Violent Threat and Property Damage on Campus."

242 Pearson, interview.

243 https://wgntv.com/news/northwestern-students-clash-with-police -in-evanston/.

244 Douglas M. Kellner, *Herbert Marcuse and the Crisis of Marxism*, 17.

245 Theodor W. Adorno, "Negative Dialektik."

246 Theodor W. Adorno, "Negative Dialektik."

247 Stanley Rothman, *The End of the Experiment: The Rise of Cultural Elites and the Decline of America's Civic Culture*, 177; Wolff et al., *A Critique of Pure Tolerance*.

248 ACLU, "ACLU Case Selection Guidelines: Conflicts between Competing Values or Priorities."

249 Richard Hanania, "It Isn't Your Imagination: Twitter Treats Conservatives More Harshly Than Liberals."

250 Natalie Escobar, "One Author's Argument 'In Defense of Looting.' "

251 "Folx" is an alternate spelling of "folks" used by radical social-justice ideologues. Some American antifa have adopted it in their writings to signal an awareness of intersectional jargon. Those who use "folx" in their writings say it is more inclusive of people of color and transgender people. A similar spelling and rationale are used for writing "Latinx" and "womxn."

252 Justin Caruso, "Yale Honors Students Who Mobbed Prof over Costume Controversy."

253 Ann M. Simmons and Jaweed Kaleem, "A Founder of Black Lives Matter Answers a Question on Many Minds: Where Did It Go?"

254 Robby Soave, "Black Lives Matter Students Shut Down the ACLU's Campus Free Speech Event Because 'Liberalism Is White Supremacy.' "

255 Alex Griswold, "Black Lives Matter Founder Claims Hate Speech Isn't Protected By First Amendment."

256 U.S. Department of Justice, *Regarding the Criminal Investigation into the Shooting Death of Michael Brown by Ferguson, Missouri Police Officer Darren Wilson: Department of Justice Report.*

257 Swain, interview.

258 Adam Tamburin, "Controversial Professor Carol Swain to Retire from Vanderbilt."

259 Assata Shakur, *Assata: An Autobiography*, 75.

260 Karl Marx and Friedrich Engels, "Communist Manifesto (Chapter 1)."

261 Crystal Lewis Brown, "#BlackLivesMatter cofounders on why the movement is more vital now than ever."

262 Black Lives Matter Global Network, "Lessons from Fidel: Black Lives Matter and the Transition of El Comandante."

263 Patrick Oppmann, "Admitted Hijacker Dreams of Home after 43 Years in Cuba."

264 Cynthia Gorney, "Mistrial Declared in Newton Murder Case."

265 Movement for Black Lives, "Invest-Divest."

266 Paige Fry, Jeremy Gorner, Peter Nickeas, Gregory Pratt, Megan Crepeau, Stacy St. Clair, Claire Hao, et al., "Police Shooting of Englewood Man Reignites Political Debate and Looting as Mag Mile Trashed, 13 Cops Injured, 2 People Shot."

267 NBC Chicago, "Black Lives Matter on Chicago Looting: Black Lives 'More Important Than Downtown Corporations.'"

268 NBC Chicago, "Black Lives Matter on Chicago Looting: Black Lives 'More Important Than Downtown Corporations.'"

269 Alicia Garza, "How do we stop 'black on black crime?'...."

270 Garza, "White supremacy and capitalism are...."

271 Opal Tometi, "For the record...."

272 Tometi, "I shared 3 core challenges...."

273 Democracy Now!, "'When They Call You a Terrorist': The Life of Black Lives Matter Co-Founder Patrisse Khan-Cullors."

274 Jeff Magalif, "Weathermen, Police Scuffle in Cambridge."

275 Alexandra Natapoff, Emma Kaufman, and Patrisse Cullors, "Abolition and Reparations: Histories of Resistance, Transformative Justice, And Accountability."

276 Real News Network, "A Short History of Black Lives Matter."

277 Swain, interview.

278 Martin Kaste, "Murder Rate Spike Could Be 'Ferguson Effect,' DOJ Study Says."

279 Richard Rosenfeld, "Documenting and Explaining the 2015 Homicide Rise: Research Directions."

280 Lindsay, interview.

281 CBS News, "'Pigs in a Blanket' Chant at Minnesota Fair Riles Police."

282 Matt Zapotosky, Adam Goldman, and Scott Higham, "Police in Dallas: 'He Wanted to Kill White People, Especially White Officers.'"

283 Advocate Staff, "Read Suicide Note Left by Gavin Eugene Long, Gunman in Deadly Baton Rouge Officer Shooting in July 2016."

284 Joy Reid, "Zero Evidence' That Black Lives Matter Has Pushed for Violence."

285 Portland State Vanguard, "Portland Black Lives Matter Protest (7/7/16)."

286 Jessica Willey, "Family of man wrongfully accused by activist Shaun King in Jazmine Barnes' shooting speaks out."

287 Shaun King, "I support ANTIFA...."

288 King, "I support the communists & socialists...."

289 King, "I've said it before & I...."

290 King, "We are told that this is the final letter...."

291 Black Lives Matter DC, "Antifa to meet up at 6pm at...."

292 Black Lives Matter DC, "STOP SPREADING THE DANGEROUS FALSE RIGHT-WING...."

293 Fox News, *Tucker Carlson*—Andy Ngo Attacked in Antifa May Day Portland Riot."

294 Portland Police Bureau, "Case No. 18-207957."

295 Joseph Bernstein, "Andy Ngo Has the Newest New Media Career. It's Made Him a Victim and a Star."

296 Portland Police Bureau, "Demonstration Events Conclude in Downtown Portland—Three Arrested."

297 Maxine Bernstein, "Police Lieutenant 'Firmly Believed' Milkshakes Thrown during June Protest 'Contained Some Form of Concrete.'"

298 Shepherd, "Is It Possible to Mix Cement into a Vegan Milkshake? We Did It."

299 Shepherd, "Portland Police Made a Dubious Claim about Protesters' Milkshakes on Twitter. What's the Evidence?"

300 Shepherd, "Portland Police Made a Dubious Claim."

301 Shepherd, "Portland Police Chief Says Antifa Protesters Used Slingshot to Launch Urine and Feces-Filled Balloons at Riot Cops."

302 The far-left Industrial Workers of the World (IWW) is a self-described "revolutionary" labor union. It is anarchist and Marxist in orientation. Many antifa members and supporters are also part of the IWW. Real News Network, "Effie Baum."

303 Alisha Berry, "Alisha Berry."

304 Jenny G. Zhang, "Milkshakes, Eggs, and Other Throwable Protest Foods, Ranked."

305 A.S.T.i, "A Worldwide Problem."

306 CNN, "Conservative Journalist Blames Antifa for Rally Attack"; Fox News, "Conservative Journalist Attacked by Antifa Protesters Speaks Out."

307 Email from art_is_freedom@protonmail.com to Bill Bradley, July 5, 2019.

308 Interview with Paul Welch. May 5, 2020. https://www.oregonlive.com/portland/2018/08/he_brought_an_american_flag_to.html.

309 Josh Meyer, Jacqueline Klimas, Wesley Morgan, and Alex Isenstadt, "FBI, Homeland Security Warn of More 'Antifa' Attacks."

310 NBC News, "Antifa Members Talk Protest Tactics: 'We Don't Depend On Cops.'"

311 Rose City Antifa, "No Pasaran! No Nazis on Our Streets!"

312 Slingshot Collective, "USA."

313 John North, "W. Asheville Crime Wave Alleged."

314 Rebecca Rosenberg, "Antifa Protester Gets 18 Months for Beating Up Trump Supporter."

315 Kim Kelly, "Hey NYC pals, if we haven't seen each other...."

316 Project Veritas, "#EXPOSEANTIFA."

317 A.M. Gittlitz, "'Make It So': 'Star Trek' and Its Debt to Revolutionary Socialism."

318 Cecilia Saixue Watt, "Redneck Revolt: The Armed Leftwing Group That Wants to Stamp out Fascism."

319 Carolina Workers Collective, Facebook post.

320 Brian Contreras and Paige Cornwell, "Armed Man Attacking Tacoma's ICE Detention Center Killed in Officer-Involved Shooting."

321 Derrick Bryson Taylor, "F.B.I. Investigating Shootings at San Antonio ICE Facilities."

322 Adam Shaw, "ICE Offices, Workers Hit by Wave of Violence and Threats: 'We Know Where All Your Children Live.'"

323 Katie Herzog, "Anti-Racist Protesters Harass Gay Asian-American Journalist."

324 Jamal Oscar Williams, Facebook post.

325 Ariel van Spronsen, "Legal Defense Fund for Will van Spronsen."

326 Tammy Mutasa, "Man Killed by Police at NW Detention Center Had Previous Arrest for Assaulting Officer."

327 Ex-Workers Collective, "On Willem van Spronsen's Action against the Northwest Detention Center in Tacoma."

328 Puget Sound Anarchists, "Mural Honoring Will van Spronsen in Exarchia."

329 Ngo, "Seattle Antifa Militia Distributes Extremist Manifesto of ICE Attacker."

330 Hannah Allam, "'I Am Antifa': One Activist's Violent Death Became a Symbol for the Right and Left."

331 KVAL, "'Nothing about Us without Us!': Oregon Students Protest University President's Speech."

332 Community Armed Self-Defense, Facebook post.

333 Michael Tobin, "FBI Releases Files Related to Deceased Activist Charlie Landeros."

334 KVAL, "DA: FBI Received Tip about Landeros 'Posting Violent Anti-Government Messages' in 2018."

335 Charles Denson, "In Memoriam: Charles (Charlie) Landeros, 1988–January 11, 2019."

336 Popular Mobilization, "Charlie Landeros, beloved comrade...."

337 Patricia Perlow, "Cascade Middle School OIS Investigation."

338 Kelly, "Comrade Boomer."

339 Kelly, "As Van Spronsen and the many other...."

340 Emily Gorcenski, "Reminder: the proper response to....'"

341 Gorcenski, "What I'm saying is armed community...."

342 Will Garbe and Hasan Karim, "Dayton Shooter Was Armed Counter-Protester at Ku Klux Klan."

343 Mitch Smith, Rick Rojas, and Campbell Robertson, "Dayton Gunman Had Been Exploring 'Violent Ideologies,' F.B.I. Says."

344 Rico Beniga, "State of Oregon vs. Michael Forest Reinoehl."

345 Ngo, "Antifa are claiming that the deceased person is...."

346 Ngo, "After finding out that it was a...."

347 Bloomberg QuickTake News, "Portland Protests: Witness Shot in the Arm during Scuffle."

348 Michael Reinoehl, "Every revolution needs people that...."

349 Megan Specia, "What We Know about the Death of the Suspect in the Portland Shooting."

350 Portland Police Bureau, "Patrick Kimmons."

351 Drew Hernandez, "For the record, this was the extreme...."

352 Hernandez, "Twisted BLM activist in Portland...."

353 Caleb Parke, "Reporter Describes 'Traumatic' Scene at Portland Assault: I Witnessed an 'Attempted Execution.'"

354 Bridget Chavez, "'They Were Looking for a Fight': Woman Describes Sunday Night Attack in Downtown Portland."

355 Lives Matter, "BLM PROTESTERS PHYSICALLY ASSAULTING AND ROBBING PEOPLE IN DOWNTOWN PORTLAND."

356 Bernstein, "Man under Investigation in Fatal Shooting of Patriot Prayer Supporter Wounded in July after Trying to Grab Gun from Stranger."

357 Bloomberg QuickTake News, "Portland Protests: Witness Shot in the Arm during Scuffle."

358 Bernstein, "Man under Investigation in Fatal Shooting of Patriot Prayer Supporter."

359 Bernstein, "Man under Investigation in Fatal Shooting of Right-Wing Demonstrator in Portland Was Outside Mayor's Condo Night Before with Daughter."

360 Vice News, "Man Linked to Killing at a Portland Protest Says He Acted in Self-Defense."

361 Neil MacFarquhar, Mike Baker, and Adam Goldman, "In His Last Hours, Portland Murder Suspect Said He Feared Arrest."

362 Evan Hill, Mike Baker, Derek Knowles, and Stella Cooper., "'Straight to Gunshots': How a U.S. Task Force Killed an Antifa Activist."

363 Ngo. "Antifa black bloc outside the Kelly Penumbra...."

364 New York City Antifa, "what the actual fuck."

365 Gorcenski, "Fuck Nazis."

366 Nate Hegyi, "Spurred by Debunked Antifa Rumors, Armed Men and Women Stand Watch Over Protests."

367 KABC, "Man Charged with Arson in Connection to Oregon Wildfire."

368 Vysotsky, *American Antifa*, 87.

369 Ngo, "Inside the Suspicious Rise of Gay Hate Crimes in Portland."

370 Shepherd, "Portland Police Refused to Respond When ICE Agents Called 911 during Protest, Letter Says."

371 Wakerell-Cruz, "ANDY? NO: Antifa Harass Asian Man for Looking like Andy Ngo."

372 Alexandria Ocasio-Cortez, 'Quick IG Q&A after Tuesday's Dem Convention Program.' "

373 Ocasio-Cortez, "Abolish ICE."; Edward Moreno, "Ocasio-Cortez Dismisses Proposed $1B Cut: 'Defunding Police Means Defunding Police' "; Christina Zhao, "NY Rep. Alexandria Ocasio-Cortez Says 'Capitalism Is Irredeemable.' "

374 Ocasio-Cortez, "One way to support the local LGBTQ...."

375 Ian Miles Cheong, "Breaking: AOC Is Fundraising for an Antifa-Affiliated Website on Instagram."

376 Tennessee Star, "Flashback: Keith Ellison Once Proposed Making a Separate Country for Blacks."

377 Keith Ellison, "At @MoonPalaceBooks and I just found...."

378 Ellison, "This man doesn't look like any civil rights...."

379 Jeremiah Ellison, "I hereby declare, officially, my support...."

380 BBC News, "George Floyd: Minneapolis Council Pledges to Dismantle Police Department."

381 Barbara Plett Usher, "George Floyd Death: A City Pledged to Abolish Its Police. Then What?"

382 Patrick Wilson, "Woody Kaine, Son of Sen. Tim Kaine, Gets Probation, Fine Stemming from Protest at Minn. Trump Rally."

383 Kshama Sawant, "The outrage on Seattle's streets today...."

384 Rantz, "This is dangerous...."

385 Gary Horcher, "SPD: Rioters Tried to Trap Officers inside Burning Precinct Using Rebar and Concrete."

386 MyNorthwest Staff, "Seattle Police Union Demands Elected Officials Condemn Violence toward Officers."

387 Portland Police Bureau, "Demonstration Education Event."

388 Kaitlin Menza, "Portland Commissioner Jo Ann Hardesty Has a Message for Trump and the Feds."

389 Wheeler, "Earlier today I directed that staff...."

390 Nick Budnick, "Portland Mayor Admonishes Police Chief after Public Clash over Tear Gas."

391 Multnomah County District Attorney, "Jeremy Joseph Christian Sentenced to Life Imprisonment without the Possibility of Release or Parole."

392 Ngo, "Popular Antifa COVID-19 Portland Fundraiser Accused of Being a Scam."

393 Olivia Louise, "RIP. Armeanio celebrating our...."

394 Jeffrey Dunn, "Portland Antifa 'Martyr' Mourned by Many Urged Terrorist Attacks, Writings Reveal."

395 Murthy, *Twitter: Social Communication in the Twitter Age.*

396 Matt Calkins, "How MLS' Ruling Allowing Iron Front Flag Might Be Pushing Away Sounders Fans."

397 Joel Moreno, "MLS Lifts Ban on Iron Front Flag Embraced by Sounders Fans."

398 Megan Burns, "Information Warfare: What and How?"

399 Kit O'Connell, "Beyond the Concrete Milkshake: Defeating Media Trolls & Grifters (Zine)."

400 Joy Reid, "Y'all Do Realize 'antifa' is just short for...."; Kyle Balluck, "CNN's Cuomo Defends Antifa: Those Who Oppose Hate 'Are on the Side of Right.'"

401 Kelly, "And one of my greatest hopes...."

402 Soave, "The Media Claimed Andy Ngo Was Complicit in a Far-Right Attack on Antifa. But the Video Doesn't Support That."

403 Alex Zielinski, "Wheeler Condemns Protest Shooting, Offers Few Solutions to Continuous Violence"; Cathell, "Left-Wing Reporter Falsely Accuses Murdered Portland Trump Supporter of Backing Terrorism."

404 Zielinski, "Lololol at Andy Ngo Being an 'expert' on...."

405 Zielinski, "Heads up all, it looks like Andy Ngo...."

406 Talia Lavin, "I wrote about the crucial role...."

407 Immigration and Customs Enforcement, "Read the full ICE statement...."

408 Lavin, "This has been a wild and difficult week...."

409 Jon Levine, "NYU Journalism School Hires Ex-New Yorker Fact Checker Who Falsely Said ICE Agent Had Nazi Tattoo."

410 Levine, "NYU Cancels Former New Yorker Fact-Checker Talia Lavin's Journalism Class."

411 Lavin, "Andy ngo is best known for providing...."

412 Ngo, "Antifa black bloc handed out flyers about me...."

413 International Workers of the World Freelance Journalists Union, "TO JOURNALISTS COVERING THE ONGOING...."

414 Robert Evans, "This is bullshit. I was...."

415 Charlie Warzel, "50 Nights of Unrest in Portland."

416 Shane Burley, "I'm a proud member of the @IWWFJU...."

417 Burley, "Opinion: What Happened When I Was the Target of Alt-Right Death Threats."

418 Burley, "Trump's Antifa Tweet Is Right-Wing Catnip—with Potentially Troubling Consequences."

419 Ngo, "Unreported conflict of interest...."

420 Sophie Peel, "Portland Protesters Say Their Lives Were Upended by the Posting of Their Mug Shots on a Conservative Twitter Account."

421 Therese Bottomly, "Letter from the Editor: You Won't See as Many Mugshots of Criminal Suspects Going Forward."
422 Ginetta Sagan and Stephen Denney, "Re-Education in Unliberated Vietnam: Loneliness, Suffering and Death."
423 Vu Thanh Thuy, " 'Boat People' Defeat Sea, but All at Visa Wall."
424 Freedom House, "Overview Fact Sheet."
425 Vysotsky, *American Antifa*, 53.
426 Eliza Theiss, "More Optimistic Than Millennials, Gen Z Is Here to Revolutionize the Housing Market."
427 Vysotsky, *American Antifa*, 146.
428 Trump, "Executive Order on Combating Race and Sex Stereotyping."
429 FOX 12 Staff, "Tips Help Police Arrest Man, Boy Accused of Attacking Bystander in Protest for George Floyd in Portland."

@JaredComrade. "Congratulations! I'm proud of you Anarchists…" Twitter, June 29, 2020. http://archive.vn/IVuq7.

@LuminaryMilan. "Proof. Also like I literally went there…." Twitter, October 2, 2020. https://archive.vn/YpSto.

@MaliceBD. "2 guys in a stolen SUV shot up…." Twitter, June 29, 2020. http://archive.is/D0fZs.

——. "I know I shouldn't glorify…." Twitter, June 29, 2020. http://archive.vn/US3K7.

@PDXDublin. "Heroe's American Café on…." Twitter, October 8, 2020. https://archive.is/W8rG3.

A.S.T.i. "A Worldwide Problem." Accessed May 11, 2020. https://www.asti.org.uk/a-worldwide-problem.html.

Aaro, David "Kenosha Sees 175 Arrested during Civil Unrest So Far; 102 Had Addresses Listed Outside City, Police Say." Fox News, August 31, 2020 https://www.foxnews.com/us/175-arrested-during-unrest-in-kenosha-including-104-outside-city-police-say.

Abedi, Maham. "Majority of Americans Think Having Neo-Nazi Views Is Unacceptable, Poll Finds." Global News, August 22, 2017. https://globalnews.ca/news/3687884/american-neo-nazi-views-poll-donald-trump/.

Abraham, David. Review of *Beating the Fascists? The German Communists and Political Violence, 1929–33* by Eve Rosenhoft. *New German Critique*, no. 42 (1987): 183–85, https://www.jstor.org/stable/488268.

Acker, Lizzy. "Who Is Jeremy Christian? Facebook Shows a Man with Nebulous Political Affiliations Who Hated Circumcision and Hillary Clinton." *The Oregonian*, 2017, 229–53.

ACLU. "ACLU Case Selection Guidelines: Conflicts between Competing Values

or Priorities." https://www.aclu.org/sites/default/files/field_document/aclu
  _case_selection_guidelines.pdf.

Adorno, Theodor W. "Negative Dialektik." *Frankfurt Am Main* 21980
  (1966): 86.

Advocate Staff. "Read Suicide Note Left by Gavin Eugene Long, Gunman in
  Deadly Baton Rouge Officer Shooting in July 2016." *The Advocate*, June
  30, 2017. https://www.theadvocate.com/baton_rouge/news/baton_rouge
  _officer_shooting/article_9748d2c0-5daa-11e7-af6d-ab3966e08d70
  .html.

Al-Anani, Khalil. *Inside the Muslim Brotherhood: Religion, Identity, and
  Politics*. Religion and Global Politics. New York, NY: Oxford University
  Press, 2016.

Alex Zielinski (@alex_zee). "Heads up all, it looks like . . . ." Twitter, June 20,
  2020. https://archive.vn/mk5JE.

———. "Lololol at Andy Ngo Being an 'expert' on . . . ." Twitter, June 28,
  2020. https://archive.vn/yx3ZH.

Allam, Hannah. " 'I Am Antifa': One Activist's Violent Death Became a
  Symbol for the Right and Left." NPR, July 23, 2020. https://www.npr
  .org/2020/07/23/893533916/i-am-antifa-one-activist-s-violent-death
  -became-a-symbol-for-the-right-and-left.

Anarchists Worldwide. "So-Called USA: Revolutionary Abolitionist Movement 10 POINTS of ACTION." Anarchists Worldwide, February 1,
  2020. http://archive.vn/YyF2b.

Andrews, Reed. "Portland Police Direct Traffic during ICE Protest Sweep,
  Mayor Wheeler Responds." KATU, June 28, 2018. https://katu.com
  /news/local/mayor-wheeler-responds-to-portland-police-directing
  -traffic-during-ice-protest-sweep.

Antifa Public Watch. "Antifa Calls Black Ice Agent the N Word Multiple
  Times." YouTube, November 27, 2018. https://www.youtube.com/watch
  ?v=-sqKhIpXV1w.

Antifa Sacramento. "Antifascist Prisoner Support." Accessed July 10, 2020.
  http://archive.vn/b2FaG.

Antifa Seven Hills (@ash_antifa). "HOW TO SUPPORT #Minneapolis
  DIRECTLY! . . . ." Twitter, May 28, 2020. http://archive.vn/Ex0tR.

Armstrong, Nicholas James (@WABlackFlag). "We can't wait till someone
  gets . . . ." Twitter, January 13, 2020. http://archive.vn/kiLUU.

Arrest Facts. "Solomon Samuel Simone." Arrest Facts, April 7, 2012. Accessed
  August 15, 2020. https://arrestfacts.com/Solomon-Simone-2p5.15.

art_is_freedom@protonmail.com. Email to Bill Bradley, July 5, 2019.

Associated Press. "Germany: Left-wing violence and extremism on the
  rise." AP News, June 20, 2018. https://apnews.com/article/2a0c3f2ee
  9b14474adea1cbef894122b

———. "Rayshard Brooks Struggled in System but Didn't Hide His Past."

Los Angeles Times, June 26, 2020. https://www.latimes.com/world
-nation/story/2020-06-26/rayshard-brooks-struggled-but-was-open
-about-his-past.

———. "Seattle Mayor Proposes $20M in Cuts to Police to Help Bud-
get." AP News, June 23, 2020. https://apnews.com/ee8ed2680ebbda
15cef8b3b899d2b7c1.

Badie, Bertrand, Dirk Berg-Schlosser, and Leonardo Morlino. "Social
Democracy." In *International Encyclopedia of Political Science.* Thousand Oaks, CA: Sage, 2011.

Baker, Andrew M. "Cardiopulmonary Arrest Complicating Law Enforcement
Subdual, Restraint, and Neck Compression." Hennepin County Medical
Examiner's Office, May 26, 2020. https://www.hennepin.us/-/media
/hennepinus/residents/public-safety/documents/floyd-autopsy-6-3-20.pdf.

Balluck, Kyle. "CNN's Cuomo Defends Antifa: Those Who Oppose Hate
'Are on the Side of Right.'" *The Hill,* August 14, 2018. https://thehill
.com/homenews/media/401699-cnns-cuomo-defends-antifa-those-who
-oppose-hate-are-on-the-side-of-right.

Banta, Mattew (@FoxAF4). "Hey you Patriot Fash…." Twitter, August 4,
2019. https://archive.vn/O32jk.

Baron, Udo. *The Victims at the Berlin Wall 1961–1989: A Biographical
Handbook.* Berlin, Germany: Verlag, 2011.

BBC News. "George Floyd: Minneapolis Council Pledges to Dismantle
Police Department." BBC, June 8, 2020. https://www.bbc.com/news/world
-us-canada-52960227.

BBC. "Berlin riot: 123 police injured in anti-gentrification protest." BBC,
July 10, 2016. https://www.bbc.com/news/world-europe-36758686.

Beckett, Lois. "Anti-Fascists Linked to Zero Murders in the US in 25 Years."
Guardian, July 27, 2020. http://www.theguardian.com/world/2020/jul
/27/us-rightwing-extremists-attacks-deaths-database-leftwing-antifa.

Beniga, Rico. "State of Oregon vs. Michael Forest Reinoehl," September 3, 2020.

Bergen, Peter, Albert Ford, Alyssa Sims, and David Sterman. New America.
"Part IV. What Is the Threat to the United States Today?" Accessed April
3, 2020. https://www.newamerica.org/in-depth/terrorism-in-america/what
-threat-united-states-today/.

Berkeleyside Staff. "Chaos Erupts, Protesters Shut Down Yiannopoulos
Events, Banks in Downtown Vandalized." *Berkeleyside,* February 2, 2017.
https://www.berkeleyside.com/2017/02/02/chaos-erupts-protesters-shut
-yiannopolous-events-banks-downtown-vandalized.

Berliner Morgenpost. "Verfassungsschutz-Chef: 'Linksextreme würden
notfalls töten.'" Morgenpost, July 11, 2017. https://www.morgenpost
.de/berlin/article211207701/Verfassungsschutz-Chef-Linksextreme
-wuerden-notfalls-toeten.html?__pwh=fo2SSawQRTIeFTZWHHQhFA
%3D%3D.

Bernstein, Joseph. "Andy Ngo Has the Newest New Media Career. It's Made Him a Victim and a Star." BuzzFeed News, July 19, 2019. https://www .buzzfeednews.com/article/josephbernstein/andy-ngo-portland-antifa.

Bernstein, Maxine. "Man under Investigation in Fatal Shooting of Patriot Prayer Supporter Wounded in July after Trying to Grab Gun from Stranger." *Oregonian*, September 1, 2020. https://www.oregonlive.com /crime/2020/09/man-under-investigation-in-fatal-shooting-of-patriot -prayer-supporter-wounded-in-july-after-trying-to-grab-gun-from -stranger.html.

———. "Man under Investigation in Fatal Shooting of Right-Wing Demon- strator in Portland Was Outside Mayor's Condo Night Before with Daughter." *Oregonian*, August 31, 2020. https://www.oregonlive.com /crime/2020/08/man-under-investigation-in-fatal-shooting-of-right -wing-demonstrator-in-portland-was-outside-mayors-condo-night -before-with-daughter.html.

———. "Police Lieutenant 'Firmly Believed' Milkshakes Thrown during June Protest 'Contained Some Form of Concrete.'" *Oregonian*, July 22, 2019. https://www.oregonlive.com/crime/2019/07/police-lieutenant -wrote-he-firmly-believed-milkshakes-thrown-during-june-protest -contained-some-form-of-concrete.html.

———. "Six Occupy ICE Protesters Charged in Federal Court Reach Set- tlement, Avoid Criminal Convictions." *Oregonian*, August 28, 2019. https://www.oregonlive.com/crime/2019/08/six-occupy-ice-protesters -charged-in-federal-court-reach-settlement-avoid-criminal-convictions.html.

Bernstein, Richard. "In Eastern Germany, 1953 Uprising Is Remembered." *New York Times*, June 16, 2003. https://www.nytimes.com/2003/06/16 /world/in-eastern-germany-1953-uprising-is-remembered.html.

Berry, Alisha. "Alisha Berry" ResearchGate. Accessed May 11, 2020, http://archive.vn/sLwVi.

Berry, Alisha (@EffieBombs). "Even better, pretending to…." Twitter, Janu- ary 3, 2020. http://archive.vn/hgtms.

———. "I'm never shutting up about…." Twitter, September 3, 2019. http://archive.vn/gwxp7.

———. "I work in medicine and…." Twitter, November 20, 2019. http://archive.vn/XZPlN.

Best, Paul. "Staffer for Top Oregon State Lawmaker Arrested during Port- land Riot." Fox News, September 9, 2020. https://www.foxnews.com /us/staffer-oregon-state-speaker-of-the-house-arrested-portland.

Biesecker, Michael, and Michael Kunzelman. "As Trump Blames Antifa, Protest Records Show Scant Evidence." Associated Press, June 6, 2020. https://apnews.com/20b9b86dba5c480bad759a3bd34cd875.

Black Lives Matter DC (@DMVBlackLives). "Antifa to meet up at 6pm at…." Twitter, September 16, 2017. https://archive.is/lK1ac.

————. "STOP SPREADING THE DANGEROUS FALSE RIGHT-WING...." Twitter, July 1, 2019. https://archive.is/REjDI.

Black Lives Matter Global Network. "Lessons from Fidel: Black Lives Matter and the Transition of El Comandante." Medium, November 27, 2016. https://medium.com/@BlackLivesMatterNetwork/lessons-from-fidel-black-lives-matter-and-the-transition-of-el-comandante-c11ee5e51fb0.

Black, Margaret. "Former College Professor Takes 3-Year Probation Plea Deal in Assault Case." Daily Californian, August 10, 2018. https://www.dailycal.org/2018/08/10/former-college-professor-takes-3-year-probation-plea-deal-assault-case/.

Bloomberg QuickTake News. "Portland Protests: Witness Shot in the Arm during Scuffle." YouTube, July 27, 2020. https://www.youtube.com/watch?v=gfMnZX7Z56o.

Boghossian, Peter. Interview by Andy Ngo, April 3, 2020.

Bokhari, Allum, and Milo Yiannopoulos. "An Establishment Conservative's Guide to the Alt-Right." Breitbart News, March 29, 2016. https://www.breitbart.com/tech/2016/03/29/an-establishment-conservatives-guide-to-the-alt-right/.

Borrud, Hillary. "Ted Wheeler to Federal Government: Revoke Permit for Portland Alt-Right Event." Oregonian, May 30, 2017. https://www.oregonlive.com/portland/2017/05/ted_wheeler_to_federal_governm.html.

Bottomly, Therese. "Letter from the Editor: You Won't See as Many Mugshots of Criminal Suspects Going Forward." Oregonian, July 12, 2020. https://www.oregonlive.com/opinion/2020/07/letter-from-the-editor-you-wont-see-as-many-mugshots-of-criminal-suspects-going-forward.html-2.

Bowles, Nellie. "Abolish the Police? Those Who Survived the Chaos in Seattle Aren't So Sure." New York Times, August 7, 2020. https://www.nytimes.com/2020/08/07/us/defund-police-seattle-protests.html.

Bray, Mark. Antifa: The Anti-Fascist Handbook. Brooklyn, NY: Melville House, 2017.

————. "Who are the antifa?" Washington Post, August 16, 2017. https://www.washingtonpost.com/news/made-by-history/wp/2017/08/16/who-are-the-antifa/.

Bromwich, Jonah Engel. "The Minnesota Freedom Fund Has $30 Million and an Identity Crisis." New York Times, June 16, 2020. https://www.nytimes.com/2020/06/16/style/minnesota-freedom-fund-donations.html.

Brown, Crystal Lewis. "#BlackLivesMatter cofounders on why the movement is more vital now than ever." SheKnows, July 17, 2015. https://archive.is/jEaqG#selection-2295.0-2295.76.

Brown, Kate (@OregonGovBrown). "After My Discussions with VP Pence A...." Twitter, July 29, 2020. https://archive.vn/RCkcd.

———. "This is a democracy, not…." Twitter, July 20, 2020. https://archive.vn/jtwD2.

Brown, Lee. "Armed Protesters Confront Armored SWAT Vehicle after Wisconsin Shooting." *New York Post*, August 24, 2020. https://nypost.com/2020/08/24/protesters-confront-armored-swat-vehicle-after-wisconsin-shooting/.

Budnick, Nick. "Portland Mayor Admonishes Police Chief after Public Clash over Tear Gas." *Portland Tribune*, September 16, 2020. https://pamplinmedia.com/pt/9-news/480993-388103-portland-mayor-admonishes-police-chief-after-public-clash-over-tear-gas?wallit_nosession=1.

Bundesamt für Verfassungsschutz. "Left-wing extremist following." https://www.verfassungsschutz.de/en/fields-of-work/left-wing-extremism/figures-and-facts-left-wing-extremism/left-wing-extremist-following-2018.

Burley, Shane (@shane_burley1). "I'm a proud member of the @IWWFJU…." Twitter, August 6, 2020. https://archive.vn/G4Rvj.

———. "Trump's Antifa Tweet Is Right-Wing Catnip—with Potentially Troubling Consequences." NBC News, June 3, 2020. https://www.nbcnews.com/think/opinion/trump-s-antifa-tweet-right-wing-catnip-potentially-troubling-consequences-ncna1222686.

Burley, Shane, and Alexander Reid Ross. "Opinion: What Happened When I Was the Target of Alt-Right Death Threats." *The Independent*, August 15, 2019. https://www.independent.co.uk/voices/alt-right-antifa-death-threats-doxxing-quillette-a8966176.html.

Burns, Asia Simone. "Police ID 8-Year-Old Shot, Killed; $10,000 Reward Offered in Case." *Atlanta Journal-Constitution*, July 5, 2020. https://www.ajc.com/news/breaking-news/police-child-shot-killed-atlanta/gePIuT0NSJFUITL5Q3eiKK/?utm_source=Iterable&utm_medium=email&utm_campaign=campaign_1337875.

Burns, Megan. "Information Warfare: What and How?" Carnegie Mellon University, School of Computer Science, 1999. https://www.cs.cmu.edu/~burnsm/InfoWarfare.html.

Caldwell-Kelly, Alice (@AliceAvizandum). "RIP Andy Ngo…." Twitter, July 1, 2019. https://archive.vn/hUV7A.

Calkins, Matt. "How MLS' Ruling Allowing Iron Front Flag Might Be Pushing Away Sounders Fans." *Seattle* Times, October 18, 2019. https://www.seattletimes.com/sports/sounders/i-have-no-supporters-home-how-mls-ruling-allowing-iron-front-flag-might-be-pushing-away-sounders-fans/.

Cameron, Ewen A. "David Powell, British Politics, 1910–35: The Crisis of the Party System." *Journal of Scottish Historical Studies*, 2005. https://doi.org/10.3366/jshs.2005.25.1.63.

Carolina Workers Collective. Facebook post, March 9, 2018. https://www.facebook.com/CarolinaWorkersCollective/posts/statement-of-carolina

-workers-collective-formerly-shelby-redneck-revoltsystems-o
/344356872721102/.

Carter, Mike. "Prosecutors Won't Retry Couple Accused in Shooting of Antifa Protester on UW Campus during Milo Yiannopoulos Event." *Seattle Times*, September 6, 2019. https://www.seattletimes.com/seattle-news /crime/prosecutors-will-not-retry-couple-accused-in-shooting-of-antifa -protester-on-uw-campus-during-milo-yiannopoulos-event/.

Caruso, Justin. "Yale Honors Students Who Mobbed Prof over Costume Controversy." May 30, 2017. https://www.campusreform.org/?ID=9238.

Cascadian Resistance. "About." Facebook post. Accessed May 2, 2020. http://archive.vn/4eKYN.

Casiano, Louis. "Seattle-Based Activists Arrested in Kenosha after Filling up Gas Cans." Fox News, August 28, 2020. https://www.foxnews.com /us/seattle-activists-arrested-kenosha-gas-cans.

———. "Seattle Father Mourning Loss of Son Killed in 'CHOP' Zone Gets Calls of Support from Trump, Mayor Durkan." Fox News, July 2, 2020. https://www.foxnews.com/us/seattle-chop-horace-lorenzo-anderson -trump-mayor-call.

Cathell, Mia. "Journalist Attacked by 'Black Bloc' Militants at Antifa Riot in Portland." *Post Millennial*, July 4, 2020. https://thepostmillennial .com/journalist-attacked-black-bloc-militants-antifa-riot-portland.

———. "Left-Wing Reporter Falsely Accuses Murdered Portland Trump Supporter of Backing Terrorism." *Post Millennial*, August 31, 2020. https:// thepostmillennial.com/left-wing-reporter-falsely-accuses-murdered -portland-trump-supporter-of-backing-terrorism.

CBC News. "WTO Protests Hit Seattle in the Pocketbook." CBC News, January 6, 2000. https://www.cbc.ca/news/world/wto-protests-hit-seattle-in -the-pocketbook-1.245428.

CBS Austin. "DPS Identifies Six Arrested during Anti-Trump Protests at Capitol on Sunday." CBS Austin, November 13, 2016. https://cbsaustin .com/news/local/anti-trump-protests-continue-at-the-capitol.

CBS, and Associated Press. "'Pigs in a Blanket' Chant at Minnesota Fair Riles Police." CBS News, August 31, 2015. https://www.cbsnews.com /news/pigs-in-a-blanket-chant-at-minnesota-fair-riles-police/.

Celona, Larry, and Vincent Barone. "Black Lives Matter Protesters Riot in Manhattan, Cause $100,000 Damage: NYPD." *New York Post*, September 5, 2020. https://nypost.com/2020/09/05/black-lives-matter-protesters -riot-in-manhattan-cause-100000-damage/.

Centers for Disease Control and Prevention. "FastStats." CDC, September 4, 2019. https://www.cdc.gov/nchs/fastats/homicide.htm.

Chang, Jung. *Wild Swans: Three Daughters of China*. Simon and Schuster, 2003.

Chavez, Bridget. "'They Were Looking for a Fight': Woman Describes Sunday Night Attack in Downtown Portland." KPTV, August 18, 2020. https://www.kptv.com/news/they-were-looking-for-a-fight-woman-describes-sunday-night-attack-in-downtown-portland/article_52eece24-e1bc-11ea-9753-c7b04b7d662a.html?utm_medium=social&utm_source=facebook&utm_campaign=user-share&fbclid=IwAR1MJLzufMNb61zaAK6GD6-aKL0qwujDg72MTG1r1Lsa0nccjQ-3jhX45pk.

Cheong, Ian Miles. "Breaking: AOC Is Fundraising for an Antifa-Affiliated Website on Instagram." Post Millennial, June 8, 2020. https://thepostmillennial.com/aoc-fundraises-antifa-unicorn-riot.

Christiansen, Rebecca. "Antifa Attacks Journalist and Right-Wing Group in Washington State." *Post Millennial*, December 9, 2019. Accessed April 10, 2020. https://www.thepostmillennial.com/watch-antifa-attack-journalist-and-right-wing-group-in-washington-state/.

Clarion Project. "The Clarion Project's Advisory Board." Accessed April 1, 2020. https://clarionproject.org/clarion-project-advisory-board/.

Cline, Sara. "Portland Protests Set Up Clash between Journalists, Police." Associated Press, September 3, 2020. https://apnews.com/article/40e2712cdfe132b6ee4e950fa42a6653.

Common Cause Ottawa. "With Allies Like These: Reflections on Privilege Reductionism." Anarchist Library, June 6, 2014. https://archive.vn/cOLex.

Community Armed Self-Defense. Facebook page. https://archive.vn/MUDMG.

Conatz, Juan. "Between Infoshops and Insurrection: U.S. Anarchism, Movement Building, and the Racial Order." August 25, 2014. https://archive.vn/VTnVP.

"Conservative Journalist Blames Antifa for Rally Attack." CNN, July 2, 2019. https://www.cnn.com/videos/us/2019/07/02/antifa-conservative-journalist-andy-ngo-bts-newday-vpx.cnn.

Contreras, Brian, and Paige Cornwell. "Armed Man Attacking Tacoma's ICE Detention Center Killed in Officer-Involved Shooting." *Seattle Times*, July 13, 2019. https://www.seattletimes.com/seattle-news/crime/tacoma-police-armed-man-throwing-incendiary-devices-shot-outside-ice-detention-center/.

"Cops Arrest 8 Occupy Portland Protesters; Reopen Street." *The Colombian*, October 12, 2011. Accessed April 11, 2020. https://www.columbian.com/news/2011/oct/12/cops-arrest-8-occupy-portland-protesters-reopen-st/.

Courtois, Stéphane, and Jean-Louis Margolin. *The Black Book of Communism: Crimes, Terror, Repression*. Cambridge, MA: Harvard University Press, 1999.

Crass, Chris. "Against Patriarchy: Tools for Men to Further Feminist Revolution." The Feminist Wire. June 25, 2013. https://archive.vn/PcuSo.

CRC Staff. "The Pro-Antifa Nonprofit Doxxing Conservatives." Capital

Research Center, March 27, 2020. https://capitalresearch.org/article
/the-pro-antifa-nonprofit-doxxing-conservatives/.

CrimethInc. "Why We Break Windows: The Effectiveness of Political Vandalism."
CrimethInc, 2018. https://crimethinc.com/zines/why-we-break-windows.

C-SPAN. "Hearing on Protests Across U.S." C-SPAN, August 4, 2020.
https://www.c-span.org/video/?474496-1/hearing-protests-us&vod=.

Cunningham, Mark D. "RE: State vs. Jeremy Christian, Provisional Report
Prepared for Bail Hearing." November 10, 2017. http://opb-imgserve
-production.s3-website-us-west-2.amazonaws.com/original/20171208
_christian_eval_ulsnmu2.pdf.

Democracy Now! " 'When They Call You a Terrorist': The Life of Black
Lives Matter Co-Founder Patrisse Khan-Cullors." Democracy Now!,
January 16, 2018. Accessed July 15, 2020. https://www.democracynow
.org/2018/1/16/when_they_call_you_a_terrorist.

Denson, Charles. "In Memoriam: Charles (Charlie) Landeros, 1988–
January 11, 2019." January 12, 2019. https://cldc.org/in-memoriam
-charles-charlie-landeros-1988-january-11-2019/.

Deutsche Welle. "East German Stasi Had 189,000 Informers, Study Says." Deutsche Welle, March 11, 2008. Accessed March 16, 2020. https://www.dw.com
/en/east-german-stasi-had-189000-informers-study-says/a-3184486-1.

———. "Leipzig police probe 'attempted murder' of officer." DW, January
1, 2020. https://www.dw.com/en/leipzig-police-probe-attempted-murder
-of-officer/a-51853772.

Dimitrov, Georgi. "The Fascist Offensive and the Tasks of the Communist
International in the Struggle of the Working Class against Fascism."
In *Speech at the VII World Congress of the Communist International*,
vol. 2, 1935. https://www.marxists.org/reference/archive/dimitrov/works
/1935/08_02.htm.

Draper, Theodore. "The Ghost of Social-Fascism." *Commentary* 47, no. 2
(1969): 29.

Dunn, Jeffrey. "Portland Antifa 'Martyr' Mourned by Many Urged Terrorist Attacks, Writings Reveal." *Post Millennial*, March 9, 2020. https://
thepostmillennial.com/portland-antifa-martyr-mourned-by-many-urged
-terrorist-attacks-writings-reveal.

Durkan, Jenny (@MayorJenny). "The Capitol Hill Autonomous Zone...."
Twitter, June 11, 2020. https://archive.vn/RSZ2l.

Ellis, Rebecca. "Portland Anti-Fascist Activist Killed in Hit and Run Outside
Cider Riot." Oregon Public Broadcasting, October 14, 2019. https://www
.opb.org/news/article/antifa-killed-homicide-cider-riot-sean-kealiher/.

———. "Portland Mayor Ted Wheeler Bans Use of CS Tear Gas in Ongoing Protests." Oregon Public Broadcasting, September 11, 2020. https://
www.opb.org/article/2020/09/10/portland-mayor-ted-wheeler-bans
-use-of-tear-gas-in-ongoing-protests/.

———. "Portland's Protests: 3 Months In, No End in Sight." Oregon Public Broadcasting, August 25, 2020. https://www.opb.org /article/2020/08/24/portlands-protests-three-months-in-no-end-in-sight/.

———. "Portland Votes to Wall Off Local Police from Federal Law Enforcement." Oregon Public Broadcasting, July 28, 2020. https://www.opb.org/news /article/portland-votes-wall-Off-police-federal-law-enforcement/.

Ellison, Jeremiah (@jeremiah4north). "I hereby declare, officially, my support…." Twitter, May 31, 2020. https://archive.vn/UjaYz.

Ellison, Keith (@keithellison). "At @MoonPalaceBooks and I just found…." Twitter, January 3, 2018. http://archive.is/irupS.

———. "This man doesn't look like any civil rights…." Twitter, May 28, 2020. https://archive.vn/RfCt8.

Equitable Workers Offering Kommunity Support (@PDXEWOKS). Twitter profile. Accessed October 2, 2020. https://archive.vn/ISAp3.

Escobar, Natalie. "One Author's Argument 'In Defense of Looting.'" NPR, August 27, 2020. https://www.npr.org/sections/codeswitch/2020/08/27 /906642178/one-authors-argument-in-defense-of-looting.

Eudaly, Chloe. "Statement from Commissioner Chloe Eudaly on Immigration & Customs Enforcement Facility 4310 SW Macadam." Press release, July 23, 2018. https://www.portlandoregon.gov/eudaly/article/691975.

Evans, Robert (@IwriteOK). "This is bullshit. I was…." Twitter, July 19, 2020. https://archive.is/K1nfU.

FBI. "Hate Crime in the U.S.: New Stats and a Continuing Mission." Federal Bureau of Investigation, November 19, 2007. Accessed October 23, 2020. https://archives.fbi.gov/archives/news/stories/2007/november /hatecrime_111907.

———. "Using Intel against Eco-Terrorists." Federal Bureau of Investigation, June 30, 2008. Accessed May 2, 2020. https://archives.fbi.gov/archives /news/stories/2008/june/ecoterror_063008.

Feis, Aaron. "Umbrella Blade Found at George Floyd Protest." *New York Post*, June 8, 2020. https://nypost.com/2020/06/08/umbrella-blade-found-at -george-floyd-protest/.

Finkelstein, Joel, Alex Goldenberg, Sean Stevens, Pamela Paresky, Lee Jussim, John Farmer, and John K. Donohue. "Network-Enabled Anarchy: How Militant Anarcho-Socialist Networks Use Social Media to Instigate Widespread Violence against Political Opponents and Law Enforcement." Rutgers, September 14, 2020.

Fiorillo, Victor. "D.C. 'Antifa Leader' Is Third Man Charged in Marine Attack in Philadelphia." *Philadelphia Magazine*, January 29, 2019. https://www.philly mag.com/news/2019/01/29/joseph-alcoff-antifa-marines-philadelphia/.

Fippel, Günter. *Antifaschisten in "antifaschistischer" Gewalt: mittel- und ostdeutsche Schicksale in den Auseinandersetzungen zwischen Demokratie und Diktatur (1945 bis 1961).* A. Peter, 2003.

Flood, Brian. "Reporter Who Had Gun Pulled on Him during Kenosha Riot Credits God for Being Alive." Fox News, August 25, 2020. https://www.foxnews.com/media/reporter-gun-pulled-on-him-kenosha-riots.

Focus. "'Bin um mein Leben gerannt': Entsetzen nach linken Krawallen in Berlin." Focus.de, November 4, 2019. https://www.focus.de/politik/deutschland/viele-polizisten-verletzt-bin-um-mein-leben-gerannt-entsetzen-nach-linken-krawallen-in-berlin_id_11305688.html.

Foley, Ryan J. "Woman, 22, Killed at Protest as Civil Unrest Roils Davenport." Associated Press, June 1, 2020. https://apnews.com/18e8ec5a9b8e7175a128254d55df41e3.

Fonrouge, Gabrielle. "This Is Why Jacob Blake Had a Warrant out for His Arrest." *New York Post*, August 28, 2020. https://nypost.com/2020/08/28/this-is-why-jacob-blake-had-a-warrant-out-for-his-arrest/.

Fosters Daily Democrat. "NH Man Gets 41 Months for Possessing Child Pornography in Maine." *Fosters Daily Democrat*. Accessed October 22, 2020. https://www.fosters.com/article/20080516/NEWS0104/48373566.

FOX 11 News. "Charges Filed against Man Accused of Defying Orders during Waupaca Protest." Fox 11, August 3, 2020. https://fox11online.com/news/local/charges-filed-against-man-accused-of-defying-orders-during-waupaca-protest.

FOX 12 Staff. "New Data Shows Surge in Portland Shootings, with 488 So Far This Year." KPTV, September 4, 2020. https://www.kptv.com/news/new-data-shows-surge-in-portland-shootings-with-488-so-far-this-year/article_9c89c710-ef08-11ea-94b6-13065376e911.html.

———. "Tips Help Police Arrest Man, Boy Accused of Attacking Bystander in Protest for George Floyd in Portland." KPTV, June 8, 2020. https://www.kptv.com/news/tips-help-police-arrest-man-boy-accused-of-attacking-bystander-in-protest-for-george-floyd/article_1083ede8-a9d7-11ea-821a-bfb5bc8b03d5.html.

Fox News. "Conservative Journalist Attacked by Antifa Protesters Speaks Out." YouTube, July 1, 2019. https://www.youtube.com/watch?v=fLgKN1ij8eM.

———. *Tucker Carlson*—Andy Ngo Attacked in Antifa May Day Portland Riot." YouTube, May 2, 2019. https://youtu.be/mtBPxDfl82I.

"Free Speech or a Vicious Crime?: Accused MAX Attacker's Lawyers Argue Legality of Rant Affects Larger Case." KGW-TV, January 2, 2020. https://www.kgw.com/article/news/local/trimet-attack/jeremy-christian-max-stabbings-trial-portland-free-speech/283-79d3cc2b-9d46-4808-b093-70833ebd820c.

FreeCapitolHill. "The Demands of the Collective Black Voices at Free Capitol Hill to the Government of Seattle, Washington." Medium, June 9, 2020. https://medium.com/@seattleblmanon3/the-demands-of-the-collective-black-voices-at-free-capitol-hill-to-the-government-of-seattle-ddaee51d3e47.

Freedom House. "Overview Fact Sheet: The Democratic Leadership Gap."

January 17, 2014. https://web.archive.org/web/20190531161947/https://freedomhouse.org/report/overview-fact-sheet.

Friedman, Gordon R. "In Response to Chaotic Street Brawls, Portland May Restrict Protests." *Oregonian*, October 16, 2018. https://www.oregonlive.com/portland/2018/10/in_response_to_street_brawls_p.html.

———. "Portland City Council Rejects Mayor Ted Wheeler's Protest Restrictions Plan." *Oregonian*, November 15, 2018. https://www.oregonlive.com/portland/2018/11/portland_city_council_rejects.html.

Fry, Paige, Jeremy Gorner, Peter Nickeas, Gregory Pratt, Megan Crepeau, Stacy St. Clair, Claire Hao, et al. "Police Shooting of Englewood Man Reignites Political Debate and Looting as Mag Mile Trashed, 13 Cops Injured, 2 People Shot." *Chicago Tribune*, August 10, 2020. https://www.chicagotribune.com/news/breaking/ct-chicago-downtown-looting-20200810-3zwa3b7zzrc5vdyb4qjqywrjvu-story.html.

Fulbrook, Mary. "Stasi. The Untold Story of the East German Secret Police John O. Koehler." *English Historical Review*, 2000. https://doi.org/10.1093/ehr/115.463.1038.

Garbe, Will, and Hasan Karim. "Dayton Shooter Was Armed Counter-Protester at Ku Klux Klan." WHIO, August 6, 2019. Accessed September 10, 2020. https://web.archive.org/web/20191129023501/https://www.whio.com/news/local/dayton-shooter-was-armed-counter-protester-klux-klan-rally/OjUttVmHRpmBGqHNRGXyoL/.

Garcia, Victor. "Ex-Antifa Member Slams Nadler for Calling Far-Left Group 'Imaginary': 'That's Just False.'" Fox News, June 27, 2020. https://www.foxnews.com/media/gabriel-nadales-jerrold-nadler-claims-antifa-imaginary.

Garza, Alicia (@aliciagarza). "How do we stop 'black on black crime?'...." Twitter, January 17, 2015. https://archive.vn/Dql77.

———. "White supremacy and capitalism are...." Twitter, July 13, 2016. https://archive.vn/Eah4s.

Gee, Taylor. "How the Middlebury Riot Really Went Down." *Politico Magazine*, May 28, 2017. https://www.politico.com/magazine/story/2017/05/28/how-donald-trump-caused-the-middlebury-melee-215195.

Gehriger, Uhrs. "America Under Siege: 'They Don't Want Law and Order. They Want Anarchy.'" Weltwoche, September 2, 2020. https://www.weltwoche.ch/ausgaben/2020-36/weltwoche-international/kalen-d-almeida-die-weltwoche-ausgabe-36-2020.html.

Gillham, Patrick F. "WTO History Project." *Journal of American History* 100, no. 2 (September 1, 2013): 615–15.

Giove, Candice M. "Occupy Wall Street Costs Local Businesses $479,400!" *New York Post*, November 13, 2011. http://www.nypost.com/p/news/local/manhattan/item_Wq8d8Q0M0W98jwaQAVPvYL.

Gittlitz, A. M. "'Make It So': 'Star Trek' and Its Debt to Revolutionary

Socialism." *New York Times*, July 24, 2017. https://www.nytimes .com/2017/07/24/opinion/make-it-so-star-trek-and-its-debt-to -revolutionary-socialism.html.

Goldberg, Zach. "America's White Saviors." Tablet Magazine, June 5, 2019. https://www.tabletmag.com/jewish-news-and-politics/284875/americas -white-saviors.

Goldberger, David. "The Skokie Case: How I Came to Represent the Free Speech Rights of Nazis." American Civil Liberties Union, March 2, 2020. https://www.aclu.org/issues/free-speech/rights-protesters/skokie-case -how-i-came-represent-free-speech-rights-nazis.

Goldsbie, Jonathan, Graeme Gordon, Kevin Sexton, and Robert Jago. "Faith Goldy Fired From The Rebel." CANADALAND, August 18, 2017. https://www.canadalandshow.com/faith-goldy-gone-rebel/.

Gorcenski, Emily (@EmilyGorcenski). "Fuck Nazis." Twitter, September 4, 2020. https://archive.vn/s2cc5.

———. "Reminder: the proper response to ….'" August 11, 2020. https:// archive.is/9MprT.

———. "What I'm saying is armed community …." Twitter, April 19, 2019. https://archive.is/Tq6Lv.

Gorney, Cynthia. "Mistrial Declared in Newton Murder Case." *Washington Post*, March 25, 1979. https://www.washingtonpost.com/archive /politics/1979/03/25/mistrial-declared-in-newton-murder-case /b6408217-1cf0-4c67-a425-9d25b6ac600f/.

Green, Aimee. "21 Protest-Related Lawsuits Have Been Filed against Portland Police: Latest 3 Accuse Police of Harassing Critics." *Oregonian*, October 14, 2020. https://www.oregonlive.com/news/2020/10/21-protest -related-lawsuits-have-been-filed-against-portland-police-latest-3-accuse -police-of-harassing-critics.html.

———. "Jeremy Christian Has No Major Mental Illness, but Is Quick to Anger over 'Trivial Issues,' Psychiatrist Testifies." *Oregonian*, February 14, 2020. https://www.oregonlive.com/news/2020/02/psychiatrist-says -jeremy-christian-doesnt-have-a-mental-illness-but-is-quick-to-become -angry-and-aggressive-over-trivial-issues.html.

Green, Sara Jean. "Capitol Hill Break-In Suspect Arrested, Tied to Crimes at So Do and White Center Auto Businesses." *Seattle Times*, June 17, 2020. https:// www.seattletimes.com/seattle-news/crime/capitol-hill-break-in-suspect -arrested-tied-to-crimes-at-sodo-and-white-center-auto-businesses/.

Griswold, Alex. "Black Lives Matter Founder Claims Hate Speech Isn't Protected by First Amendment." *Washington Free Beacon*, August 14, 2017. https://freebeacon.com/issues/black-lives-matter-founder-claims-hate -speech-isnt-protected-by-first-amendment/.

Grossman, Andrew. "Man Arrested in Sex Assaults at Occupy Wall

Street." *Wall Street Journal*, November 2, 2011. http://blogs.wsj.com/metropolis/2011/11/02/man-arrested-in-sex-assaults-at-occupy-wall-street/.

Guarente, Gabe. "What It's Like to Eat Inside Seattle's Much-Discussed Protest Space." Eater Seattle, June 18, 2020. https://seattle.eater.com/2020/6/18/21293916/seattle-protest-zone-chop-chaz-capitol-hill-food-eating.

Gutman, David. "Durkan Proposes $20 Million in Cuts to Seattle Police as Part of Proposal to Balance Budget." *Seattle Times*, June 23, 2020. https://www.seattletimes.com/seattle-news/politics/durkan-proposes-20-million-in-cuts-to-seattle-police-as-part-of-proposal-to-balance-budget/.

Hamerquist, Don, J. Sakai, and Xtn. *Confronting Fascism: Discussion Documents for a Militant Movement*. Kersplebedeb, 2017.

Hampe, Blake David (br0k3nr0b0t). "I was marching very close...." Reddit post, August 14, 2020. http://archive.vn/AHu6E.

Hanania, Richard. "It Isn't Your Imagination: Twitter Treats Conservatives More Harshly Than Liberals." *Quillette*, February 12, 2019. https://quillette.com/2019/02/12/it-isnt-your-imagination-twitter-treats-conservatives-more-harshly-than-liberals/.

Hegyi, Nate. "Spurred by Debunked Antifa Rumors, Armed Men and Women Stand Watch Over Protests." Boise State Public Radio, June 8, 2020. https://www.boisestatepublicradio.org/post/spurred-debunked-antifa-rumors-armed-men-and-women-stand-watch-over-protests#stream/0.

Heim, Joe. "Charlottesville Response to White Supremacist Rally Is Sharply Criticized in Report." Washington Post, December 1, 2017. https://www.washingtonpost.com/local/charlottesville-response-to-white-supremacist-rally-sharply-criticized-in-new-report/2017/12/01/9c59fe98-d6a3-11e7-a986-d0a9770d9a3e_story.html.

Hernandez, Drew. "BLM PROTESTERS PHYSICALLY ASSAULTING AND ROBBING PEOPLE IN DOWNTOWN PORTLAND (FULL)." YouTube, August 19, 2020. https://www.youtube.com/watch?v=JCKcYSQAP6U.

———. "For the record, this was the extreme...." Twitter, August 17, 2020. https://archive.vn/i870Z.

———. Interview by Andy Ngo. October 2020.

———. "Twisted BLM activist in Portland...." Twitter, August 17, 2020. https://archive.vn/GG8oX.

Herzog, Katie. "Anti-Racist Protesters Harass Gay Asian-American Journalist." The Stranger, December 7, 2018. Accessed September 3, 2020. https://www.thestranger.com/slog/2018/12/07/36874512/anti-racist-protesters-harass-gay-asian-american-journalist.

Heye, Bob. "Former Portland ICE Protest Campsite Reopens to Public." KATU News, July 26, 2018. https://katu.com/news/local/former-portland-ice-protest-camp-site-reopens-to-public.

Hill, Christian. "Fatal Police Shooting in Front of Cascade Middle School Was Justified, DA Rules." *Register-Guard*, January 24, 2019. Accessed September 7, 2020. https://www.registerguard.com/news/20190124/fatal -police-shooting-in-front-of-cascade-middle-school-was-justified-da -rules.

Hill, Evan, Mike Baker, Derek Knowles, and Stella Cooper. "'Straight to Gunshots': How a U.S. Task Force Killed an Antifa Activist." *New York Times*, October 13, 2020. https://www.nytimes.com/2020/10/13/us/ michael-reinoehl-antifa-portland-shooting.html.

Hogg, David (@davidhogg111). "While white men stomp around with...." Twitter, May 7, 2020. https://archive.vn/NXas9.

Hoppe, Bert. *In Stalins Gefolgschaft: Moskau und die KPD 1928–1933*. Oldenbourg Verlag, 2011.

Horcher, Gary. "SPD: Rioters Tried to Trap Officers inside Burning Precinct Using Rebar and Concrete." August 26, 2020. https://www.kiro7.com /news/local/spd-rioters-tried-trap-officers-inside-burning-precinct-using -rebar-concrete/5AERWGBGYJE7DC6CLW3PEKKAEE/.

Horowitz, Ami. "Inside CHAZ (the Capitol Hill Autonomous Zone)." YouTube, June 17, 2020, https://www.youtube.com/watch?v=ZpW _QLWrubE.

Hubbard, Wayne. "Justice for Sean Reed!" Change.org. Accessed May 27, 2020. https://www.change.org/p/mayor-joe-hogsett-justice-for-sean-reed.

Iannarone, Sarah (@sarahforpdx). "To those who say Antifa are...." Twitter, January 27, 2019. https://archive.is/A0SVG.

Immigration and Customs Enforcement (@ICEgov). "Read the full ICE statement...." Twitter, June 18, 2018. https://archive.vn/3sqOG#selection -3941.0-4009.8.

Incite! "Why Misogynists Make Great Informants: How Gender Violence on the Left Enables State Violence in Radical Movements." Incite!, July 15, 2010. https://archive.vn/fSaUm.

Indianapolis Metropolitan Police Department. "IMPD Officer Involved Shooting." Press release, May 7, 2020. https://archive.vn/x4ir6.

Indigenous Action Media. "Accomplices not allies: Abolishing the ally industrial complex." Accessed September 29, 2020. https://archive.vn/do5zg.

Influence Watch. "National Lawyers Guild." Accessed October 21, 2020. https://www.influencewatch.org/non-profit/national-lawyers-guild/.

International Workers of the World Freelance Journalists Union (@IWWFJU). "TO JOURNALISTS COVERING THE ONGOING...." Twitter, August 5, 2020. https://archive.vn/CTQaR.

Ioffee, Karina. "FBI Investigates Threat against Berkeley School after Teacher's Counterprotest at Neo-Nazi Rally." *East Bay Times*, June 28, 2016. https://www.eastbaytimes.com/2016/06/28/fbi-investigates-threat -against-berkeley-school-after-teachers-counterprotest-at-neo-nazi-rally/.

It's Going Down (@IGD_News). Twitter profile. Accessed October 7, 2020. https://archive.is/rCU9s.

It's Going Down. "Call to Action Border Resistance Tour and Convergence," It's Going Down, July 29, 2019. https://web.archive.org/web/20190804220709/https://itsgoingdown.org/call-to-action-border-resistance-tour-and-convergence/

———. "Time to Beef Up Defense against Far-Right Doxxing." ItsGoing Down.org, February 6, 2017. https://itsgoingdown.org/time-beef-defense-against-far-right-doxxing/.

Jany, Libor. "Minneapolis police say 'Umbrella Man' was a white supremacist trying to incite George Floyd rioting." StarTribune, July 28, 2020. https://www.startribune.com/police-umbrella-man-was-a-white-supremacist-trying-to-incite-floyd-rioting/571932272/.

Joe Rogan Experience #1323—Andy Ngo. YouTube, 2019. https://youtu.be/cI2EHMy1lgs.

Jones, Jeremy. "Gregory McMichael Murderer Ahmaud Arbery Seen at KKK Rally in 2016." GAFollowers, May 9, 2020. http://archive.is/FpN98.

Jones, Nigel. Mosley. Haus Publishing, 2004.

JoshWho News. "CHAZ Shooting Victim's Brother Claims Criminal Protesters 'Hid' His Brother from Him while He Was Dying." JoshWho News, June 21, 2020. https://www.joshwho.net/chaz-shooting-victims-brother-claims-criminal-protesters-hid-his-brother-from-him-while-he-was-dying/.

"Joy Reid: 'Zero Evidence' That Black Lives Matter Has Pushed for Violence." MSNBC, October 22, 2020. https://www.msnbc.com/the-reidout/watch/joy-reid-zero-evidence-that-black-lives-matter-has-pushed-for-violence-94450245781.

KABC. "Man Charged with Arson in Connection to Oregon Wildfire." KABC-TV, September 12, 2020. https://abc7.com/wildfire-oregon-fire-in-arson/6420067/.

Kalbaugh, Brad. "State of Oregon v. Amelia Joan Shamrowicz," June 1, 2020.

Kasprak, Alex. "Does This Video Show Raz Simone Handing Out Guns in Seattle's CHOP?" Snopes, June 23, 2020. https://www.snopes.com/fact-check/raz-simone-guns/.

Kaste, Martin. "Murder Rate Spike Could Be 'Ferguson Effect,' DOJ Study Says." NPR, June 15, 2016. https://www.npr.org/2016/06/15/482123552/murder-rate-spike-attributed-to-ferguson-effect-doj-study-says.

KATU Staff. "Police: Man Charged with Keying Patrol Car at SE Portland Protest." KATU-TV, October 16, 2015. https://katu.com/news/local/police-man-charged-with-keying-patrol-car-at-se-portland-protest.

———. "Protests Cost $23 Million in Damage, Lost Business, Portland Police Say." KATU-TV, July 8, 2020. https://katu.com/news/local/portland-police-plan-to-address-nightly-protests.

Kellner, Douglas M. *Herbert Marcuse and the Crisis of Marxism*. London: Palgrave, 1984.

Kelly, George, and Rick Hurd. "Bay Area College Professor Used U-Shaped Bike Lock in Beating, Police Say." *East Bay Times*, May 25, 2017. https://www.eastbaytimes.com/2017/05/24/berkeley-college-professor-arrested-as-assault-suspect/.

Kelly, Kim (@GrimKim). "And one of my greatest hopes...." Twitter, November 7, 2019. http://web.archive.org/web/20191107194718/https://twitter.com/GrimKim/status/1192526839585095680.

———. "As Van Spronsen and the many other...." Twitter, July 15, 2019. http://web.archive.org/web/20190715005051if_/http://twitter.com/grimkim.

———. "Comrade Boomer." Twitter, November 7, 2019. http://web.archive.org/web/20191107232938/https://twitter.com/GrimKim/status/1192583246732767236.

———. "Hey NYC pals, if we haven't seen each other...." Twitter, January 23, 2020. https://archive.is/Kdfoo.

Kelly, Meg, and Elyse Samuels. "Who caused the violence at protests? It wasn't antifa." *Washington Post*, June 22, 2020. https://www.washingtonpost.com/politics/2020/06/22/who-caused-violence-protests-its-not-antifa/.

KGW. "82nd Avenue of Roses Parade Canceled due to Threats." KGW-TV, April 26, 2017, https://www.kgw.com/article/news/local/82nd-avenue-of-roses-parade-canceled-due-to-threats/283-434090945.

———. "'ICE Is Stupid': Portland Commissioner to Occupy ICE PDX Protesters." KGW-TV, 2018, https://www.kgw.com/article/news/special-reports/at-the-border/ice-is-stupid-portland-commissioner-to-occupy-ice-pdx-protesters/283-568226290.

King, Angela, Casey Martin, and Gil Aegerter. "1 Teen Dead, 1 Wounded in Shooting at Seattle's CHOP." KUOW-FM, June 29, 2020. https://www.kuow.org/stories/shooting-in-seattle-s-chop-leaves-one-man-dead-one-wounded.

King, Shaun (@shaunking). "I Support ANTIFA...." Twitter, August 16, 2017. http://archive.is/UOn0J.

———. "I support the communists & socialists...." Twitter, August 16, 2017. http://archive.is/ifd8k.

———. "I've said it before & I...." Twitter, March 5, 2018. https://web.archive.org/web/20200826112713/https://twitter.com/shaunking/status/970865184209297408.

———. "We are told that this is the final letter...." Twitter, July 15, 2019. https://archive.fo/xQ1DG.

Kohn, Sally (@sallykohn). "My sense is that if Trump...." Twitter, November 8, 2016. https://archive.vn/LJwxD.

KOMO News Staff. "Best: SPD Response Times Have Tripled since Loss of East Precinct." KOMO, June 11, 2020. https://komonews.com/news/local/best-spd-response-times-have-tripled-since-loss-of-east-precinct.

Krasner, Stephen D. *Organized Hypocrisy*. Princeton, NJ: Princeton University Press, 1999.

Kruse, Brandi. "CHOP: Seattle Mayor Walks Back 'Summer of Love' Comment." Q13 FOX, June 22, 2020. https://www.q13fox.com/news/chop-seattle-mayor-walks-back-summer-of-love-comment.

KVAL. "DA: FBI Received Tip about Landeros 'Posting Violent Anti-Government Messages' in 2018." KVAL-TV, January 24, 2019. https://kval.com/news/local/da-fbi-received-tip-about-landeros-posting-violent-anti-government-messages-in-2018.

———. " 'Nothing about Us without Us!': Oregon Students Protest University President's Speech." KVAL-TV, October 6, 2017. https://kval.com/news/local/nothing-about-us-without-us-oregon-students-protest-university-presidents-address.

Lavin, Talia (@chick_in_kiev). "Andy ngo is best known for providing...." Twitter, June 27, 2020. http://archive.is/WzZHa.

———. "I wrote about the crucial role...." Twitter, June 5, 2020. https://archive.is/MIi3n.

———. "This has been a wild and difficult week...." Twitter, June 21, 2018. http://archive.is/h3nyd.

Levin, Jack, and Jack McDevitt. "Hate Crimes." In *International Encyclopedia of the Social & Behavioral Sciences*, 540–45. Elsevier, 2015.

Levine, Jon. "NYU Cancels Former New Yorker Fact-Checker Talia Lavin's Journalism Class." The Wrap, May 30, 2019. https://www.thewrap.com/nyu-cancels-former-new-yorker-fact-checker-talia-lavins-journalism-class/.

———. "NYU Journalism School Hires Ex-New Yorker Fact Checker Who Falsely Said ICE Agent Had Nazi Tattoo." The Wrap, March 20, 2019. https://www.thewrap.com/nyu-journalism-talia-lavin-new-yorker-fact-checker-false-ice-agent-nazi-tattoo/.

Lindsay, James. Interview by Andy Ngo, April 22, 2020.

Louise, Olivia. "RIP. Armeanio celebrating our...." Facebook post, October 15, 2019. https://archive.vn/PgIn5.

Lucas, Fred. "Antifa Activist Facing Assault Charges Was Tied to Democratic Policymakers." Fox News, February 11, 2019. https://www.foxnews.com/politics/antifa-activist-facing-assault-charges-was-tied-to-democratic-policymakers.

MacFarquhar, Neil. "Minneapolis Police Link 'Umbrella Man' to White Supremacy Group." *New York Times*, July 28, 2020. https://www.nytimes.com/2020/07/28/us/umbrella-man-identified-minneapolis.html.

MacFarquhar, Neil, Alan Feuer, and Adam Goldman. "Federal Arrests Show No Sign That Antifa Plotted Protests." *New York Times*, June 11, 2020. https://www.nytimes.com/2020/06/11/us/antifa-protests-george-floyd.html.

MacFarquhar, Neil, Mike Baker, and Adam Goldman. "In His Last Hours, Portland Murder Suspect Said He Feared Arrest." *New York Times*, September 4, 2020. https://www.nytimes.com/2020/09/04/us/portland-shooting-michael-reinoehl.html.

Magalif, Jeff. "Weathermen, Police Scuffle in Cambridge." *Harvard Crimson*, November 20, 1969. Accessed July 14, 2020. https://www.thecrimson.com/article/1969/11/20/weathermen-police-scuffle-in-cambridge-pweathermen/.

Marx, Karl, and Friedrich Engels. "Communist Manifesto (Chapter 1)." Marxists.org archive, 1848. https://www.marxists.org/archive/marx/works/1848/communist-manifesto/ch04.htm.

Mathew, Benita. "Neenah Man Charged with Bringing Smoke Grenades to Green Bay Rally, Accused of Pointing Rifle at Police in Waupaca." *Green Bay Press Gazette*, August 31, 2020. https://www.greenbaypressgazette.com/story/news/2020/08/31/neenah-man-charged-bringing-smoke-grenades-green-bay-rally-accused-pointing-rifle-police-waupaca/3448722001/.

Mayer, M. "The Career of Urban Social Movements in West Germany." In *Mobilizing the Community: Local Politics in the Era of the Global City*, edited by R. Fisher and J. Kling. Newbury Park, CA: Sage, 1993.

McDermott, Kevin, and Jeremy Agnew. *The Comintern: A History of International Communism from Lenin to Stalin*. Red Globe Press, 1996.

McEvoy, Jemima. "14 Days of Protests, 19 Dead." *Forbes Magazine*, June 8, 2020. https://www.forbes.com/sites/jemimamcevoy/2020/06/08/14-days-of-protests-19-dead/.

McGowan, Rory. "Claim No Easy Victories: An Anarchist Analysis of ARA and Its Contributions to the Building of a Radical Anti-Racist Movement." Libcom, September 29, 2020. https://archive.vn/gnwqk.

McLaughlin, Sarah. "City College of New York Reverses Cancellation of Pro-Palestine Event after Pressure from Legal Groups." FIRE, May 2, 2018. https://www.thefire.org/city-college-of-new-york-reverses-cancellation-of-pro-palestine-event-after-pressure-from-legal-groups/.

Menza, Kaitlin. "Portland Commissioner Jo Ann Hardesty Has a Message for Trump and the Feds." *Marie Claire*, July 22, 2020. https://www.marieclaire.com/politics/a33385651/portland-jo-ann-hardesty-protests/?fbclid=IwAR3I6VvPjn9a8DMZOvaDD6ZRNh7sI16HPMOg2XQU603xe26wK3dFDFmnRhs.

Merkel, Wolfgang. "Embedded and Defective Democracies." *Democratization* 11, no. 5 (December 1, 2004): 33–58.

Mesh, Aaron, and Corey Pein. "White Supremacists Are Brawling with Masked Leftists in the Portland Streets. Homeland Security Is Watching." *Willamette Week*, May 23, 2017. https://www.wweek.com/news/2017/05/23/white-supremacists-are-brawling-with-masked-leftists-in-the-portland-streets-homeland-security-is-watching/.

Meyer, Josh, Jacqueline Klimas, Wesley Morgan, and Alex Isenstadt. "FBI, Homeland Security Warn of More 'Antifa' Attacks." *Politico*, September 1, 2017. https://www.politico.com/story/2017/09/01/antifa-charlottesville-violence-fbi-242235.

Miller, Joshua Rhett. "Federal Agents Likely Permanently Blinded by Portland Protesters' Lasers, White House Says." *New York Post*, July 24, 2020. https://nypost.com/2020/07/24/3-fed-agents-likely-blinded-by-lasers-pointed-at-them-in-portland-wh/.

Milwaukee Coalition Against Trump. "As protesters milled along the side of...." Facebook post, September 3, 2020. https://archive.vn/ukRjd.

Moreau, Patrick, and Rita Schorpp-Grabiak. *Man muß so radikal sein wie die Wirklichkeit—Die PDS: eine Bilanz*. Nomos Verlagsgesellschaft, 2002.

Moreno, J. Edward. "Ocasio-Cortez Dismisses Proposed $1B Cut: 'Defunding Police Means Defunding Police.'" *The Hill*, June 30, 2020. https://thehill.com/homenews/house/505307-ocasio-cortez-dismisses-proposed-1b-cut-defunding-police-means-defunding.

Moreno, Joel. "MLS Lifts Ban on Iron Front Flag Embraced by Sounders Fans." KOMO-AM, September 25, 2019. https://komonews.com/news/local/mls-lifts-ban-on-iron-front-flag-embraced-by-sounders-fans.

Movement for Black Lives, "Invest-Divest." Accessed April 29, 2020. https://archive.is/JNyWd.

Multnomah County District Attorney. "District Attorney Mike Schmidt Announces Policy Regarding Protest-Related Cases." Press release, August 11, 2020. Accessed October 5, 2020. https://www.mcda.us/index.php/news/district-attorney-mike-schmidt-announces-policy-regarding-protest-related-cases/.

———. "Jeremy Joseph Christian Sentenced to Life Imprisonment without the Possibility of Release or Parole." Press release, June 24, 2020. Accessed October 27, 2020. https://www.mcda.us/index.php/news/jeremy-joseph-christian-sentenced-to-life-imprisonment-without-the-possibility-of-release-or-parole/.

———. "Protest Cases." Accessed October 7, 2020. https://www.mcda.us/index.php/protest-cases/.

Multnomah County Sheriff's Office. "Blake David Hampe Booking." July 25, 2020. http://archive.vn/UJFen.

———. "Unified Command: Individuals target a City Commissioner's home, set fire at Portland City Hall." Press release, November 6, 2020. https://flashalert.net/id/MCSO/139816.

———. "Unified Command press release on Nov. 4 unlawful assembly and riot." Press release, November 5, 2020. https://flashalert.net/id/MCSO/139773.

Murthy, Dhiraj. *Twitter: Social Communication in the Twitter Age*. Cambridge: Polity Press, 2018.

Mutasa, Tammy. "Man Killed by Police at NW Detention Center Had

Previous Arrest for Assaulting Officer." KOMO-FM, July 13, 2019. https://
komonews.com/news/local/man-killed-by-police-at-nw-detention-center
-had-previous-arrest-for-assaulting-officer.

MyNorthwest Staff. "Seattle Police Union Demands Elected Officials Condemn Violence toward Officers." MyNorthwest.com, June 8, 2020.
https://mynorthwest.com/1929274/spog-safety-officers-seattle-protests/?

Nachrichten. "'Dann war Stille im Schanzenviertel.'" n-tv.de, July 13, 2017.
https://www.n-tv.de/politik/Dann-war-Stille-im-Schanzenviertel-article
19934632.html.

Natapoff, Alexandra, Emma Kaufman, and Patrisse Cullors. "Abolition
and Reparations: Histories of Resistance, Transformative Justice, and
Accountability." *Harvard Law Review*, April 10, 2019. Accessed April 30,
2020. https://harvardlawreview.org/2019/04/abolition-and-reparations
-histories-of-resistance-transformative-justice-and-accountability/.

NBC Chicago, "Black Lives Matter on Chicago Looting: Black Lives
'More Important Than Downtown Corporations.'" NBC Chicago,
August 11, 2020. https://www.nbcchicago.com/news/local/black-lives
-matter-on-chicago-looting-black-lives-more-important-than-downtown
-corporations/2320685/.

NBC News. "Antifa Members Talk Protest Tactics: 'We Don't Depend
On Cops.'" YouTube, August 19, 2019. https://www.youtube.com
/watch?v=af5o-4eI9PA.

New York City Antifa (@NYCAntifa). "Solidarity from NYC to...." Twitter, May 27, 2020. http://archive.is/xO5Mx.

———. "What the actual fuck." Twitter, September 3, 2020. https://archive
.vn/jEe6Q.

Ngo, Andy. "Antifa Militant Seen with Illegal Gun in the 'CHAZ.'" YouTube,
June 20, 2020. https://www.youtube.com/watch?v=oSVhBlvIxv8.

———. "Inside the Suspicious Rise of Gay Hate Crimes in Portland." *New
York Post*, March 30, 2019. https://nypost.com/2019/03/30/inside-the
-suspicious-rise-of-gay-hate-crimes-in-portland/.

Ngo, Andy (@MrAndyNgo). "After finding out that it was a...." Twitter,
August 29, 2020. https://archive.vn/t6uz1.

———. "Antifa are claiming that the deceased person is...." Twitter, August
29, 2020. https://archive.vn/dEKZe.

———. "Antifa black bloc handed out flyers about me...." Twitter, November 5, 2019. https://archive.vn/tYHnz.

———. "Antifa black bloc outside the Kelly Penumbra...." Twitter, September 4, 2020. https://archive.vn/3weIr.

———. "Blake David Hampe, the accused #antifa stabber...." Twitter,
August 19, 2020. https://archive.vn/77TmI.

———. "For those who say I am lying about the 'mom'...." Twitter, July 21,
2020. https://archive.vn/TsK7L.

———. "In downtown Portland, rioters...." Twitter, May 30, 2020. https://archive.vn/ljkfE.

———. "Masked militants ransacking the Justice Center...." Twitter, May 29, 2020. https://archive.vn/jyuLI.

———. "Nicholas James Armstrong/Nikki Jameson was seen...." Twitter, June 9, 2020. http://archive.vn/gDBK8.

———. "Popular Antifa COVID-19 Portland Fundraiser Accused of Being a Scam." *Post Millennial*, June 14, 2020. https://thepostmillennial.com/popular-antifa-covid-19-portland-fundraiser-accused-of-being-a-scam.

———. "Portland: Hundreds are led in a chant by a man...." Twitter, May 29, 2020. https://archive.vn/gDlcr.

———. "Seattle Antifa Militia Distributes Extremist Manifesto of ICE Attacker." *Post Millennial*, March 9, 2020. https://thepostmillennial.com/seattle-antifa-militia-distributes-extremist-manifesto-of-ice-attacker/.

———. "Trump-Loving Grandma Outs Portland 'bomber' to Feds—and It's Her Own Grandson." *New York Post*, August 1, 2020. https://nypost.com/2020/08/01/trump-loving-grandma-outs-her-own-grandson-as-portland-bomber/.

———. "Unreported conflict of interest...." Twitter, June 29, 2020. https://archive.vn/0mAZ3.

Ngo, Andy, and Mia Cathell. "Portland District Attorney Brings Charges Following Week of BLM-Antifa Arson Attacks." *Post Millennial*, September 27, 2020. https://thepostmillennial.com/portland-district-attorney-brings-charges-following-week-of-blm-antifa-arson-attacks.

Ngo, Andy, Serina Hersey, and Jon Raby. "Portland Black Lives Matter Protest (7/7/16)." Portland State Vanguard and YouTube, July 10, 2016. https://www.youtube.com/watch?v=XURLNqphQuY.

North Carolina Piece Corps. "The divorce of thought from deed: a compilation of writings on social conflict, white supremacy, and the mythology of free speech at UNC." Anarchist Zine Library. Accessed September 29, 2020. https://archive.vn/EYbOZ.

North, John. "W. Asheville Crime Wave Alleged." *Asheville Daily Planet*, December 2, 2019. Accessed August 28, 2020. http://www.ashevilledailyplanet.com/news/4617-w-asheville-crime-wave-alleged-.

O'Connell, Kit. "Beyond the Concrete Milkshake: Defeating Media Trolls & Grifters (Zine)." Kit O'Connell, June 22, 2020. https://kitoconnell.com/2020/06/22/beyond-the-concrete-milkshake-media-trolls-zine/.

Ocasio-Cortez, Alexandria (@AOC). "Quick IG Q&A after Tuesday's Dem Convention Program." Instagram post, August 18, 2020. https://www.instagram.com/tv/CEDqrtFn1-v/?hl=en.

———. "Abolish ICE." Twitter, November 27, 2019. https://archive.vn/BuIZO.

———. "One way to support the local LGBTQ...." Twitter, August 31, 2019. https://archive.vn/xHKSP.

OHSU4BLM (@OHSU4BLM). "Dear Community, We are so proud...." Twitter, August 4, 2020. http://archive.vn/fUdBe.

Oloffson, Kristi. "Food Vendors Find Few Customers during Protest." *Wall Street Journal*, October 12, 2011. https://blogs.wsj.com/metropolis/2011 /10/12/food-vendors-find-few-customers-during-protest/.

"On Willem van Spronsen's Action against the Northwest Detention Center in Tacoma." CrimethInc, July 14, 2019. Accessed September 3, 2020. https://crimethinc.com/2019/07/14/on-willem-van-spronsens-action -against-the-northwest-detention-center-in-tacoma-including-the-full -text-of-his-final-statement.

Oppmann, Patrick. "Admitted Hijacker Dreams of Home after 43 Years in Cuba." CNN, April 9, 2015. https://www.cnn.com/2015/04/09/americas /us-cuba-fugitive-charlie-hill/index.html.

Oregon Secretary of State. "General Election November 3, 2020." Oregon Secretary of State, November 16, 2020. https://archive.vn/QuPUv.

"Outnumbered Sacramento Spartans Rout Leftist Scum; A Call For Nationalist Solidarity." Traditionalist Youth Network, June 29, 2016. https://web.archive.org/web/20160702072724/http://www.tradyouth .org/2016/06/outnumbered-sacramento-spartans-rout-leftist-scum/.

Pacific Northwest Youth Liberation Front (@PNWYLF). "BOOSTING Portland: Vigil for...." Twitter, May 27, 2020. http://archive.vn/MnDKW.

———. "For real tho, the cops...." Twitter, July 21, 2020. https://archive .is/aJNbU.

———. "From Portland to Minneapolis, for Youth Liberation!...." Twitter, May 27, 2020. https://archive.vn/OU7mw.

———. "Livestreamers are doing the...." Twitter, July 26, 2020. https:// archive.is/8bw8z.

Parke, Caleb. "Reporter Describes 'Traumatic' Scene at Portland Assault: I Witnessed an 'Attempted Execution.'" Fox News, August 19, 2020. https://www.foxnews.com/us/portland-assault-witness-video-search -police-drew-hernandez.

Parks, Bradley W. "Portland Mayor Ted Wheeler Calls for Shutdown of 'Trump Free Speech,' Anti-Muslim Rallies." Oregon Public Broadcasting, May 29, 2017. https://www.opb.org/news/article/portland-free-speech -march-sharia-wheeler-permit/.

PDX Community Jail Support (@PDXJail_Support). Twitter profile. https:// archive.vn/hFhR8.

PDX Hydration Station & Umbrellacrosse Sticks (@PDXCarMedic). "As #Beans and @riotribs have...." Twitter, July 27, 2020. https://archive .vn/2DbLd.

"PDX Protest Bail Fund." GoFundMe, May 30, 2020. https://archive.vn/ke6UJ.

PDX Shieldsmiths (@ShieldPDX). Twitter profile. https://archive.vn/kcQI5.

Pearson, Alex. Interview by Andy Ngo, June 15, 2017.

Peel, Sophie. "Portland Protesters Say Their Lives Were Upended by the Post-ing of Their Mug Shots on a Conservative Twitter Account." *Willamette Week*, September 16, 2020. https://www.wweek.com/news/2020/09/16/portland-protesters-say-their-lives-were-upended-by-the-posting-of-their-mug-shots-on-a-conservative-twitter-account/.

Peninsula Daily News. "Family Reportedly Harassed in Forks after Being Accused of Being Members of Antifa." *Peninsula Daily News*, June 4, 2020. https://www.peninsuladailynews.com/crime/family-harassed-in-forks-after-being-accused-of-being-members-of-antifa/.

Perlow, Patricia W. "Cascade Middle School OIS Investigation." Letter to Lane County Media, January 11, 2019." January 24, 2019. https://lanecounty.org/UserFiles/Servers/Server_3585797/File/OIS%20press.website.pdf.

Peterson, Jordan. "The Fatal Flaw Lurking in American Leftist Politics." Big Think, April 11, 2018. https://bigthink.com/videos/jordan-peterson-the-fatal-flaw-lurking-in-american-leftist-politics.

Planned Parenthood Advocates of Oregon. "Congratulations to Jacinda Padilla,…." Facebook post. February 12, 2020. https://archive.vn/uSv4F.

Popular Mobilization (@PopMobPDX). "Charlie Landeros, beloved com-rade…." http://web.archive.org/web/20190113165808/https://twitter.com/PopMobPDX/status/1084494781617627136.

Porter, Laural. "On Straight Talk, Portland mayoral candidate Sarah Iann-arone declines to denounce violent protests, says protesters' outrage with police is valid." KGW, August 7, 2020. https://www.kgw.com/article/entertainment/television/programs/straight-talk/straight-talk-sarah-iannarone/283-72b3ce7d-88f1-42c2-86c5-10189d2c2d17.

Portland City Council. "City Council 2017-03-22 PM." YouTube, March 22, 2017. https://youtu.be/XRcgE6v8PEM.

Portland General Defense Committee. "GoFundMe Transparency." Accessed October 8, 2020. https://archive.vn/8dQOO.

Portland Police Association. "A letter to the editor…." Facebook post, November 8, 2018. https://www.facebook.com/PortlandPoliceAssociation/photos/a.386709091352814/2233132546710450.

Portland Police Bureau. "12 Adults Arrested, 1 Juvenile Detained-New Criminal Tactic Used on Police Vehicles, Spike Devices Seized." Press release, August 7, 2020. https://archive.vn/W1SFN.

———. "24 Arrested, Officer Injured by Large Rock during Unlawful Assembly." Press release, August 8, 2020. https://archive.vn/SNR7L.

———. "59 Arrested during Riot." Press release, September 6, 2020. https://archive.vn/OTNZL.

———. "Ammunition and Destructive Devices Recovered at Lownsdale Square Park." July 27, 2020. https://archive.vn/DVaH5.

———. "Arrests Made for July 4th Demonstrations." Press release, July 5, 2020. https://archive.vn/k9OIK.

———. "Arson Fire in Building, Riot Declared." Press release, August 9, 2020. https://archive.vn/WIH98.

———. "Case No. 18-207957." Portland report, June 2018.

———. "Demonstration Education Event." YouTube, August 15, 2019. https://www.youtube.com/watch?v=VJYvDIe2Isk.

———. "Demonstration Events Conclude in Downtown Portland—Three Arrested." Press release, June 29, 2019. https://archive.vn/9qXRe.

———. "Destructive Crowd Topples Historic Statues in South Park Blocks, Breaks Windows, Arrests Made." Press release, October 12, 2020. https://archive.vn/owAk3.

———. "During June 1st Demonstration 10 Adults Arrested and 6 Adults Cited." Press release, June 2, 2020. Accessed October 2, 2020. https://archive.vn/KLaWR.

———. "Justice Center—Police Raw Video." YouTube, July 6, 2020. https://www.youtube.com/watch?v=5FOgwZOgjrs.

———. "Mass Gathering Vandalizes Building in Laurelhurst Neighborhood." Press release, November 9, 2020. https://archive.vn/DA1XL.

———. "Multiple Suspects Charged with Assaulting Officers, Other Charges." Press release, August 16, 2020. https://archive.vn/VZIFM.

———. "Patrick Kimmons." Press release, September 30, 2018. https://www.portlandoregon.gov/police/article/701715.

———. "Protest Blocks Streets, Officers Assaulted, Pelted with Rocks, Glass Bottles, Other Objects." Press release, August 15, 2020. https://archive.vn/dbA8q.

———. "Protesters Break Windows, Burglarize Business, Start Fire in Apartment Building; Riot Declared." Press release, September 1, 2020. https://archive.vn/7WiTG.

———. "Saturday Demonstrations Have Concluded in Downtown Portland." Press release, July 2, 2018. http://archive.is/EYgzO.

———. "Several Weapons Seized Related to Downtown Demonstrations." Press release, June 7, 2020. Accessed October 2, 2020. https://archive.vn/8jbkP.

———. "Update: Information About Additional Arrests from May 30 Riot." Press release, May 31, 2020. https://archive.vn/32Rtr.

———. "Update: List of Arrests Made during North Precinct Riot." Press release, August 22, 2020. https://archive.vn/TGQJU.

Portland Police Bureau (@PortlandPolice). "To the group near N. Mississippi Avenue...." Twitter, August 14, 2020. http://archive.vn/KLw6S.

Portland Police Bureau and Portland Fire and Rescue. "Arson Fires 5/29/2020 to 6/8/2020." Press release, June 13, 2020. https://archive.vn/8vvQL.

"Portland State Ronald E. McNair Scholars Program." Portland State University, 2004. Accessed September 29, 2020. https://web.archive.org/web/20181010081713/https://www.pdx.edu/mcnair-program/adam-carpinelli.

Project Veritas. "#EXPOSEANTIFA." YouTube, June 5, 2020. https://www
.youtube.com/watch?v=fIp1pcbRsCI.

———. "Militia Wing of ANTIFA Believes in Complete Abolition of the
System Itself, Including Police." Project Veritas, June 9, 2020. Accessed
August 11, 2020. https://www.projectveritas.com/news/militia-wing-of
-antifa-we-believe-in-complete-abolition-of-the-system-itself/.

PubliCola. "FBI Says There Was Specific Threat against East Precinct; Durkan
Letter Dodges Protesters' Three Demands." PubliCola, July 7, 2020.
https://publicola.com/2020/07/06/fbi-says-there-was-specific-threat
-against-east-precinct-durkan-letter-dodges-protesters-three-demands/.

Puget Sound Anarchists. "Mural Honoring Will van Spronsen in Exarchia."
September 1, 2019. https://pugetsoundanarchists.org/mural-honoring
-will-van-spronsen-in-exarchia/.

Queally, James. "Violence in Sacramento Shows Old and New Faces of White
Extremism." Los Angeles Times, June 27, 2016. https://www.latimes
.com/local/lanow/la-me-ln-california-white-nationalists-sacramento
-20160627-snap-story.html.

Racine County Eye. "Police: K9 Dozer Helps Subdue Man Who Pulled Gun
at Bar." Racine County Eye, September 22, 2015. https://racinecounty
eye.com/police-k9-dozer-helps-subdue-man-who-pulled-gun-at-bar/.

Raguso, Emilie. "UCPD Chief at Berkeley: 'Crowd Control Situations Are
Different." Berkeleyside, February 4, 2017. https://www.berkeleyside
.com/2017/02/04/ucpd-chief-berkeley-crowd-control-situations-different.

Raice, Shayndi. "Jacob Blake Shooting: What Happened in Kenosha, Wisconsin?" Wall Street Journal, August 25, 2020. https://www.wsj.com
/articles/jacob-blake-shooting-what-happened-in-kenosha-wisconsin
-11598368824.

Raiford, Teressa (@TeressaLRaiford). "We should abolish period." Twitter,
June 10, 2020. https://archive.vn/w6xOg.

Rantz, Jason. "Rantz: Alleged Seattle Arsonist near CHOP Arrested, AK-47
Found Nearby." MyNorthwest, June 18, 2020. https://mynorthwest
.com/1959063/rantz-seattle-chop-arsonist-arrested-weapons-found/.

———. "Rantz: Rioters Tried to Burn Seattle Police Alive, Sealed Door during
Fire at East Precinct." MyNorthwest, August 25, 2020. https://mynorth
west.com/2114190/rantz-rioters-burn-seattle-police-alive-sealed-door/.

Ranzt, Jason (@jasonrantz). "This is dangerous…." Twitter, June 1, 2020.
https://archive.vn/nS1FV.

Ray Lambert, Hannah. "Policing Portland's protests: 1,000 arrests, handful
of prosecutions." KOIN, https://www.koin.com/news/protests/policing
-portlands-protests-1000-arrests-handful-of-prosecutions/

Real News Network. "A Short History of Black Lives Matter." YouTube,
July 22, 2015. https://www.youtube.com/watch?v=kCghDx5qN4s.

————. "Effie Baum." Accessed May 10, 2020. https://web.archive.org/web/20200722075813/https://therealnews.com/bios/effie-baum.

Redden, Jim. "'Police Overtime Costs City about $2 Million for Protests.'" *Portland Tribune*, February 22, 2012. https://pamplinmedia.com/pt/9-news/20178-police-overtime-costs-city-about-$2-million-for-protests.

Reed, Dreasjon (@shelov3sean). "Just say the word I'm on they block...." Twitter, April 2, 2020. http://archive.is/kZpwz.

Reid, Joy (@JoyAnnReid). "Y'all Do Realize 'antifa' is just short for...." Twitter, May 30, 2020. https://archive.vn/QAHWI.

Reinoehl, Michael (@michael_reinoehl). "Every revolution needs people that...." Instagram post, June 16, 2020. https://archive.is/qdc90.

Remnick, David. "An American Uprising." *The New Yorker*, May 31, 2020. https://www.newyorker.com/news/daily-comment/an-american-uprising-george-floyd-minneapolis-protests.

Revolutionary Abolitionist Movement NYC (@RevAbolitionNY). Twitter profile. Accessed August 8, 2020. http://archive.vn/t7rOF.

Riot Ribs (@riotribs). "FOR IMMEDIATE RELEASE...." Twitter, July 28, 2020. https://archive.vn/HBF8W.

————. Twitter profile. Accessed July 28, 2020. https://archive.vn/Q0Jmo.

Riski, Tess. "New Multnomah County District Attorney Mike Schmidt Must Decide Who Faces Criminal Charges Amid Portland's Protests." *Willamette Week*, July 15, 2020. Accessed October 5, 2020. https://www.wweek.com/news/courts/2020/07/15/new-multnomah-county-district-attorney-mike-schmidt-must-decide-who-faces-criminal-charges-amid-portlands-protests/.

Robinson, Nathan J. "The Southern Poverty Law Center Is Everything That's Wrong with Liberalism." *Current Affairs*, March 26, 2019, https://www.currentaffairs.org/2019/03/the-southern-poverty-law-center-is-everything-thats-wrong-with-liberalism.

Rogers, Laura, and Karen Moore. "Crowd Gathers in Indianapolis to Protest Death of Sean Reed in Police Shooting." *Fort Worth Star-Telegram*, May 7, 2020. https://www.star-telegram.com/news/article242584271.html.

Rose City Antifa. Letter to "Lion"/Project Veritas. September 22, 2017.

————. "No Pasaran! No Nazis on Our Streets!" Facebook post, May 25, 2017. http://archive.vn/lZf8t.

————. "Statement about June 29, 2019." Rose City Antifa, July 3, 2019. Accessed July 10, 2020. https://web.archive.org/web/20191013081127/https://rosecityantifa.org/articles/june-29-statement/.

Rosenberg, Rebecca. "Antifa Protester Gets 18 Months for Beating Up Trump Supporter." *New York Post*, October 23, 2019. https://nypost.com/2019/10/23/antifa-protester-gets-18-months-for-beating-up-trump-supporter/.

Rosenfeld, Richard. "Documenting and Explaining the 2015 Homicide Rise:

Research Directions." *National Institute of Justice*, 2016. https://pdfs
.semanticscholar.org/ecf0/8cbbfd1cd07aaeb99df0a741ef9cdcd105f8.pdf.

Ross, Alexander Reid (@areidross). "Andy Ngo contacted me about a book
talk...." Twitter, September 24, 2020. https://archive.vn/3D9e5.

Ross, Alexander Reid. "Curriculum Vitae." http://archive.vn/AuyVN.

Ross, Chuck. "Look Who Funds the Group Behind the Call to Arms
at Milo's Berkeley Event." Daily Caller, February 3, 2017. https://
dailycaller.com/2017/02/03/look-who-funds-the-group-behind-the
-call-to-arms-at-milos-berkeley-event/.

Rothman, Stanley. *The End of the Experiment: The Rise of Cultural Elites
and the Decline of America's Civic Culture*. New York: Routledge, 2017.

Rothstein, Adam. "Adam Rothstein's Info and CV." Poszu. Accessed June 4,
2020. http://archive.vn/m8pKz.

Rubin, Bret. "The Rise and Fall of British Fascism: Sir Oswald Mosley and
the British Union of Fascists." *Intersections* 11, no. 2 (2010): 323–80.

Ruptly. "USA: Scuffles Erupt between Patriot Prayer and Antifa." YouTube.
Accessed May 1, 2020. https://www.youtube.com/watch?v=b3WRrM81FbI.

Ryan, Jim. "Portland's Anti-Trump Protest Turns Violent, as Rioters Rampage in Pearl." *Oregonian*, November 11, 2016. https://www.oregonlive
.com/portland/2016/11/anti-trump_protests_held_for_f.html.

Sagan, Ginetta, and Stephen Denney. "Re-Education in Unliberated Vietnam: Loneliness, Suffering and Death." *The Indochina Newsletter*, 1982.

Salo, Jackie. "New York Times Reporter Says Destroying Property Is 'Not
Violence.'" *New York Post*, June 3, 2020. https://nypost.com/2020/06/03
/ny-times-reporter-says-destroying-property-is-not-violence/.

Sandberg, Diane. "Family of George Floyd Seeks Independent Autopsy."
KARE, 2020. https://www.kare11.com/article/news/local/george-floyd
/george-floyd-family-seeks-independent-autopsy-minnneapolis/89
-8661d16f-2a8e-44bf-a9fa-d72e9e274dcf.

Sarlin, Benjy. "Antifa Violence Is Ethical? This Author Explains Why."
NBC News, August 26, 2017. https://www.nbcnews.com/politics/white
-house/antifa-violence-ethical-author-explains-why-n796106.

Satterberg, Daniel T. "The State of Washington v. Jacob Bennet Greenburg,
Danielle E. McMillan." October 16, 2020.

Sawant, Kshama (@cmkshama). "The outrage on Seattle's streets today...."
Twitter, May 30, 2020. https://archive.vn/FtM35.

Schaffer, Elijah. Interview by Andy Ngo. October 2020.

Schmeidel, John. "My Enemy's Enemy: Twenty Years of Co-operation
between West Germany's Red Army Faction and the GDR Ministry for
State Security." *Intelligence & National Security* 8, no. 4 (October 1,
1993): 59–72.

Schoffstall, Joe. "Southern Poverty Surpasses Half Billion in Assets."
Washington Free Beacon, March 12, 2019. https://freebeacon.com

/issues/southern-poverty-surpasses-half-billion-in-assets-121-million
-now-offshore/.

Schultz, Marisa. "Dem Senator Walks Out of Ted Cruz's Antifa Hearing: 'I Don't
Think You Listen.'" Fox News, August 4, 2020. https://www.foxnews.com
/politics/dem-senator-mazie-hirono-walks-out-ted-cruz-antifa-hearing.

Schwartz, Joseph, and Jason Schulman. "Toward Freedom: Democratic
Socialist Theory and Practice." Democratic Socialists of America,
December 21, 2012 https://www.dsausa.org/strategy/toward_freedom/.

Seattle Antifascists (@RainCityAntifa). "We need more people with guns…."
Twitter, June 9, 2020. http://archive.is/zaGqc.

Seattle Police Department. "East Precinct Protest Update." SPD Blotter, June 7,
2020. https://spdblotter.seattle.gov/2020/06/07/east-precinct-protest-update/.

———. "Group Causes Significant Property Damage and Commits Arson in
Capitol Hill Neighborhood." SPD Blotter, July 23, 2020. https://spdblotter
.seattle.gov/2020/07/23/group-causes-significant-property-damage-and
-commits-arson-in-capitol-hill-neighborhood/.

———. "Homicide Investigation Inside Protest Area." SPD Blotter, June 20,
2020, https://spdblotter.seattle.gov/2020/06/20/homicide-investigation
-inside-protest-area/.

———. "Officer Injuries, Precinct Damage, Arrest Updates." SPD Blotter,
July 26, 2020, https://spdblotter.seattle.gov/2020/07/26/officer-injuries
-precinct-damage-arrest-updates/.

———. "Officer Involved Shootings (OIS) Dashboard." Accessed October
20, 2020. https://www.seattle.gov/police/information-and-data/use-of
-force-data/officer-involved-shootings-dashboard.

———. "Updated: Officers Injured, 18 Arrested during Riot in SODO."
SPD Blotter, August 17, 2020. https://spdblotter.seattle.gov/2020/08
/17/officers-injured-18-arrested-during-riot-in-sodo/.

Shakur, Assata. *Assata: An Autobiography*. Westport, CT: Lawrence Hill,
1974.

Shankbone, David. "Satanism: An Interview with Church of Satan High
Priest Peter Gilmore." 2007. https://en.wikinews.org/wiki/Satanism:_An
_interview_with_Church_of_Satan_High_Priest_Peter_Gilmore.

Shaw, Adam. "ICE Offices, Workers Hit by Wave of Violence and Threats: 'We
Know Where All Your Children Live.'" Fox News, August 14, 2019. https://
www.foxnews.com/politics/ice-offices-workers-wave-of-violence-threats.

Shepherd, Katie (@katemshepherd). "At IRE One of the tips from the…."
Twitter, June 30, 2019. https://web.archive.org/web/20190701063401
/https://twitter.com/katemshepherd/status/1145399931533840384.

Shepherd, Katie. "Is It Possible to Mix Cement into a Vegan Milkshake?
We Did It." *Willamette Week*, July 10, 2019. Accessed May 8, 2020.
https://www.wweek.com/news/courts/2019/07/10/is-it-possible-to-mix
-cement-into-a-vegan-milkshake-we-did-it/.

———. "Portland Police Chief Says Antifa Protesters Used Slingshot to Launch Urine and Feces-Filled Balloons at Riot Cops." *Willamette Week*, June 23, 2017. Accessed May 8, 2020. https://www.wweek.com /news/city/2017/06/23/portland-police-chief-says-antifa-protesters-used -slingshot-to-launch-urine-and-feces-filled-balloons-at-riot-cops/.

———. "Portland Police Made a Dubious Claim about Protesters' Milkshakes on Twitter. What's the Evidence?" *Willamette Week*, July 2, 2019. Accessed May 8, 2020. https://www.wweek.com/news/city/2019 /07/02/portland-police-made-a-dubious-claim-about-protesters -milkshakes-on-twitter-whats-the-evidence/.

———. "Portland Police Refused to Respond When ICE Agents Called 911 during Protest, Letter Says." *Willamette Week*, July 30, 2018. Accessed April 7, 2020. https://www.wweek.com/news/courts/2018/07/30/ice -agents-say-portland-mayor-violated-the-u-s-constitution-by-barring -police-from-responding-to-the-feds-calls-for-help/.

SHUTTERSHOT45. "Trump Supporter Smashed in the Head with U-Lock by Masked Antifa Thug in Berkeley." YouTube, April 16, 2017. https:// www.youtube.com/watch?v=9qKCl9NL1Cg.

Silverstein, Jason. "Kamala Harris Meets with Jacob Blake's Family in Wisconsin." CBS News, September 8, 2020. https://www.cbsnews.com /news/kamala-harris-meets-jacob-blake-family-wisconsin/.

Simmons, Ann M., and Jaweed Kaleem. "A Founder of Black Lives Matter Answers a Question on Many Minds: Where Did It Go?" *Los Angeles Times*, August 25, 2017. https://www.latimes.com/nation/la-na-patrisse -cullors-black-lives-matter-2017-htmlstory.html.

Simone, Solomon (@RazSimone). "The President really put a hit on my head…." Twitter, June 11, 2020. http://archive.vn/Fo4VN.

Skovlund, Joshua. "How a Marine Corps Veteran Disarmed a Rioter during Seattle Protest." *Coffee or Die*, June 3, 2020. https://coffeeordie .com/marine-seattle-protest/.

Slingshot Collective. "USA." Accessed August 29, 2020. https://slingshot collective.org/usa/.

Smale, Alison. "60 Years Later, Germany Recalls Its Anti-Soviet Revolt." *New York Times*, June 18, 2013. https://www.nytimes.com/2013/06/18 /world/europe/germany-puts-spotlight-on-its-own-anti-soviet-revolt.html.

Smith, Mitch, Rick Rojas, and Campbell Robertson. "Dayton Gunman Had Been Exploring 'Violent Ideologies,' F.B.I. Says." *New York Times*, August 6, 2019. https://www.nytimes.com/2019/08/06/us/mass -shootings.html.

Soave, Robby. "Black Lives Matter Students Shut Down the ACLU's Campus Free Speech Event Because 'Liberalism Is White Supremacy.'" *Reason*, October 4, 2017. https://reason.com/2017/10/04/black-lives-matter-students -shut-down-th/.

———. "The Media Claimed Andy Ngo Was Complicit in a Far-Right Attack on Antifa. But the Video Doesn't Support That." *Reason*, September 3, 2019. https://reason.com/2019/09/03/andy-ngo-video-antifa -patriot-prayer-attack-media/.

Solan, Mike. Interview by Andy Ngo. August 23, 2020.

Southern Poverty Law Center. "Active Hate Groups 2016." Accessed May, 2017. https://www.splcenter.org/fighting-hate/intelligence-report/2017/active -hate-groups-2016.

———. "Charles Murray." Accessed April 26, 2020. https://www.splcenter .org/fighting-hate/extremist-files/individual/charles-murray.

———. "District of Columbia." Accessed April 1, 2020. https://www.splcenter .org/states/district-columbia.

———. "Texas." Accessed March 31, 2020. https://www.splcenter.org /states/texas.

Specia, Megan. "What We Know about the Death of the Suspect in the Portland Shooting." *New York Times*, September 4, 2020. https://www .nytimes.com/2020/09/04/us/michael-forest-reinoehl-portland.html.

Spiegel. "Polizei richtet Sonderkommission ein." Spiegel, July 10, 2017. https://www.spiegel.de/panorama/justiz/hamburg-polizei-richtet-nach -g20-krawalle-soko-ein-a-1156977.html.

Spronsen, Ariel van. "Legal Defense Fund for Will van Spronsen." Indiegogo .com, June 5, 2013. https://www.indiegogo.com/projects/legal-defense -fund-for-will-van-spronsen#/.

Sprout Anarchist Collective. "What is security culture? A guide to staying safe…" Accessed September 29, 2020. https://archive.vn/RJj5t.

Sprout Distro. "Accomplices Not Allies: Abolishing the Ally Industrial Complex." Accessed October 20, 2020. https://www.sproutdistro.com/catalog /zines/anti-oppression/accomplices-allies-abolishing-ally-industrial-complex.

———. "An Activist's Guide to Information Security," accessed September 29, 2020, https://www.sproutdistro.com/catalog/zines/security/activists -guide-information-security.

———. "Blockade, Occupy, Strike Back." Accessed October 19, 2020. https://www.sproutdistro.com/catalog/zines/direct-action/blockade -occupy-strike-back.

Steven. "1985–2001: A Short History of Anti-Fascist Action (AFA)." Libcom .org. April 20, 2020 http://libcom.org/history/1985-2001-anti-fascist -action-afa.

Svriuga, Susan. "Evergreen State College Reopens after Violent Threat and Property Damage on Campus." *Washington Post*, June 5, 2017. https://www .washingtonpost.com/news/grade-point/wp/2017/06/05/evergreen-state -college-reopens-after-violent-threat-and-property-damage-on-campus/.

Swain, Carol. Interview by Andy Ngo, May 1, 2020.

Sylvester, Terray. "Suspect in Fatal Portland Attack Yells about 'Free Speech' at Hearing." *Reuters*, May 31, 2017. https://www.reuters.com/article/us-usa-muslims-portland-idUSKBN18Q11F.

Talcott, Shelby. " 'I've Been Scared Every Day': Seattle Resident Speaks Out about Life on the Border of CHAZ." Daily Caller, June 14, 2020. https://dailycaller.com/2020/06/13/exclusive-seattle-resident-life-border-capitol-hill-autonomous-zone-chaz/.

Tamburin, Adam. "Controversial Professor Carol Swain to Retire from Vanderbilt." *Tennessean*, January 23, 2017. https://www.tennessean.com/story/news/education/2017/01/23/carol-swain-announces-retirement-vanderbilt-university/96959004/.

Taylor, Derrick Bryson. "F.B.I. Investigating Shootings at San Antonio ICE Facilities." *New York Times*, August 14, 2019. https://www.nytimes.com/2019/08/14/us/ice-san-antonio-shooting.html.

Tennessee Star. "Flashback: Keith Ellison Once Proposed Making a Separate Country for Blacks." *Tennessee Star*, September 16, 2018. https://tennesseestar.com/2018/09/16/flashback-keith-ellison-once-proposed-making-a-separate-country-for-blacks/.

The Witches (@TheWitchesPDX). Twitter profile. Accessed September 14, 2020. https://archive.vn/6XH9W.

thegiver@riseup.net. Letter to Dianne Gill, April 22, 2017. https://www.scribd.com/document/346378772/Threat-against-Multnomah-County-Republican-Party-during-Avenue-of-Roses-Parade.

Theiss, Eliza. "More Optimistic Than Millennials, Gen Z Is Here to Revolutionize the Housing Market." PropertyShark, September 4, 2018. https://www.propertyshark.com/Real-Estate-Reports/2018/09/04/more-optimistic-than-millennials-gen-z-is-here-to-revolutionize-the-housing-market/.

Thurlow, Richard C. *Fascism in Britain: A History, 1918–1985*. Olympic Marketing Corp, 1987.

Thuy, Vu Thanh. "Boat People' Defeat Sea, but All at Visa Wall." *San Diego Union*, July 20, 1986.

Tobin, Michael. "FBI Releases Files Related to Deceased Activist Charlie Landeros." *Daily Emerald*, July 23, 2019. https://www.dailyemerald.com/news/fbi-releases-files-related-to-deceased-activist-charlie-landeros/article_7f53b6ba-ad8c-11e9-aee7-eb7c58383b02.html.

Tometi, Opal (@opalayo). "For the record...." Twitter, August 28, 2015. https://archive.vn/m2JVY.

———. "I shared 3 core challenges...." Twitter, July 12, 2016. https://archive.vn/IUCMQ.

Torch Network. "About." Accessed June 2, 2020 https://archive.vn/pEQmD.

———. "Points of Unity." Torch Network. Accessed August 2, 2019. https://archive.vn/dgdbM.

Torres, Libby. "Drake, Chrissy Teigen, and Steve Carell Are Just Some of the Stars Who've Donated to Bail-Relief Funds across the US." Insider,

May 29, 2020. https://www.insider.com/minnesota-protests-celebrity -donations-george-floyd-reactions-2020-5.

Treloar, M. "Portland History in Review: A Hundred Little Hitlers." Rose City Antifa, 2009. https://archive.vn/RMQ1F.

Trump, Donald J. (@realDonaldTrump). "Major consideration is being given...." Twitter, August 17, 2019. http://archive.vn/I3TGi.

Trump, Donald J. "Executive Order on Combating Race and Sex Stereo-typing." White House, September 22, 2020. Accessed October 6, 2020. https://www.whitehouse.gov/presidential-actions/executive-order -combating-race-sex-stereotyping/.

Turner, Kris. "Local terrorist activity suspected." State News, August 30, 2005. https://web.archive.org/web/20060530134437/http://www.statenews .com:80/article.phtml?pk=31230.

U.S. Department of Justice. "Department of Justice Identifies New York City, Portland and Seattle as Jurisdictions Permitting Violence and Destruction of Property." Press release, September 21, 2020. https://www.justice .gov/opa/pr/department-justice-identifies-new-york-city-portland-and -seattle-jurisdictions-permitting.

———. "Man Charged with Arson for Setting Fire to Seattle's East Police Precinct during Capitol Hill Protest." Press release, July 15, 2020. https://www.justice.gov/usao-wdwa/pr/man-charged-arson-setting-fire -seattle-s-east-police-precinct-during-capitol-hill.

———. Regarding the Criminal Investigation into the Shooting Death of Michael Brown by Ferguson, Missouri Police Officer Darren Wilson: Department of Justice Report. Memorandum, March 4, 2015.

———. "Seven Arrested, Facing Federal Charges After Weekend Riots at Hatfield Federal Courthouse (Photo)." Press release, July 7, 2020. https:// www.justice.gov/usao-or/pr/seven-arrested-facing-federal-charges-after -weekend-riots-hatfield-federal-courthouse.

———. "Texas Man Charged with Assaulting Deputy U.S. Marshal with Hammer during Weekend Protests in Portland (Photo)." Press release, July 13, 2020. https://www.justice.gov/usao-or/pr/texas-man-charged -assaulting-deputy-us-marshal-hammer-during-weekend-protests -portland.

"UCB News: Campus Investigates Damage from Feb. 1 Violence." Berke-leyside, February 2, 2017. https://www.berkeleyside.com/2017/02/02 /ucb-news-campus-investigates-damage-feb-1-violence.

University of California, Berkeley. "Milo Yiannopoulos Event Canceled after Violence Erupts." Berkeley News, February 2, 2017, https://news .berkeley.edu/2017/02/01/yiannopoulos-event-canceled/.

Univision. " 'Se Me Partió El Alma Al Ver La Foto': Padre de La Niña Que Llora Mientras Arrestan a Su Madre." Univision, June 18, 2018. https://www.univision.com/noticias/inmigracion-infantil/se-me

-partio-el-alma-al-ver-la-foto-padre-de-la-nina-que-llora-mientras-arrestan-a-su-madre-video.

Usher, Barbara Plett. "George Floyd Death: A City Pledged to Abolish Its Police. Then What?" BBC, October 23, 2020. https://www.bbc.com/news/world-us-canada-54665665.

Varon, Jeremy Peter. *Bringing the War Home: The Weather Underground, the Red Army Faction, and, Revolutionary Violence in the Sixties and Seventies*. Berkeley: University of California Press, 2004.

Vice News. "Man Linked to Killing at a Portland Protest Says He Acted in Self-Defense." VICE, September 3, 2020. Accessed September 13, 2020. https://www.vice.com/en_us/article/v7g8vb/man-linked-to-killing-at-a-portland-protest-says-he-acted-in-self-defense.

Victorin, Caroline. "Johan's Green Card Fund." GoFundMe, December 14, 2015. Accessed June 4, 2020. https://archive.vn/S8qyC.

Vysotsky, Stanislav. *American Antifa: The Tactics, Culture, and Practice of Militant Antifascism*. Fascism and the Far Right. New York: Routledge, 2020.

Wakerell-Cruz, Roberto. "ANDY? NO: Antifa Harass Asian Man for Looking like Andy Ngo." *Post Millennial*, July 14, 2020. https://thepostmillennial.com/watch-antifa-harass-asian-man-for-looking-like-andy-ngo.

———. "Oregon Man Part of Radical Left-Wing Antifascist Group Sues His Grandmother over Rent Disagreement." *Post Millennial*, April 26, 2020. https://thepostmillennial.com/oregon-man-part-of-radical-left-wing-group-sues-his-grandmother-over-rent-disagreement.

Wamsley, Laurel. "White Supremacist Charged with Killing 2 in Portland, Ore., Knife Attack." NPR, May 27, 2017. https://www.npr.org/sections/thetwo-way/2017/05/27/530351468/2-dead-1-injured-after-stabbing-in-portland-ore.

"War of the Skinheads." *Chicago Tribune*, May 11, 1989. https://www.chicagotribune.com/news/ct-xpm-1989-05-11-8904110718-story.html.

Warzel, Charlie. "50 Nights of Unrest in Portland." *New York Times*. July 18, 2020. https://www.nytimes.com/2020/07/17/opinion/portland-protests-federal-agents.html.

Warzone Distro. "Against the Police and the Prison World They Maintain." Warzone Distro, September 8, 2017. Accessed October 20, 2020. https://warzonedistro.noblogs.org/post/2017/09/08/against-the-police-and-the-prison-world-they-maintain/.

Waters, Tony, and Dagmar Waters. "Politics as Vocation." In *Weber's Rationalism and Modern Society: New Translations on Politics, Bureaucracy, and Social Stratification*, edited by Tony Waters and Dagmar Waters, 129–98. New York, NY: Palgrave Macmillan, 2015.

Watt, Cecilia Saixue. "Redneck Revolt: The Armed Leftwing Group That Wants

to Stamp out Fascism." *Guardian*, July 11, 2017. http://www.theguardian
.com/us-news/2017/jul/11/redneck-revolt-guns-anti-racism-fascism-far-left.

Weill, Kelly. "Local Businesses Love the 'Domestic Terror' Zone in Seattle,
Actually." Daily Beast, June 12, 2020. https://www.thedailybeast.com/local
-businesses-love-the-domestic-terror-autonomous-zone-in-seattle-actually.

West, Robert. "Protester Admits He Was Called up by Rose City ANTIFA to
Disrupt Meeting." YouTube, March 6, 2019. https://www.youtube.com
/watch?v=PFceZ5DJG88.

Wheeler, Ted (@tedwheeler). "A number of people have asked...." Twitter,
July 16, 2020. https://archive.vn/Dke8q.

———. "Earlier today I directed that staff...." Twitter, July 18, 2020.
https://archive.vn/82ke8.

———. "We talked about agitation...." Twitter, May 31, 2020. https://
archive.vn/PtOd8.

Willey, Jessica. "Family of man wrongfully accused by activist Shaun King in
Jazmine Barnes' shooting speaks out." ABC 7 Chicago, January 8, 2019.
https://abc7chicago.com/family-of-wrongfully-accused-man-receiving
-violent-threats/5034081/.

Williams, Jamal Oscar. Facebook post, May 1, 2018. https://archive.vn/Ujo5y.

Wilson, Jason. "Landlord of Portland ICE Offices Admits He Was
at the Wheel of a Mercedes That Struck a Protester." *Willamette
Week*, June 21, 2018. Accessed April 9, 2020. https://www.wweek
.com/news/courts/2018/06/21/landlord-of-portland-ice-offices
-admits-he-was-at-the-wheel-of-a-mercedes-that-struck-a-protester/.

———. "Revealed: Pro-Trump Activists Plotted Violence ahead of Portland
Rallies." *Guardian*, September 23, 2020. http://www.theguardian.com
/world/2020/sep/23/oregon-portland-pro-trump-protests-violence-texts.

Wilson, Patrick. "Woody Kaine, Son of Sen. Tim Kaine, Gets Probation, Fine Stemming from Protest at Minn. Trump Rally." *Richmond
Times-Dispatch*, December 28, 2017. https://richmond.com/news/local
/government-politics/woody-kaine-son-of-sen-tim-kaine-gets-probation
-fine-stemming-from-protest-at-minn/article_ddf24b77-1bdc-542a
-840b-8c9721e080ba.html.

Wolff, Robert Paul, Barrington Moore, and Herbert Marcuse. *A Critique of
Pure Tolerance*, 1966. https://philarchive.org/rec/RACO-5.

Wyden, Ron (@RonWyden). "The consequences of Donald Trump unilaterally...." Twitter, July 12, 2020. https://archive.is/mIcpp.

Yahoo Finance. "Seattle Police Chief Carmen Best Plans to Announce Her
Resignation." YouTube, August 11, 2020. https://www.youtube.com
/watch?v=ORz9vfklmNA.

Yoder, Traci. "Legal Support for Anti-Fascist Action." National Lawyers Guild,
July 10, 2017. https://www.nlg.org/legal-support-for-anti-fascist-action/.

Zapotosky, Matt, Adam Goldman, and Scott Higham. "Police in Dallas: 'He Wanted to Kill White People, Especially White Officers.'" *Washington Post*, July 8, 2016. https://www.washingtonpost.com/world/national -security/police-in-dallas-he-wanted-to-kill-white-people-especially-white -officers/2016/07/08/fe66fe52-4553-11e6-88d0-6adee48be8bc_story.html.

Zhang, Jenny G. "Milkshakes, Eggs, and Other Throwable Protest Foods, Ranked." Eater, June 10, 2019. https://www.eater.com/2019/6/10/18652472/ milkshakes-eggs-throwable-protest-foods-ranked.

Zhao, Christina. "NY Rep. Alexandria Ocasio-Cortez Says 'Capitalism Is Irredeemable.'" *Newsweek*, March 10, 2019. https://www.newsweek .com/alexandria-ocasio-cortez-says-capitalism-irredeemable-1357720.

Zielinski, Alex. "Wheeler Condemns Protest Shooting, Offers Few Solutions to Continuous Violence." Portland Mercury, August 30, 2020. Accessed September 23, 2020. http://web.archive.org/web/20200901005436/https:// webcache.googleusercontent.com/search?q=cache%3Ahttps%3A%2F %2Fwww.portlandmercury.com%2Fblogtown%2F2020%2F08%2F30 %2F28782169%2Fwheeler-condemns-protest-shooting-offers-little -solutions-to-continuous-violence.

Zindulka, Kurt. "Three Arrested as Extinction Rebellion Violently Clash with Police." Breitbart, February 15, 2020. https://www.breitbart.com /europe/2020/02/15/exclusive-video-climate-strike-chaos-as-antifa -extinction-rebellion-clash-with-london-police/.

ACKNOWLEDGMENTS

Before 2019, few had heard of me or the reporting I do. I was a small regional figure in the American Pacific Northwest who developed a small online following for my reporting on Portland and antifa riots. I still remember what it was like to send pitch after pitch to publications only to be rejected—or worse, ignored. But more importantly, I remember those who stood by me, helped and mentored me each step of the way toward becoming the journalist and writer I am today, even as my detractors brought increasing social pressure for those who dared associate with me.

I am grateful to my family for the sacrifices they've made. I often take for granted the freedom and security they risked life and limb to find.

I would like to thank the following for their role in the development of this book and/or the personal development in my life: James O'Keefe and Project Veritas, Asra Nomani, Douglas Murray, Michelle Malkin, Harmeet Dhillion, John D., Brittany, Chelly Bouferrache, Keith Urbahn and Javelin, and the editors and staff at Center Street.

I am enormously grateful to those who support my work and legal justice efforts through pledges and donations. There are endless noble causes to donate to in a zero-sum world, and yet, you find what I do of value and worth. Thank you. I am truly privileged to have your following, feedback, and support.

ABOUT THE AUTHOR

ANDY CUONG NGO is an American journalist best known for covering protests and riots in Portland, Oregon. He has written columns in the *Wall Street Journal*, the *New York Post*, *Newsweek*, and others. He drew national attention when he was attacked by antifa on the streets of Portland in the summer of 2019.